MEN AND DEEDS

MEN AND DEEDS

BY

JOHN BUCHAN

Essay Index Reprint Series

 BOOKS FOR LIBRARIES PRESS
FREEPORT, NEW YORK

First Published 1935
Reprinted 1969

63101

LIBRARY OF CONGRESS CATALOG CARD NUMBER:
69-17567

PRINTED IN THE UNITED STATES OF AMERICA

PREFACE

OF the papers in this collection, the first was the Rede Lecture at Cambridge in the autumn of 1929. The second appeared as a volume in Mr. Peter Davies' Series of *Short Biographies*, the third and fourth as volumes in the same publisher's Series of *Great Occasions*. The fifth was the Walker Lecture delivered before the University of St. Andrews in January 1932. The sixth is from the Proceedings of the British Academy. The seventh is a chapter from a little book published by Messrs. Hodder and Stoughton, and written in collaboration with Sir George Adam Smith at the request of the Church of Scotland to commemorate the Union of 1929. I would offer my thanks to the different authorities concerned for their permission to reprint.

J. B.

August 1935.

CONTENTS

I
THE CAUSAL AND THE CASUAL IN HISTORY

I

THE CAUSAL AND THE CASUAL
IN HISTORY

A VISITOR to Cambridge from the sister University, especially a visitor on such an errand as mine, is not likely to be forgetful of the special genius of the place. He remembers that for some centuries Cambridge has been the chosen home of the natural sciences; that, while keeping a shrewd eye upon practical applications, she has not allowed the lure of immediate rewards to divert her from the quest of truth; and that one of her traditional toasts has been 'God bless the higher mathematics and may they never be of the slightest use to anybody.' Here, if anywhere on the globe, he may expect to find a proper notion of what constitutes a science. He will also, if he have historical interests, remember that within recent years Cambridge has been fruitful in pronouncements on the meaning of history. In 1903 Professor Bury proclaimed: 'History is a science—no less and no more'; while it has been the happy task of your present Regius Professor to emphasise the other side of the truth—that Clio is a Muse, the daughter of Zeus and Mnemosyne, and the mother of Orpheus.

I propose, with Cambridge's scientific fame in my mind, and with these sayings of two of her most eminent historians to guide me, to make some further observations on the Muse of History. She is a lady of many parts. She has her laboratory, no doubt, and her record office; she has, beyond question, her lyre and her singing robes. But the character in which I would exhibit her this afternoon is homelier than these. I can picture Clio with knitted brows, striving to disentangle the why and the wherefore of things. I can picture her with rapt eyes, making epic and drama out of the past. But I can picture her most easily with the puzzled and curious face of a child, staring at the kaleidoscope of the centuries, and laughing—yes, laughing—at an inconsequence that defies logic, and whimsicalities too fantastic for art.

3

I

Let me begin by making concessions to every school. History is an art, and it is also a science; we may say that it is an art which is always trying to become more of a science. As a science it is concerned with causation. The past, if it is to satisfy intelligent minds, must be presented as a sequence of effects and causes. History is not content with an accumulation of facts; it seeks to establish relations between facts. Like every other science, it is a form of thought, and, like every other science, it aims at the attainment of truth. The past cannot be regarded as a mere pageant. Events do not follow each other only in succession of time. Even from the point of view of art, history must have its own inevitableness; and, from the point of view of science, it must aim at representing the whole complex of the past as a chain, each link riveted to the other by a causal necessity.

That is an ideal which we may well admire. It represents an instinct at which we dare not cavil—one of the oldest of human instincts, the instinct to rationalise. For some time there has been a movement on foot towards what is called the 'rationalising' of industry, and there is no reason why the modest labours of Clio's domain should be exempt from the impulse. History must be more than a chronicle; it must be synoptic and interpretative.

In practice, rationalisation may take many forms. To begin with, there are the high philosophers, the professional metaphysicians. If Bolingbroke was right, and history is philosophy teaching by examples, it is clearly most important to get at the philosophy. Then there are those who fix their eyes upon scientific method, and, like Taine, believe that by means of a number of categories of determinable causes every historical event can be mathematically explained. Others are content to seek a formula, and there are many kinds of formulas. There is the formula derived from metaphysics—the Hegelian dialectic, for example, with its sequence of thesis and antithesis and synthesis; or, in a simpler form, Louis Blanc's succession of authority, individualism and fraternity; or, simpler still, the mysticism which finds the key in a single aspect, like Karl Marx's economic interpretation. Or you may have the unifying notion in the shape of a metaphor, a pictorial conception, such as the idea of the past as a cyclic or a spiral process. You may get a loose interpretative principle in something akin to biological evolution, or you may find it in an ethical or theological purpose. Lord Acton saw in history the working of the moral law, and Bishop Stubbs the revelation of the 'Almighty Ruler of the world' busied with 'leading the world on to the better, but never forcing, and out of the evil of man's working bringing continually that which is good.'

There is no word to be said against the ambition of philosophers and scientists and even theologians to bring light and order into the dark places of the past. Every historian must have a thesis, some principle of illumination to guide him, and the value of his work will largely depend upon the sanity and profundity of that thesis. But I would suggest that, the subject-matter of history being what it is, we should be chary of becoming too dogmatic about any principle of interpretation which we put forward. For history works under conditions wholly unlike those of the natural sciences, and historic truth must be something very different from mathematical truth, or even from biological truth.

The philosophers need not trouble us. The awful gambols of a metaphysical doctrine are apt now and then to make nonsense of history, as when Hegel contemplated the stately process of the Absolute Will, and found its final expression in Germany before 1840—a view more flattering to Germany than to the Absolute Will. But if the metaphysician likes to explain everything by some such process, he is welcome to try, so long as he admits that he cannot expound its precise working.

The scientific historian is more dangerous. The older school, of the type of Buckle and Guizot, believed that they had established historical laws of universal validity, and provided a clockwork uniformity of effects and causes. It would appear that they misunderstood the kind of material with which they had to deal. M. Bergson has shown us that half the blunders of philosophy are due to the application of the methods and ideals of physical science to spheres of thought where they are strictly inapplicable. In the kaleidoscope of the past we cannot, as a rule, sort out effects and causes with any precision, nor can we weigh events in the meticulous scales which science demands. Even when causes are reasonably plain, their classification eludes us. We cannot tell which is the *causa causans*, which are proximate, or efficient, or final. We must be content with generalisations which are only generalisations and not laws, with broad effects and massed colours. The weakness of the scientific historian is that he underrates the complexity of human nature. He would turn mankind into automata, motives into a few elementary emotions, and the infinitely varied web of life into a simple geometrical pattern. Order and simplicity are great things, but they must be natural to the subject and not due to the blindness of the historian. You remember Sainte-Beuve's comment on Guizot:

'I am one of those who doubt if it is given to man to embrace the causes and sources of his history with this completeness and certitude. It is as much as he can do to reach an imperfect understanding of the presènt. . . . History seen from a distance undergoes a strange metamorphosis; it produces the illusion— most dangerous of all—that it is rational. The perversities, the follies, the ambitions, the thousand queer accidents which compose it, all these disappear. Every accident becomes a necessity. . . . Such history is far too logical to be true.'

On this point we are perhaps a little more modest to-day than our fathers were. But we are always apt to forget that history cannot give us the precise and continuous causal connections which we look for in the physical sciences. All that we get are a number of causal suggestions, with a good many gaps in them, and if we try to get more we shall do violence to historical truth. We shall be in danger of writing history in order to prove something, and thereby missing that disinterested intellectual curiosity which is the only avenue to truth. We shall try to make the accidental the inevitable, and to explain the inexplicable. We shall refuse to recognise the fundamental irrationality of a large part of Clio's domain.

An example of this fallacy is the attitude of the would-be scientific historian towards great men. The hero in history is a terrible nuisance to the lover of dapper generalities. He breaks the symmetry and spoils the syllogism. What is to be done with him? The scientific mind likes to deal with human nature in the lump, for it is aware that you can generalise with reasonable accuracy about the behaviour of masses of people, when you cannot dogmatise about any single one of them. But what about the daimonic figures who obstinately refuse to be merged in the mass? The embarrassed scientist is driven to one of two courses. Either he declares that the great people had but little influence on the course of events, that the real motive force was this or that intellectual movement or economic grouping. But in many cases this is simply not the truth. The great individuals— Alexander, Caesar, Mohammed, Charlemagne, Luther, Calvin, Peter the Great, Napoleon,—cannot be explained in the terms of any contemporary movement. They are in a sense the children of their age, but they bring to their age more than they draw from it; they seem to be, like Melchizedek, without recognisable ancestry, and by the sheer force of personality and mind they lift the world to a new plane. . . . Or he will try to submerge them in the mass by arguing that they were not so great after all. This necessity may partly account for the sansculottism of a certain type of historian, who is always attempting to deflate the majestic reputations of history, and to reduce the great figures of the past to a drab level of mediocrity. Partly, no doubt, these essays in belittlement are the result of what is called in the jargon of to-day an 'inferiority complex,' the jealousy of small minds perturbed by the spectacle of something beyond their compass. They see a chance of winning an easy notoriety. An old Cambridge friend of mine had a simile for such people; he said that they were like some Greek of the decadence who broke the nose of an Apollo of Pheidias in order to make the Goths laugh. But, for the honour of human nature, I like to think it is partly the desire of the embarrassed scientist to have less truculent material to work with. Once again, the trouble is that the result is not the truth. Such denigratory efforts may explain many things in a great man, but not his greatness.

The fault, of course, is that of undue simplification. It is the application by a false analogy of the ideals and methods of certain physical sciences to a domain where they are not relevant. In physics we reduce a complex to the operations of constant and measurable forces, but no such mechanical simplification is possible with the inconstants of human history. The movement of mankind is not by a single-gauge track; there is a network of tracks, and the one actually taken may owe its choice to the blindest chance. Rationalise the facts as much as you please—and you can often carry the process a long way—there will remain things which you cannot rationalise, things which you can only call accidents, and which cannot be explained in any logical terms. Instead of the causal we find the casual. I do not for one moment argue that these incomprehensible factors are incapable of rationalisation by some higher intelligence than our own; I only say that we cannot fit them into any mortal scheme of effects and causes. The President of the Immortals has not chosen to take us into his confidence.

Explanation and interpretation, let me repeat, are the essence of history. An historical event can be partially explained by many causes, but there may be some little thing without which it could not have happened, and that little thing may come out of the void, without any apparent justification for its existence. Nevertheless, but for it the history of a decade or a century would have gone differently. Everywhere in the record of the past we find those sparks which fire the powder mines, and in the absence of which the powder might have become useless and never have exploded at all. Let us be a little chary about accepting the so-called 'streams of inevitable tendency' which are the delight in each generation of simple souls, and give them the opportunity of posing as minor prophets and announcing the 'decline of the West' or the 'recrudescence of barbarism,' or some such journalistic slogan. The historian is wise if, like the Romans of the early Empire, he admits Fortuna and even Sors to a place in his Pantheon, and concedes the eternal presence of the irrational and the inexplicable.

It is a recognition which encourages intellectual humility. I venture to think, too, that our sense of the mystery and variousness of life is enlarged, when we realise that the very great may spring from the very small. How does Edmund Burke put it? 'A common soldier, a child, a girl at the door of an inn, have changed the face of fortune, and almost of Nature.' History is full of these momentous trifles—the accident which kills or preserves in life some figure of destiny; the weather on some critical battlefield, like the fog at Lützen or the snow at Towton; the change of wind which brings two fleets to a decisive action; the severe winter of 1788 which produces the famine of 1789, and thereby perhaps the French Revolution; the birth or the death of a child; a sudden idea which results in some potent invention. Let me give you an instance from recent history. The success of Turkish Nationalism under Kemal was due to the complete rout of the Greek armies in 1922 in Asia Minor. That ill-omened Greek campaign was largely due to the restoration in 1920 of King Constantine, which led to the Western Allies dissociating themselves from Greek policy and leaving Greece to her own devices. King Constantine was recalled as a consequence of a general election when M. Venizelos was defeated, and that election was held because young King Alexander, the *protégé* of the Allies, died early in the autumn of 1920. The cause of his death was blood-poisoning due to the bite of a pet monkey in the palace gardens. I cannot better Mr. Churchill's comment: 'A quarter of a million persons died of that monkey's bite.'

To look for such pregnant trifles is an instructive game, very suitable for academic circles in the winter season. But it must be played according to the rules. The business is to find the momentous accident, and obviously the smaller you make the accident, the more you reduce it to its ultimate elements, the more startling will be the disproportion between the vast consequence and the minute cause. The accident must be small, and it must be a true parent of consequences. Not every one will serve our purpose. Take Pascal's query—as to what would have happened to the world had Cleopatra's nose been a little shorter? The answer, I think, is—Not very much. Egypt, as the granary of the Roman world, was obviously a trump card for ambition to seize, and its importance did not depend upon the profile of its queen. Take another familiar speculation— what difference would it have made if Clive's pistol had not missed fire when, as a young man, he attempted suicide? Again, I think, the right answer is—Not a great deal. India was ripe for British conquest; if Clive had not led the way, some other would. In the middle decades of the sixteenth century a great deal seemed to depend upon the appearance of royal heirs, and historians have speculated as to what would have happened if Anne Boleyn had borne a male child, or Mary Tudor, or Mary of Scotland when she was the wife of the Dauphin of France. I doubt if there would have been any substantial change. The main lines of the future had been already determined by the complex of economic and intellectual forces which were responsible for the Reformation.

But let me offer to you—in the spirit of the game which I have suggested—one or two cases where destiny does seem for one moment to have trembled in the balance.

II

The first is a November day in London in the year 1612. There is a curious hush in the city. Men and women go about with soft feet and grave faces. People whisper anxiously at street corners; even the noise in the taverns is stilled. The only sound is a melancholy wind howling up the river. Suddenly above the wind rises the tolling of a bell, and at the sound women cover their heads and weep, and men uncover theirs and pray. For it is the Great Bell of Paul's, which tolls only for a royal death. It means that Henry, Prince of Wales, at the age of eighteen is dead. . . . He died of a malignant fever which puzzled the doctors. It was an age of strange diseases, but a prince was jealously guarded against them, and I think he must have caught the infection on one of his visits to Sir Walter Raleigh in the Bloody Tower, when he went to talk of high politics and hear tales of the Indies, and admire the model ship called *The Prince*, which Raleigh and Keymis had made for him. Prisons in those days, even prisons reserved for grandees, were haunts of pestilence, and in some alley of the Tower, in that heavy autumn weather, he may have caught the germ which brought him to his death. A chance breath drew the malignant micro-organism into his body, and he was doomed.

Suppose that breath had not been drawn, and that the Prince had lived the full span of life, for there was uncommon tenacity in his stock. So far as we can judge, he resembled his sister, Elizabeth of the Palatine, who was for many years the star to adventurous youth. In no respect did he resemble his brother

Charles. He was a *revenant* from the Elizabethan Age, and his chief mentor was Walter Raleigh himself. He was a Protestant enthusiast, to whom Protestantism was identified with patriotism, after the stalwart fashion of Cromwell thirty years later. Not for him any philandering with Spain. He would have gladly warned England as Cromwell did in 1656: 'Truly your great enemy is the Spaniard! He is naturally so—by reason of that enmity which is in him against whatsoever is of God.' When a French marriage was proposed to him he told his father that 'he was resolved that two religions should not lie in his bed.'

Had Henry lived, what might have happened? In European politics he would have made Britain the leader of the struggle against the Counter-Reformation. We cannot assess his abilities in the field, but, judging from the respect in which Raleigh held his brains, it is possible that he might have taken the place of Gustavus Adolphus. In any case Britain was a greater power than Sweden, and almost certainly he would have led the Continental Protestants. As for domestic affairs, it is clear that he had that indefinable magnetism which his sister had, and which attracted easily and instantly a universal popularity. He would have been a people's king. More, he would have shared the politics of the vast bulk of his subjects, their uncompromising Protestantism, their nascent imperialism. In ecclesiastical matters he would have found the *via media* which Charles missed. He would not have quarrelled with his Parliaments, for his views were theirs. They would have followed him voluntarily and raised no question of rights against the Crown, because the Crown thought as they did, and one does not question the rights of a willingly accepted leader. The change from the Tudor to the modern monarchy would have been of a very different kind. There would have been no Civil War. Cromwell might have died the first general in Europe and Duke of Huntingdon, while the guide of the monarchy into new constitutional paths might have been a great Scotsman, James Graham, the first Duke of Montrose, who some time about the year 1645 effected the union of the Scottish and English Parliaments.

Let us slip a hundred years and take the summer of 1711, when Marlborough was facing Villars before the famous *Ne Plus*

Ultra line of trenches. His classic victories were behind him, and the campaign of that summer is not familiar to the world like the campaigns of Blenheim and Ramillies and Malplaquet. Yet I think the most wonderful of all the great Duke's exploits fell in that year, when he outwitted Villars and planted himself beyond the Scheldt at Oisy, between Villars and France, and within easy reach of Arras and Cambrai. Had he had his country behind him, I cannot but believe that he was in a position to take Paris and bring the French monarchy to its knees. But, as all the world knows, his country was not behind him. He had lost the Queen's favour. Some small thing—an increasing arrogance in the manners of the Duchess Sarah, an extra adroitness in the diplomacy of Mrs. Masham—had wrought the change. Marlborough saw his triumphant career in the field cut short, and two years later came the Peace of Utrecht.

What might have happened had Mrs. Masham been less persuasive and the Duchess Sarah less domineering? As I have said, I do not think that anything could have kept Paris from Marlborough. With its capture would have come the degradation of the French monarchy, and the downfall from his pedestal of the Grand Monarque. With such a cataclysm there was bound to be a complete revision of the French system of government. There would also have come one of those stirrings of national pride which have always made France one of the most formidable nations in the world, and, I think, a rallying of her people to some sort of national and popular kingship. After that? Well, there would have been no French Revolution, for there would have been no need for it. But something akin to the French Revolution was inevitable somewhere in Europe towards the close of the eighteenth century, for it was the only way to get rid of a certain amount of mediaeval lumber. Where would it have taken place? Possibly in Britain. It was fortunate, perhaps, that in the intrigues of Queen Anne's bedchamber, Mrs. Masham got the better of the Duchess Sarah.

My next scene is in the last year of the century. I pass with reluctance over the intervening years, for they include many critical hours. In particular there was that hour some time during a December night in the year 1745, in the town of

Derby, when it was decided that Prince Charles should not march on London, but should retreat with his Highland army across the Border. Had the decision been otherwise, the Rebellion of the Forty-five might have succeeded, and much in British history might have been different. But I pass to a greater issue than the dynastic settlement of Britain—the French Revolution and the career of Napoleon. Professor Trevelyan, in a delightful essay, has expounded what might have been the course of history had Napoleon won the battle of Waterloo. That is not quite the kind of case we are in quest of, for the loss or winning of Waterloo was not a small thing. Let us go further back in Napoleon's career, to a day when the issue was not less momentous and the balance hung on a hair—the 19th day of Brumaire—the 9th day of November in the year 1799. The Government of the Directory was rotten; France was ripe for a change, for any policy or any leader that would give her what, after the first day or two, every revolution yearns for, order and peace. Napoleon, with his dubious Egyptian laurels fresh upon him, had arrived in Paris. The plot had been hatched and the conspirators assembled. The two Councils, the Council of the Ancients and the Council of the Five Hundred, had been summoned on that day, the 19th day of Brumaire, to meet at Saint-Cloud, and Sieyès and Napoleon had decided that by these assemblies the new Consulate should be formally authorised.

It is never wise to protract a *coup d'état*, and this one had been staged to occupy two days. On the afternoon of November 9, at Saint-Cloud, Napoleon was in a fever of impatience. His journey from Egypt, and the strain he had lately gone through, had caused an irritation in the skin of his sallow face, and now and then, in his excitement, he scratched it. He was a strange figure as he paced the little room facing on the park, while the Ancients assembled upstairs in the Salle Apollo, and the Five Hundred in the Orangerie below. At half-past three he made a silly, rambling speech to the Ancients, which none of them understood, and Bourrienne had to drag him away in the midst of general laughter. Then he proceeded to the Five Hundred, accompanied by a handful of grenadiers. He was shouted down, hustled about, and only extricated by his bodyguard. The game seemed irretrievably lost. . . . But in the meantime he had been scratching his inflamed face, and had caused it to bleed. Leaving his brother, Lucien, in the presidential chair to watch his interests, he went out of doors, and showed himself with his bleeding face to the soldiers. At once the rumour flew that there had been daggers used on the General, and that his life was in danger from loquacious civilians. It was enough. Presently Lucien joined him, and in a burning harangue to the troops made the most of that bleeding cheek. Murat, with a file of Guards, cleared out the Five Hundred, and, ere the November evening fell, Napoleon was not only the leader of the French Army, but the civilian head of the French people.

On one point among the wild events of that day all authorities are agreed. Napoleon fumbled and blundered, and the situation was saved by Lucien. But would Lucien have succeeded in his appeal to the troops but for the blood on his brother's face? It seems to me unlikely, as I read the story of that day. I am inclined to think that it was that fortunate affection of the skin, and the nervous excitement that caused him to scratch his face, which at a critical moment made plain Napoleon's path to the control of France.

Let us make another leap—to the hour of nine o'clock on the evening of May 2 in the year 1863. The place is among the scrub and the rough meadows of that part of Virginia called the Wilderness, near the hamlet of Chancellorsville. General Hooker, 'Fighting Joe Hooker,' is in command of the Federal Army of the Potomac, which comprises something like 130,000 men. He is the last hope of the Government in Washington, who have not been having much luck with their generals. He has promised them a crushing victory, and Lincoln, in the War Department there, is sitting anxiously at the end of the telegraph wire. Hooker has crossed the Rappahannock, and believes that the road is open before him to Richmond. In front of him lies a Confederate Army, the Army of Northern Virginia; it numbers not much more than 62,000 men, less than half the Federal force, but its commander is Robert Lee, and his chief lieutenant is Stonewall Jackson.

Hooker has followed a dangerous plan. He has divided his big army into two separate wings, thereby giving the small

Confederate force the advantage of the interior lines.   Jeb Stuart with his cavalry has given Lee prompt information about every Federal move. . . . Very early it became clear that Hooker intended to turn the Confederate left.   Lee, with the audacity of supreme genius, decided that, on the contrary, he would turn the Federal right, and make the outflanker the outflanked. Secretly, silently, Jackson made his way through the thick bush and the swamps of the Wilderness forest, and by the late afternoon of May 2, Hooker's right, utterly unsuspicious, suddenly became aware, by the rush of small deer and birds from the woods, that Jackson was upon them. . . . By seven o'clock the battle of Chancellorsville had been won.   Hooker was in full retreat. . . . But in a rout strange things may happen.   Detachments of the Federals straggled about in the darkness, and in the gloom of the woods came into conflict with Confederate detachments, and there was much wild firing.   Jackson and his staff, galloping to direct the pursuit, ran into the 18th North Carolina regiment, and were taken for the enemy.   The Carolinians fired a volley in the confusion, and Jackson fell with three bullets in him.   Eight days later he died.

It was the blindest mischance, but it had momentous consequences.   In Jackson, Lee lost his right hand and a third of his brains.   Two months after Chancellorsville he fought the indecisive action of Gettysburg, an action in which the absence of complete victory meant defeat.   Lee always said that if he had had Jackson with him he would have won the battle, and I believe that he was right.   If Lee had won Gettysburg then I am convinced that there would have been a negotiated peace. The North was sick to death of the war, and a Southern victory in Pennsylvania would have broken the last remnant of Washington's nerve.   Lincoln's stern determination to accept nothing less than complete victory and unconditional surrender would have been overruled. . . .   What would have happened then? Lincoln would not have been assassinated;   there would have been little bitterness left over on either side, since neither was the conqueror.   In the inevitable reconstruction which must have followed it is difficult to believe that two such men as Lincoln and Lee would not have achieved a reasonable compromise, and a reconstituted United States.   There must have been drastic, and probably beneficial, changes in that most cumbrous instrument, the American Constitution. Slavery would have been abolished on equitable terms, for Lee was at least as eager in that cause as Lincoln. Beyond that we need not penetrate. But we can at least say that America's development, economic, political, constitutional and spiritual, would have been very different from what it is to-day. That North Carolina volley, fired blindly in the woodland dusk on that May evening, was one of the most fateful in history.

Half a century more and we come to the Great War. I suppose we must rank the First Battle of the Marne as one of the two or three decisive battles of the world. If Germany had won, she would have attained the victory of which she dreamed 'before the leaves fell.' What was the *causa causans*, the little extra weighting of the scales, which turned the balance on that long battle front between the suburbs of Paris and the hills of Nancy? It is impossible to be certain. The Germans say that it was the disastrous visit of Colonel Hentsch, the plenipotentiary of Great Headquarters, to Bülow and Kluck at noon on Wednesday, September 9. The French say that it was the march of the French 42nd Division under Foch on the evening of the 8th. It may also be argued that it was the advance of the British 2nd Corps north of the Marne early on the 9th, which by good fortune touched the most sensitive portion of the German front. I think that the right answer is that there was no one such cause; there were half a dozen.

But let us take a moment seven months later—the attack of the British fleet on the Dardanelles. On Thursday, March 18, Admiral John de Robeck launched his assault on the Narrows. He silenced most of the forts, and the attack seemed to be proceeding well, until suddenly he began to lose ships from mines; first the *Bouvet*, then the *Irresistible*, then the *Ocean*. But when he broke off the action he intended to resume it later, and he and the Government in London were still confident that it would be carried presently to a successful issue.

Then something happened to change his view. In the second volume of his book, *The World Crisis*, Mr. Winston Churchill has told dramatically the tale of that see-saw of hopes and fears. On the 23rd Admiral de Robeck, after a talk with Sir Ian Hamilton, telegraphed to London that he could not continue the naval attack till the army was ready to co-operate, and that that would not be before April 14. Lord Fisher promptly swung round to his side, his argument being that we need not lose any more ships when Britain was bound to win in any case, seeing that the British were the lost ten tribes of Israel! The other Admirals, as Mr. Churchill says, 'stuck their toes in.' Mr. Asquith, though inclined to Mr. Churchill's view, was not prepared to intervene and override naval opinion both at home and on the spot. The naval attack was dropped, and we waited for a month to land an army, with results which are only too well remembered. Turkey was at her last gasp, and to her amazement was given a breathing space, of which she made brilliant use.

What made Admiral de Robeck change his mind, for it is clear that it was his change of mind which was the determining factor? It may have been his talk with Sir Ian Hamilton which opened to him a prospect of combined operations against the Gallipoli Peninsula, a prospect which he had not realised before, and which relieved him of a share of his heavy responsibilities. But we can narrow down the cause to something still smaller. What made his responsibilities seem so heavy? It was the presence of unsuspected mines in the Narrows on March 18 that caused our losses and thereby shook the nerve of the naval staff. How did the mines get there? Ten days earlier a little Turkish steamer called the *Nousret* had dodged the British night patrol of destroyers, and laid a new line of twenty mines in Eren Kui Bay. On March 16 three of these mines were destroyed by our sweepers, but we did not realise that they were part of a *line* of mines, and so we did not look for more. If we had made a different deduction there would have been no casualties on the 18th, and de Robeck on the 19th or 20th must have taken his fleet into the Sea of Marmora.

The officer in charge of the little *Nousret* did not know, probably—if he is still alive—does not yet know, the fatefulness of his deed. It altered the whole course of the War, for at that moment Turkey was in the most literal truth at her last gasp. We have the evidence of Enver; we have the evidence of half a dozen Germans on the spot. She was almost out of munitions,

B

and her resistance in the Narrows that day was the last effort of which she was capable in defence. Her Government had its papers packed, and was about to leave for the uplands of Asia Minor. I have talked to a distinguished German diplomatist who was then in Constantinople, and he has described to me the complete despair of the Turkish Government and their German advisers. They believed that it was mathematically certain that in a day or two Constantinople would be in British hands. When they heard that the British fleet had given up the attack they could not believe their ears; it seemed to them the most insane renunciation of a certain victory.

The occupation of Constantinople would have meant that Turkey fell out of the War. It would have meant much more. Bulgaria would never have become an ally of the Central Powers. The way would have been prepared to supply the needs of Russia, and Russia would have been kept in close touch with her Western allies. There would have been no Russian Revolution, or, if revolution had come, it would have taken a very different form. Austria would have been caught in flank and presently put out of action. It would have meant that in all human likelihood the Allies would have been victorious early in the year 1916. What oceans of blood and treasure would have been saved, what a different world we should be living in to-day, had an obscure Turkish sailorman not laid his mines in the way he did on that March evening!

III

I have put before you a few crucial moments in history, when a great event has been determined by some small thing which it is difficult to describe as anything but an accident—something which we cannot explain by reference to profound causes, something which it is not easy to rationalise. My argument is a modest one: simply that we should not attempt to impress our modern whim upon the immutable past, and press our theories of historical processes too far. We must have these theories, and they explain a great deal, but they do not explain everything. We must interpret as well as chronicle, we must attempt to show the interconnection of events; but let us be chary about large mechanical principles of interpretation which explain too much.

Let us by all means accept the doctrine of predestination, whether in its metaphysical or theological form, so long as we do not try to show in detail how it works. The danger is not with it, for at bottom it is a poetic or religious conception rather than a scientific. The danger is rather with the pseudo-scientists, the Buckles and Guizots and Taines and their modern counterparts, who dogmatise about the details, and believe that they can provide a neat explanation of everything in the past by subsuming it under a dozen categories; and with the doctrinaires, like Marx and his school, who would fit the centuries into the iron bed of a single formula. The answer is an appeal to facts, to the stubborn nodules of the unrelated and the inexplicable which everywhere confront us. The romantic accident cannot be expelled by the mechanical doctrine. It will still come out of the void, alter the course of history, and disappear before it can be classified.

This parlour game, which I suggest to you for a winter fireside, has its own seriousness. To reflect how easily the course of things might have been different is to learn perspective and humility. The world is bigger and more intricate than we thought, and there are more things in heaven and earth than we can bring within the pale of any copy-book philosophy. To-day, physical science is in a modest mood. It admits frankly a large hinterland of mystery. 'While Newton,' David Hume wrote in his *Dialogues*, 'seemed to draw off the veil from the mystery of Nature, he showed at the same time the imperfections of the mechanical philosophy; and thereby restored her ultimate secrets to that obscurity in which they ever did, and ever will, remain.' The physical scientist of to-day, though he may not approve the scepticism of Hume's last sentence, is well aware of the imperfections of a mechanical creed. Philosophy, too, has, I think, learned humility. At any rate she has abated something of her exclusive arrogance, and the lines of Pope have almost become true:

> ' Physic of Metaphysic begs defence,
> And Metaphysic calls for aid on Sense.'

Surely the Muse of History, whose domain has not the rigour of the natural sciences, or the ancient right of metaphysics to dogmatise, should not be behind her sisters in this noble modesty.

I suggest as a suitable motto for Clio's servants some words of one of the greatest of them, a passage of Burke in his *Letters on a Regicide Peace*:

'It is often impossible, in these political enquiries, to find any proportion between the apparent force of any moral causes we may assign, and their known operation. We are therefore obliged to deliver up that operation to mere chance; or, more piously (perhaps more rationally), to the occasional interposition and the irresistible hand of the Great Disposer.'

II
JULIUS CAESAR

To

MY FRIEND

AIRCRAFTMAN T. E. SHAW

Two main types may be discerned in the inner circle of human greatness. One is the cyclopean architect, the daimonic force who swings the world into a new orbit, whose work is as plain as the result of some convulsion of nature, but whose personality is hard to discover behind the colossal façade of his achievements, and at whose mental processes we can only guess. Such are the conquerors, the men of the sword, the Alexanders and Charlemagnes. The second is the man whose business is directly with souls, the thinker, the priest, and the prophet. His influence is to be looked for in no solid concrete creation, but must be traced through a thousand intricate channels, like the advent of spring. The minds of such we know fully, for the mind was their tool, and the mind of man was the object on which they wrought.

Caesar belongs to neither type. He performed the greatest constructive task ever achieved by human hands. He drew the habitable earth into an empire which lasted for five centuries, and he laid the foundations of a fabric of law and government which is still standing after two thousand years. He made the world possible for the Christian faith, so that there was reason in the mediaeval belief which saw in him a Bishop and a Father of the Church. He gave humanity order and peace, and thereby prepared the ground for many precious seeds. His genius as soldier and law-maker is amply proven. The greatest of poets called him 'the noblest man that ever lived in the tide of times.' But although we can come under the spell of his magnificence and appraise his character, we cannot probe to its inner springs. About the mind of this man, his inmost thoughts and dreams, there is still a mystery. We know the things that he did, but not why he did them.

He emerges from the clouds of mythology, lives his life in clear air, and then disappears in a divine mist. He was sprung from the ancient kings of Rome, and had the Goddess of Love herself as an ancestress. Before his death he was regarded by the Roman populace as a god, and later he was believed to have

legal phrase went, 'in arbitratu, dicione, potestate, amicitiave
populi Romani.' By the beginning of the third century before
Christ, Rome had become mistress of the Italian peninsula. In
the second century the Macedonian and Punic wars had given
her Greece and part of North Africa, and by its close she controlled the whole Mediterranean basin and had fallen heir to the
greater part of the empire of Alexander. It was an uneasy
suzerainty; her new empire was not integrated under any plan,
but presented a baffling collection of diverse polities, and even
in Italy itself there was no complete acceptance of her rule. The
frontiers, too, were still fluid; in the east, Anatolia was a mutter-
ing volcano; beyond it, stretching into the dim spaces of Asia,
the Parthian power hung like a thunder-cloud; while to the
north and west lay the unconquered Celtic and Germanic peoples,
whose strange tumultuous mass movements had already threatened her very citadel.

This miraculous expansion was achieved rather by accident
than by design. A bold and adventurous spirit like the elder
Scipio accepted it with open eyes; but the majority of Romans
drifted into it by the sheer compulsion of facts, and there were
not wanting men like the elder Cato, who would have confined
the Roman rule to Italy. But the pressure of circumstance was
too strong; conquests brought wealth, and money is a potent
argument; the governing aristocracy became rapidly a plutocracy, its appetite growing with each success. In spite of itself
the City-State had become the Great-State.

Yet it retained its antique urban constitution, and the forms
which had sufficed for a simple community of farmers were
strained so as to embrace the inhabited globe. A city with less
than half a million free denizens, a city-state with less than a
million voters, attempted to control a greater domain than
Alexander's. This paradox was matched by the paradox of the
constitution itself. The Roman people reigned but did not
govern. The permanent governing power was the Senate,
which had steered the republic through the great wars of defence
and conquest. It prepared the laws for the people to ratify, and
received into its body the magistrates whom the people elected.
By the end of the second century it had become virtually an
oligarchy of office-holding families. The Assembly, the legal

sovereign, had less actual power than a king in the most limited of monarchies. The senatorial oligarchy, who gave themselves the name of Optimates as embodying all the traditional wisdom of the state, were resolute to retain their privileges, and exclude from their ranks all 'new men' who did not come within that sacred circle which could count curule magistrates in its ancestry. As against it, there grew up the party of the Populares, who laid the emphasis on the rule of the whole community; but the opposition was illusory, since they too accepted the machine of the old city-state, which made impossible any serious popular government. How could the whole nation assemble in the narrow limits of the Field of Mars, and vote intelligently on a question obscurely propounded by a magistrate? The power of the people lay only in the election of officials, and not in decisions on policy, and elections tended consequently to be a sordid business of personal influence and lavish bribes. A superior magistracy carried with it the government of one of the overseas provinces, and therefore ample opportunities for enrichment; so the functions of the sovereign people were limited to deciding which members of the oligarchy should be given the privilege and in return for what largesse.

Such a constitution would have worked badly in a small self-contained state. There was no easy mechanism of change, and emergencies had to be met by special appointments and by the suspension of laws—expedients which brought the normal law into contempt. The Senate was perpetually, as Tacitus said of Pompey, 'suarum legum auctor ac subversor.' The administration of the foreign domains was little better than a farce. There was no principle of provincial government, and therefore no continuity; everything depended upon the character of the proconsul. There was no permanent civil service at home or abroad, and the ordering of the city itself was as casual as the administration of Greece and Macedonia. As for public finance, it was naked chaos. The state domains and the tribute due from foreign possessions were farmed out to joint-stock companies of Roman capitalists. The Roman polity at the close of the second century before Christ has been described not unfairly as 'government by the unpaid aristocrat and exploitation by the irresponsible profiteer.'

In such a commonwealth much will depend upon the armed forces. Rome had travelled far from the citizen militia which had built up her greatness. There is no such guarantee for sobriety in public affairs as the fact that any citizen may have to risk his life for the policy which he approves. Armies were now no longer conscript but volunteer, and the soldier was a professional, enlisted under a particular general for a particular campaign, and looking to that general for his reward. His loyalty was owed to him and not to the state, and the *sacramentum*, or military oath, was his charter. Such an army of mercenaries put into the hand of a great commander a most potent weapon, for it was his personal following and could be readily used to cut the knots in political dispute.

If the ancient polity of Rome was proving inadequate to the new duties laid upon it, the spirit which had created that polity and had given it value was rapidly disappearing. The strength of the antique Roman character lay in its narrowness, its Calvinistic sense of sin, its austere conception of civic and personal duty, its hardy asceticism, its rigid family ties. Such a type could not adjust itself to novel conditions; if the traditional sanctions were once weakened the whole fabric must crumble. The new Roman had not the *gravitas* of his ancestors. The opening up to him of Greece and the East had induced new tastes and appetites, and he had fallen under the spell of both the refinements and the luxuries of the Hellenic world. His strict domestic discipline had broken down, and popular opinion admitted extravagances and vices which would have been unthinkable in the old republic. The traditional *pietas* had largely gone, for Greek philosophy was a sceptical dissolvent of the antique religion. What had once been a faith which governed the homeliest incidents of daily life was now only an antiquarian tradition retained for political purposes. The masses fell back upon blind superstition and exotic cults, and the finer minds sought a refuge in the cosmic speculations of the Greek thinkers, or, like Lucretius, in an austere intellectualism which was a near neighbour to despair. A vague belief in the *anima mundi* had not the same influence on conduct as the concrete faith which was intertwined with household laws. Doubtless there were many both among the patricians and the new middle class who still stood in the old ways, for it is easy to paint too dark a picture of Roman decadence. There were still those to whom the home was a dominant loyalty, and who could say with Cicero—'Hic arae sunt, hic foci, hic di penates; hic sacra, religiones, caerimoniae continentur.' But for the bulk of the people the past was dead, and they had to face new seas and tides without chart or compass.

The older aristocracy, at the close of the second century, had either relapsed upon a barren pride of birth, drawing in their skirts from an unfamiliar world, or had joined with the 'new men' in the frantic race for wealth. It was the rise of these new men that made the chief feature of the epoch. The Equites, the upper middle class, were the great capitalists of the day. They farmed the state rents and taxes, contracted for the armies, made fortunes in the slave trade, and controlled the banks. Usury was one of the main industries of the Roman world, which speculated on a gigantic scale and was perpetually in debt. To be a banker was the readiest way to fortune. The big joint-stock companies made advances to rich and poor, accepted deposits, and by means of a cheque system transferred cash throughout the empire. They played a useful, indeed an indispensable, part, but they were the main agents in furthering the systematic plunder of the provinces by Roman officials, and in encouraging the insensate speculative mania in Rome herself. They were responsible for the fact that half the people were always in debt, and that the cry of repudiation was the stock-in-trade of every demagogue.

Below the business class came the Roman populace, now very mixed in blood. Paying no taxes and bearing no civic burdens, they had nevertheless their votes in the Assembly and were a dangerous powder-magazine for sparks. A city like Rome had no corn lands within easy reach, transport was difficult and slow, so it became necessary to organise the food supply. The import and supply of cheap food was a necessity if the people were not to starve, and it was only a step from selling corn below the market-price to distributing it free. The masses lived in huge warrens of slum-tenements (a favourite investment of the new capitalists), and spent most of their time in the Forum and in the streets. The old free artificers and tradesmen were fewer in number, since the great houses with their slaves and freedmen were self-contained economic units, and most of the workers were unskilled labourers. The police system was rudimentary, and both life and property were insecure. The poorer freemen of Rome had become little better than parasites, living largely on doles, kept amused by free shows, accustomed to rioting with little police interference. No demagogue had ever better material for his purpose, so small wonder that demagogy became a recognised profession. The masses were told that they were the real rulers of the world, and, since their life was brutish and uncertain, they would readily welcome any revolution which might give them the fruits of that rule. They had nothing to lose by disorder and much to gain.

At the bottom of the social pyramid were the hordes of slaves, that canker of the ancient world. Slavery under the old rural regime had been often a tolerable rule of life with its own dignity; but in the welter of the new capitalist society it was an unmitigated evil. The slaves crowded the freemen out of the arts and crafts, and many of them acquired a potent secret influence over their masters and the conduct of private and public business. In town and country alike they did all the menial work and most of the superior management. In Rome itself they numbered over a quarter of a million. They were of every type, from the artistic and scholarly Greeks to the roughs of the cattle ranches. Here was a vast population of which the state had no control, a private army over which the masters had powers of life and death, a race who owed no loyalty to the commonwealth. Such an element was not only a perpetual danger to the state, but it perverted the moral sense of the best citizens. In it we may find the chief source of the instability of ancient societies, and of that coarseness of fibre which offends us even in what we most deeply admire. With slavery as a sinister background there could be no true *humanitas*.

The close of the second century was, therefore, for Rome a time of unsettlement and doubt, when to the wisest minds it seemed that the commonwealth had entered upon a decline. It was a period of immense material progress. Rome had most of the world at her feet, and her citizens were growing rich with the accumulated wealth of eastern despotisms. The little town of tufa and stucco, sprawled over its many hills, was rapidly becoming a city of marble. But behind this splendid façade there were signs of decay. The great patrician houses produced either haughty and half-witted reactionaries—'homines prae-posteri'—or degenerates who joined in the scramble for wealth. The middle classes had built up a capitalistic system which was oppressing the overseas provinces, ruining the free agriculture of Italy, and winding the whole people in coils of debt. A false imperialism, based on the interests of the capitalists, regarded the provinces as mere milch-cows from which tribute could be drawn. In Rome herself, a mongrel population, petted and pampered and yet eternally on the verge of famine, had taken the place of the old stalwart freemen, while the slave masses were a perilous undigested element in the body politic. Worse still, the ancient moral standards of personal continence and discipline and of public loyalty were gravely weakened. The aristocracy had become an oligarchy and largely a plutocracy; the Senate was losing the power to govern; and the whole machinery of the state was cracking under burdens for which it had not been designed.

To wise men it was becoming clear that three reforms were overdue. The central government must be put into stronger and cleaner hands; the power of the capitalists to mismanage the public finances and oppress the masses must be curbed; and some means must be found of organising the new empire not as a bundle of alien tributary states, but as one great organic polity. These ideas had scarcely yet come to birth, but they were in the germ, and they meant the renunciation of the former Roman doctrines of government and the narrow bounds of the city-state. The conquests of Alexander and the lessons taught by the Greek political theorists pointed the same moral, for they involved the conception of the earth as one universal society, in which all free men were equal citizens, and of the state not as a city but as a cosmopolis. They involved something more—some opportunism about the nature of the central power, and the abandonment of the old republican rigidity. It was plain to the wise that the affairs of Rome, for all her apparent splendour, were moving fast to a crisis, and the words spoken by Cicero half a century later were already being whispered in secret: 'No issue can be looked for from discords among the leading men except either universal ruin, or the rule of a conqueror, or a monarchy.'

II

THE FORERUNNERS

IN the last century of the republic there was no dearth of would-be reformers. The ills of the state were not hard to diagnose, but there was little agreement about the cure. There were the idolaters of the past, the antiquarians, who tried to achieve the impossible and revive creeds and manners that had gone. There were the enlightened aristocrats who strove to marry what was best in the old and new cultures, and to create a type of Roman in whom a liberal philosophy should not weaken the ancient fibre. Such an one was the younger Scipio, the perfect example of a Roman gentleman, wise, moderate, urbane, clear-sighted; but he was as ineffective to cure the mischief as was Lord Falkland to stem the tide of the English Civil War. The trouble needed more drastic surgery.

The first of the rough surgeons were the two Gracchi, the grandsons of the great Scipio Africanus. The elder, Tiberius, who was born in 163, grappled with the eternal land question, and as tribune carried an agrarian law to make state lands, illegally held by the big landowners, available for settlement by landless citizens. When the opposition to his policy proved too strong to be met by constitutional methods, he summoned a bodyguard from the pavement, and at the age of thirty was crushed in that arbitrament of force to which he had appealed. He tried to build his authority on the popular Assembly, but no serious democracy could be based on what had become a farcical piece of mechanism. Gaius, the younger brother, carried on the work of the dead Tiberius, but with a bolder hand and a wider vision. As tribune he stretched the tribunician power to its extreme limits, and presently passed beyond them into what was constitutionally rebellion. There is scarcely a conception of the later reformers which is not to be found in the policy of Gaius Gracchus. His aim seems to have been to create a perpetual magistracy based on the tribunician power, to transfer the practical sovereignty from the Senate to the popular Assembly and the middle classes, and to replace the city-state by an Italian nation. But such a course meant a defiance of the existing law, and he had not the force behind him for successful revolution. The varied antagonisms which he had roused coalesced against him, and his end was a violent death. One lesson stood out from the failure of the brothers for all to read. For a reformer a bodyguard from the pavement was not enough; he must have behind him an army.

Presently appeared the popular leader with the army, but he was not the stuff of which revolutionary statesmen are made. Gaius Marius, the son of a Latin farmer, rose from the ranks to be commander-in-chief against Jugurtha, and became consul fourteen years after the death of the younger Gracchus. He recast the army on a democratic basis, rolled back the invasion of the Cimbri and the Teutons, and became the virtual dictator of Rome. But Marius was only a peasant of genius, slow-witted, inelastic, a good soldier but a blundering politician. Seven times he was consul, and when he returned to Rome as conqueror he was naturally called to the leadership of the Populares. But he was in the hands of demagogues, who professed to carry out the dreams of Gaius Gracchus without comprehending their true purpose. The uneasy alliance dissolved, Marius dropped out of public life, and the senatorial party won the triumph which falls to those who know their own minds. An attempt at reform from the side of the moderate aristocrats succeeded no better, and its leader, Livius Drusus, went the way of the Gracchi. But the silencing of protesting voices could not bring peace; the incompetence of the Senate, the greed of the capitalists, the unrest of the Roman mob, and the discontent of the unenfranchised Italians remained; and at the close of the first decade of the last century before Christ all Italy was in the throes of insurrection.

Some reconstruction was inevitable, even if it were only temporary and partial, and to this task a remarkable man set his hand. Lucius Cornelius Sulla was sprung from one of the oldest of the patrician houses, and had spent his youth as a dissolute man of fashion and an amateur of art and letters. But the war with Jugurtha revealed to him his exceptional military talent,

C

and thenceforth he was above all things a soldier, with a soldier's contempt for political squabbles. The honours of the last phase of the North African campaign fell to him, he played a leading part in the defeat of the Cimbri and the Teutons and in quelling the Italian revolt, and earlier he had, as propraetor in Asia, patched up a truce with Mithridates of Pontus. He was consul when Mithridates took the field again and crossed the Bosphorus and overran Greece, and he was appointed to command against the most formidable foe that Rome had known since Hannibal. But he was suspected by the popular party, and by a decree of the people the charge of the war against Mithridates was entrusted to Marius.

Sulla did not hesitate. He had little respect for aristocracy, capitalists or rabble, but he was determined to defend his country, and he had no belief in his old leader. He marched his six legions on Rome, took the city, and lit his watch-fires in the market-place, while Marius fled to the salt marshes of Minturnae. He proceeded to put together an interim constitution, the basis of which was the degradation of the Assembly and the restoration of the right of initiative to the Senate. Otherwise he allowed the Gracchan innovations to stand. Then, leaving as he well knew no secure settlement behind him, he embarked his legions for the East. This contemptuous grandee, with his piercing blue eyes and blotched face 'like a floury mulberry,' was cynical about all things but one: he hated cant and bungling, and was resolute to face realities. The major problem was to crush Mithridates, and he was ready to let politics at Rome drift into chaos so long as this task was accomplished. So with 30,000 men and no fleet he set out against a conqueror who had command of the sea and of armies unnumbered, and already controlled every Roman domain east of the Adriatic except a fragment of Macedonia.

Sulla was absent for four years, and meantime Rome was in anarchy. The popular party, with Cinna at its head, repealed the Sullan acts, old Marius returned from exile, and there followed a great massacre of opponents. Marius, savage, drunken and now half insane, passed in 86 to a dishonoured death, and till 84 Cinna was virtually tyrant of Rome. He had no serious policy, beyond revenge upon his enemies and sops to the mob, but under

his rule the rights of citizenship were finally confirmed to all Italy
south of the Po. Anxiously he kept his eyes on the East, where
month by month Sulla was moving steadily on his career of
conquest. Nothing perturbed that extraordinary man. When
Rome sent a general to replace him, he won over the general's
troops, and he made his own armies his loyal personal following.
He finished his immediate task, made terms with Mithridates,
and in 83 returned to Italy, with a veteran army and ample
treasure. Some of the ablest of the officers who had taken
service under Cinna joined him, like the young Pompey and the
young Marcus Crassus, the government levies melted before
him, and in a battle at the very gates of Rome the last stand of
the Populares was broken. Sulla was made dictator for such
time as he pleased to hold office, with absolute power over the
lives of Romans and the laws of Rome.

He was too humorous and too cynical to be cruel for cruelty's
sake, and the terrible proscription which followed had a reasoned
purpose—to get rid for good of troublesome opponents, and to
discourage for the future performances like those of Marius and
Cinna. Then, before retiring to the leisure which he had amply
earned and the pleasures which were his main interest in life, he
set to work to remake the constitution. He despised alike the
mob and the aristocracy, but concluded that the latter was 'the
more natural beast of the twain,' so the object of his changes was
to aggrandise the Senate, teach the middle class its place, and
put the rabble in bonds. One thing he did not touch; he left
the Roman citizenship to the Italians, for he saw the folly of again
stirring up that secular strife. Also, like the Gracchi, he established many new colonies, chiefly of his former soldiers, who, he
believed, would act as a guard for his new regime. He increased
the numbers of the Senate, made it an oligarchy of officials by
confining its membership to those who had held the higher
magistracies, and secured to it the legislative initiative. He
established a strict *cursus honorum*, and weakened the tribunate
by imposing a heavy fine for the improper use of the veto, and
laying it down that a tribune was disqualified from standing for a
higher office. He abolished the corn doles. He took the jury-
courts away from the Equites and restored them to the Senate,
and he dealt a heavy and just blow at the capitalists by putting

an end to the farming of the revenues of Asia and making each province levy its own tribute.

There was much that was good in his reconstruction. If Sulla is to be credited with any principle, it was a belief in the republic, and he sincerely thought that he was restoring republican institutions. He had given the Roman oligarchy a last chance. It was not an aristocratic restoration, for there was no real aristocracy left, but it was an attempt to create an efficient bureaucracy backed by an efficient police. It solved no one of Rome's greater problems, such as the relation of the new mercenary armies to the civil power, or the absorption of the provinces into the Roman polity. But Sulla was not concerned with the dim future; it was enough for him to set the old machine going again, so that he could withdraw to the life of ease which he loved. A cynic to the core, he feared danger no more than he feared the mouthings of the demagogues. Though many thousands desired his death, he laid down his dictator's power and retired calmly to the life of the sportsman, the epicure, and the literary dilettante. A year later, fortunate to the last, he died peacefully in his bed. All Italy stood around his pyre, and the women of Rome mourned him for a year.

The Sullan reconstruction left, as I have said, the main blemishes in the state untouched. It put the government into the hands of an official oligarchy who had lost the talent for government, and had in any case at their disposal a most unworkable machine. The narrow city-state had gone, but a body of citizens scattered throughout the Italian peninsula were no better fitted to administer an empire. Moreover, the credulous and undisciplined urban mob had still ample power to make mischief. It did not take from the capitalists the opportunities of public plunder. It did not diminish the opposition between Optimates and Populares, between those who had and those who had not, but the opposition had become merely opportunist and had no serious basis of principle. Cicero defined the Optimates as those who said and did what pleased the best men, but the word 'best' was equivocal. There were among the Optimates stiff relic-worshippers, republicans of the old rock, who had forgotten nothing and learned nothing; but there were also moderate men, especially among the jurists, who saw the necessity of reform. In the ranks of the Populares were shallow radicals who worshipped phrases and bankrupts who hungered for revolution, but there were also many solid citizens who resented the contempt of the aristocrats, and all the classes proscribed by Sulla, and the aspiring young men who always draw to an opposition. One thing was clear. Politics had become the profession of every ambitious Roman, and everywhere political clubs and coteries were springing up like weeds. Through politics alone a man could win to wealth and high civil and military command.

Such was the view of a young cadet of the great Julian house just back from the East, whose candid eyes were now surveying the Roman scene.

III

THE YOUTH OF CAESAR

THIS young man, Gaius Julius Caesar, was born on the 12th of July 102, the year when at Aquae Sextiae Marius checked the advance of the Teutons in Gaul. He belonged to a branch of the patrician Julian family, which traced descent from Aeneas and so from the gods, and his grandmother Marcia claimed the blood of Ancus Marcius, the fourth of the early Roman kings. His mother, Aurelia, was also of the inner circle of the aristocracy. His branch of the Julii had held in recent generations many high public offices, but had produced no figure of the first importance. They were patricians of the moderate school, and his aunt Julia had broken with the traditions of her caste and married the plebeian Marius.

When he was not yet eighteen his father died, for the Caesars were a short-lived race. His mother lived for thirty years more, long enough to see her son the conqueror of Gaul, and it would appear that Aurelia was the chief formative influence of his youth. To the end of her life she was his friend and counsellor, a gentler figure than the mother of the Gracchi, but with much of the antique Roman discipline. Of his education we know little. He had as tutor not a Greek but a Cisalpine Gaul, but, according to the fashion, most of his training must have been on Greek lines, since the Latin schools of rhetoric were closed when he was ten years old. For Hellenic culture he cherished an abiding love; when in 48 Athens surrendered to him after Pharsalus, he spared the people 'because of their dead'; nevertheless he was always more Roman than Greek in his habits of thought. He dabbled in literature, and wrote a tragedy and some boyish love-songs, which long afterwards Augustus took pains to suppress, believing that they would not add to his fame; he also acquired two hobbies which never left him, astronomy and an eager curiosity about the undiscovered regions of the globe, and he pored over the Alexandrian geographers.

Quite early he seems to have developed an interest in politics, and to have leaned, through the influence of his mother, and of the Marian circle to which his aunt's marriage introduced him, to the side of the Populares. When he was sixteen Marius and Cinna nominated him as *flamen dialis*, or priest of Jupiter, and his father, who was then living, did not object. When he was nineteen he married Cornelia, Cinna's daughter, a bold step, for Cinna's power was crumbling and the avenging Sulla was on the seas. A year later his cousin, the younger Marius, died at Praeneste, and had his head spiked in the market-place to the accompaniment of Sulla's caustic epigram, 'One must first become an oarsman before handling the rudder.' Presently the conqueror set about rearranging Roman society. Pompey obediently divorced his wife at Sulla's command and accepted the hand of his step-daughter. But the young Caesar defied him. He refused to divorce Cinna's daughter, with the con-sequence that he lost his priesthood and his wife's dowry, and was compelled to hide in fever-stricken nooks of the Apennines, being saved only by the influence of his mother's house and the intercession of the college of the Vestal Virgins. It was a bold act for a young man of twenty, but Caesar never throughout his life knew the meaning of fear.

His politics were still a boy's politics, based on personalities and romance. Old Marius his kinsman, of whose ugly side he knew little, had been the hero of his youth, and his cousin, the younger Marius, was a picturesque adventurer. A boy takes sides in any quarrel, and Caesar's side was predestined. He was brought daily into contact with the leaders of the Populares, and also with the rising capitalist classes. His father had tried to marry him to a financier's daughter, and his niece had espoused one Gaius Octavius, the son of a rich country banker. He heard the talk of these people, their complaints of the inefficiency of the Senate and the blundering arrogance of the oligarchy, and it sank deep into his mind. He may also have suffered personally from the boorishness of the elder senatorians and the raffish insolence of the younger. But he was a young man with whom no one took liberties, very courteous and with a pleasant wit of his own, but not inclined to air his opinions or reveal his heart. Cicero, who knew him as a boy, makes fun in his

letters of every other contemporary, but he never trifles with
Caesar.

From earliest youth he cast a curious spell over all who met
him. He had a genius for attracting people to him, and doing
kindnesses with a graciousness which left no sting. Already he
was schooling himself to discover men's souls and play on them
as on an instrument of music. He ranked as tall among the
small-boned Romans—perhaps five foot eight; he was very slim,
but his figure was wiry and athletic, and he excelled in swimming,
riding, and swordsmanship. In a gluttonous age he was noted
for his moderation in both food and wine. He dressed carefully
and always kept his body in hard condition. His head was large,
beautifully shaped, and set on a sinewy neck; his forehead was
broad, his nose strong and aquiline, his complexion a healthy
pallor, and his eye dark and piercing like an eagle's. He was
capable of feats of great endurance, but constitutionally he was
always a little delicate, suffering from recurring bouts of fever.
Altogether a formidable young man, whose eyes revealed nothing
and missed nothing, a puzzle alike to strenuous *arrivistes* like
Cicero and to the apolaustic youth of his own class. He was
biding his time and forming himself, for he remembered Sulla's
gibe about his cousin Marius.

When he escaped the Sullan proscription he went to the East
for his term of military service. He served under one of Sulla's
lieutenants at the siege of Mytilene, and won the 'civic crown'
for saving a soldier's life. He was despatched on duty to Bithynia,
whose king, Nicomedes, had been restored to the throne. A
quarter of a century later Roman gossip credited him with in-
dulging at Nicomedes' court in orgies of oriental vice. There
is no reason to believe the slander, for it was one regularly spread
in the Roman world about every great figure in public life, just
as charges of incontinence were automatically levied by the
Puritans against every Cavalier. Exotic debaucheries had no
attraction for Caesar, and it is to be noted that in a plea for
certain Bithynians, made when he was Pontifex Maximus, he
spoke most frankly and naturally of his dealings with Nicomedes,
which scarcely suggests a guilty conscience. After Mytilene he
joined the fleet of Servilius Isauricus in its campaign against the
Cilician pirates. While there he heard of Sulla's death, and

returned to Rome to see if the political world was now ripe for his entrance.

He arrived in time for the abortive rebellion of Lepidus, a light-headed enterprise with which, though solicited by young Cinna his brother-in-law, he would have nothing to do. Instead he turned to the law-courts. He was not rich, but Aurelia had carefully conserved his inheritance, and he had enough to launch him in public life. He prosecuted the ex-proconsul of Macedonia on a charge of extortion, and, though he failed to secure a conviction, he won a certain amount of repute. Next year he attacked another malefactor of the same type and failed again. Clearly he required more training, so, characteristically, he went to seek it where it could best be got. At the age of twenty-eight he sailed for Rhodes to study under Apollonius Molo, who had been Cicero's master. He had no cause to lose heart because of his comparative failure in the law-courts. Cicero, who had a complete professional training, undertook no political case till he was thirty-six.

But the next year was not to be one of academic study, but an interlude of wild adventure. On the way to Rhodes he was captured by pirates. While his friends were sent off to raise the necessary ransom, Caesar remained as a hostage, and for twenty-eight days was the life and soul of the company. He promised cheerfully to hang them all, a promise which he faithfully kept, when the ransom arrived and he could hire ships at Miletus. Apollonius must have had an unsatisfactory pupil, for the next we hear is of Caesar raising troops to repel the new invasion of Mithridates. Meantime, in his absence he had been elected through the influence of his mother's family to a place in the college of *pontifices*, and he felt that, in Napoleon's phrase, he had done enough 'pour chauffer la gloire' and should return home. He knew that he would get short shrift if pirates captured him a second time, so he hired a vessel which could outsail any pirate craft, and reached Rome at the end of 74. There he won his first elective office, that of military tribune, and as such he may have served against Spartacus in the Slave insurrection which presently broke out. He was living in a modest establishment with his mother and his wife, improving daily in his oratory in spite of his high-pitched voice, and circumspectly surveying the political field. He was now entering his thirtieth year.

IV

The Party Game

The first two years of Caesar's life in Rome as an aspirant to a political career gave him ample material for thought. The Sullan regime had produced the inevitable reaction, for it contented nobody except the inner circle of the Senate; the more enlightened of the aristocracy, the lawyers, the middle class and the mob were alike dissatisfied. The opposition of the Populares became suddenly respectable. The supple mind of the young Caesar, which may once have dreamed of a Periclean democracy in Rome, a government of the Many who should be also the Best, was now engaged not with visions of a Platonic republic but with the dingy realities of the 'cesspool of Romulus.' He was clear about two things—that the aristocracy was no longer fit to govern, and that the traditional constitution of Rome was inadequate to its new duties. But it seems to me idle to hold, with some of his hero-worshippers, that he had already conceived a plan of reconstruction, and that he worked throughout his life on the dream 'that pleased his boyish thought.' That is not how a realistic intelligence behaves, and Caesar was the supreme realist of history. He was ambitious to succeed in the fashionable game of politics, and he cast about him for the best methods.

These were years of war. The Slave revolt under Spartacus was brought to an end by Marcus Crassus. The ex-Marian Sertorius, one of the most enlightened and attractive figures in Roman records, was at long last crushed in Spain by Pompey. Mithridates was checked in his conquering progress by Lucius Lucullus, who was making war with a free hand and performing miracles of which political hatred was to deprive him of the credit. Caesar saw that in the chaos of the Roman state the decisive word would lie with the man who had an army at his back. Especially was he interested in the commander in Spain, who was only four years his senior. Pompey was the luckiest of mortals. Sulla had saluted him as Imperator when he was twenty-three, and had called him 'the Great,' and he had been permitted the honour of a triumph at the age of twenty-seven, before he was even a senator. He was a friendly, courteous person, not too puffed up by his successes; handsome in the fleshy Roman way, with melting eyes which women found irresistible. Something might be made of him, for he was not likely to be a docile tool of the Senate. But Caesar had no belief in Pompey's brains. He saw in him talent, but not genius. If such a man could be a successful soldier, why should not he also win the same laurels and the same power? Moreover, the law and custom of the constitution had been broken by giving Pompey a high command overseas before he had entered on the *cursus honorum*. Marius had been right; the laws were silent when confronted with arms; the only way to get rid of antiquarian lumber was to have an army behind one.

But Caesar realised that he had a long road to travel before he could win Pompey's power, and in the meantime he must use the weapons which lay to his hand. The first of these was the mob—the great mass of the dispossessed and discontented who filled the city kennels. He had no leaning to equalitarian whimsies; the Roman populace was to him a rabble, a squalid thing which had its rights under an antiquated constitution, and might be used to intimidate the oligarchy. Till he could fit himself with a disciplined army he would make shift with a bodyguard from the pavement. This meant that he must play a large part in the democratic clubs, and make himself a popular favourite. There is no reason to believe that Caesar's début in the part of a radical leader had any but a tactical motive.

It meant also that he must spend a great deal of money, which his modest patrimony could not provide. Therefore he must cultivate the new monied classes with whom he had already family connections. He must not champion the mob so as to lose the confidence of the capitalists. These were immensely powerful, and it was largely owing to their opposition that Lucullus's brilliant achievements were decried. The most important was Crassus, who had finished the Slave war. Crassus was the eternal type of money-spinner, who in the interests of his business had not attached himself too closely to any party. His fortune ran to several millions sterling, and he had the equivalent of a million and a half invested in land alone. He was a poor speaker, an indifferent soldier, and with little political aptitude, but he was insatiably ambitious. He belonged to an ancient house, and he was also the recognised leader of the rich bourgeoisie, so he naturally believed that he had it in him to head a coalition of what Cicero called 'honest men.' Caesar saw it otherwise. He would make this bustling and not too intelligent plutocrat at once the milch-cow and the stalking-horse of the radicals, and in particular the means of providing his own campaign fund.

The events of the year 70 seemed to favour these views. Pompey and Crassus were consuls, the one in virtue of his military prestige and the other because of his wealth and largesses; each, it was remarked, had legions behind him to enforce his claims, if necessary. Both consuls inclined for the moment against the Optimates. That was the year of the trial of Verres, the restoration of the tribunician power, the recovery by the Equites of a predominant share in the jury-courts and of the farming of the Asian taxes, the revival of the censorship and the consequent striking off of sixty-four members from the roster of the Senate. These changes were brought about by a union of the capitalists and the popular party; Cicero supported them, and Caesar played some part in the restoration of the tribunate, and probably made his first speech in the Forum to a public gathering. The oligarchy was for the moment discredited, and Pompey and Crassus, having undone most of Sulla's work, showed no inclination to go further, but disbanded their forces and retired into private life. The time seemed opportune for the entry into politics of a young man on the popular side.

Two years later Caesar attained his first important office, the quaestorship, in virtue of which he entered the Senate. The post gave him some insight into the details of public business, for it was a kind of secretaryship to the treasury, and involved the management of the municipal supply of corn and water. That year his aunt Julia and his wife Cornelia died, and, in the public eulogies on them which he delivered according to custom, he seized the opportunity of displaying his political colours. He had the bust of Marius carried in Julia's funeral procession, and the people wildly applauded the effigy of the man whose name a decade before they had been forbidden to speak. In his oration Caesar lauded his aunt's divine and royal ancestry, and he proceeded to marry a girl Pompeia, young and well-dowered, who was Sulla's granddaughter. If the rôle of demagogue was to be his, he was determined that the patrician should not be forgotten.

Presently, according to the Roman ritual of office, he went abroad attached to the propraetor of Farther Spain. This, his first foreign journey on duty, was one of the formative episodes in his life. At Cadiz he is said to have meditated with bitterness that he was now thirty-four and that before that age Alexander had conquered the world. The thought may have quickened his power of reflection and receptivity. He came to understand the meaning of Sertorius's work, for Sertorius was the first Roman to think of provincials as Roman citizens and not as chattels. He fell in love with this land in the West, and saw in its people the stuff of a strong nation. On his way home overland he spent some time in Cisalpine Gaul, and heard at first hand the grievances of the dwellers north of the Po who were denied the full citizenship. Into his shrewd tactical schemes there came new ideas which stretched far beyond the Roman party game. Rome had a great heritage, human and territorial, outside her city walls, and some day, if the gods were kind, it might fall to his lot to shape it to high purpose.

He returned early in 67 to find politics at their liveliest. Foreign affairs were in chaos, Mithridates was not conquered, and pirates had so dominated the Mediterranean that the Roman corn supply was imperilled. Pompey, tired of a quiet life, was growing restless, and the people were demanding that some use should be made of the foremost soldier of the day. It was proposed to give him an extraordinary command for three years with an adequate army to suppress piracy, and to recall Lucullus, and when the Senate would have none of it, the tribune Gabinius introduced and carried the measure by a plebiscite. Later, another tribune, Manilius, carried a second plebiscite which entrusted Pompey with the governments of Bithynia, Pontus, and Cilicia, and gave him the sole conduct of the war in the East. These proceedings were a defiance of the custom of the constitution. The burgesses might confirm a special appointment, but hitherto the Senate had made it. But now not only was the Senate roughly set aside, but Pompey was given unlimited financial and military power, which was wholly inconsistent with republican principles. The Senate was furious and impotent, the capitalists were alarmed, and Crassus was sulky; but the need was urgent, for Rome was faced with starvation, and even a moderate like Cicero accepted the Manilian law and spoke in its favour. Caesar and his radicals welcomed it for another reason; they saw that the appointment of Pompey meant the beginning of the end of the old regime.

In 66 Caesar was elected aedile, and took up office on the first day of the following year. Owing to his popular canvassing he had fallen into debt before his quaestorship, and Pompeia's dowry had not cleared his feet. Now with the most expensive of all magistracies on his hands—it meant virtually the administration of the Roman municipality—his borrowings reached a colossal figure. He had to give public games, and in his extravagance he outdid all predecessors, for the very cages of the wild beasts were of silver, and he produced three hundred and twenty pairs of gladiators. He erected costly public buildings, and, greatly daring, he restored and regilded the trophies and statues of Marius on the Capitol. Old Marian veterans wept at the sight, and the young patrician of thirty-seven became as never before the darling of the mob. The result was that he owed some hundreds of thousands of pounds, which he could scarcely have raised if Crassus had not backed his bills.

Caesar had now emerged into the full glare of publicity. To the Senate he was the chief mark for hostility, the real leader of the Populares, vigilant, intrepid, and resourceful. They had feared Pompey, but Pompey was a formal, supine being compared to this audacious meteor. The hope of the old men like Catulus was that he would wear himself out in debaucheries, like other aristocrats who had forsworn their class, and they whispered slanders which have ever since found credence. Most were patently untrue. Caesar was living at the time the life of a man of fashion, but his body was always subject to his mind and his pleasures subordinated to his ambition. He preferred good talk to drunken orgies, and the society of cultivated women to that of the ordinary male glutton. Women indeed had a peculiar fascination for him, and he for them, but he was no casual libertine. Roman morals on this point were of the easiest, for family life was in decay. The elder Cato had the lowest view of the female sex, and the younger Cato was not above divorcing his wife to give her to Hortensius, and remarrying her as Hortensius's well-dowered widow; Cicero plumed himself on flirting with disreputable actresses; Pompey divorced Mucia on account of an intrigue with Caesar, and promptly married the daughter of his wife's seducer. Caesar had a host of women friends, of whom the closest was Servilia, the mother of Marcus Brutus, but there is no evidence that any one of them was his mistress except Pompey's wife. In continence he did not fall below the average standard of his day. As for friends of his own sex, the exigencies of the political game impelled him to have many dealings with blackguards, but he had no taste for raffish company, and even in politics he would have nothing to do with the irredeemable degenerate.

He was tolerant of most men, and able to handle every variety. But there was one exception, Servilia's half-brother, Marcus Porcius Cato, who was seven years his junior, and who followed him steadily at a little distance in the *cursus honorum*. Every type has its anti-type, and to Caesar Cato was eternally antipathetic. He was a man of mediocre intelligence and unshakable self-conceit. New ideas, new facts beat vainly against the shuttered casements of his soul. His moral sense in many ways was no higher than that of others, as he showed in his mission to Cyprus, but to himself he was the one virtuous man in a world of rogues. His strength lay in this sincere conviction, which made him intolerable but also formidable. He was the unyielding reactionary, who may be broken but cannot be bent. His intellect was, as Cicero said of another senator, a mere desert island, 'shore and sky and utter desolation,' but dim as his lights were, he lived stoutly up to them. To Caesar he was the only contemporary whom he genuinely detested; he never forgave him, especially for dying prematurely and so preventing him from punishing an old foe by magnanimity. It was no small achievement to have incurred Caesar's unhesitating dislike.

Meantime in that year of extravagance strange things were going on underground, and Caesar had other relations with Crassus than those of debtor and creditor. The first elected consuls in 66 had been unseated for corrupt practices, and had planned a *coup d'état* to make Crassus dictator and Caesar master of the horse. Crassus was becoming utterly malcontent. He saw his ex-colleague Pompey driving the pirates from the seas, and defeating Mithridates and Tigranes, while he himself languished in wealthy obscurity at home. His irritable ambition revived, and he dreamed of a dictatorship on his own account, with Egypt and its treasures as his special province. The conspiracy failed, and the storm blew over, but for Caesar it was a difficult moment. He was very much in Crassus's debt, and dare not quarrel with him, but at the same time he had no wish to break with Pompey, who was still the best card which the radicals held against the Senate. Besides, he was not ready to play a master-stroke, having only reached the aedileship. Nevertheless the abortive conspiracy had brought Crassus nearer to the radicals, and the radicals nearer to what might be called the anarchists, the underground world of bankrupts and libertines who had nothing to lose by violence. Chief of these latter was the late praetor Catiline, who in 64 was a candidate for the consulship.

In 64, while Pompey was playing the part of conquistador and marching through Syria, the consular elections offered some excitement. Cicero, who had won fame by his prosecution of Verres, the Sullan propraetor of Sicily, and was known as a friend of Pompey, was supported reluctantly by the Optimates, though he had toyed with the Populares and had the confidence of the bourgeoisie of the capital and the country towns. Caesar and Crassus took the side of his rivals Catiline and Antonius, whom they considered with reason to be better tools for their purpose; but the alarm excited by Catiline's appearance was so general that Cicero was elected by a handsome majority, with Antonius as his colleague.

Thus entered into high politics one of the most versatile and gifted of Romans and the supreme master of the Latin tongue. So far Cicero had been only the leader of the bar and a famous man of letters; he had neither wealth nor family behind him, and he was the first to reach the highest office solely by his intellectual attainments. He was honourable, affectionate, and loyal, and he had that finest kind of courage which means the habitual suppression of temperamental fears. He saw as clearly as any man the canker in the state, but he could not be its surgeon, for to him the republic was too dear and ancient a thing for a harsh knife. His physical traits, the big head, the thin neck, the mobile mouth, were an index to his character. Sentiment ruled him, the sentiment of a provincial for the old aristocracy, and for the forms which he had been schooled to reverence. He could not take a hand in plucking down a proud class which it had been the dream of his boyhood to enter, for its destruction would take all the pleasure from his laborious career. This innocent snobbishness was joined to an equally innocent vanity, and to a morbid sensitiveness. He was not vain of his true endowments—his oratory, his prose style, his legal and philosophical learning; but the scholar was apt to strut like a peacock after any little success in the alien world of action. He was far more than a mere man of phrases, for in an emergency he could be very bold; but he lacked the two chief qualities of a leader, a knowledge of what he wanted and an eye for things as they were. The first lack made him waver all his life between the upper and the middle classes, between Optimates and Populares, between Caesar and Pompey; the second bound him to a sterile antiquarianism. He wished to restore the rule of all honest men, to link together the Senate and the Equites in a *concordia ordinum*, and to preserve the traditional republican fabric, and he would not admit to himself, except in moments of exasperated candour, that it was a baseless dream. In this he was the exact opposite of Caesar, who was accustomed to look at facts in all their grimness, and who had no sentimental attachment to the aristocracy, since he came from the heart of it and knew its rottenness.

The year 63 was a hard trial for the lawyer-consul. The radicals began briskly with a new agrarian law, promulgated by

D

the tribune Rullus. The measure had no great popular appeal, and Cicero's eloquence easily defeated it. Then they tried another tack. Titus Labienus, one of Caesar's henchmen, indicted for high treason an aged senator, Rabirius, who thirty-seven years before had been concerned in the killing of the tribune Saturninus. This was purely a political demonstration, for the trial was not allowed to come to a verdict, but it was a shrewd assault upon the citadel of the senatorial power; it emphasised the tribunes' right of inviolability for all to mark, and it repudiated the Senate's claim to declare a state of siege, the famous *senatus consultum ultimum*, which put the lives and liberties of the people temporarily in its hands.

There followed a still more notable radical success. The office of Pontifex Maximus fell vacant, an office which carried with it not only high distinction, but considerable revenues, an official residence, and the right of personal immunity, things most valuable to a demagogue who was walking in dangerous ways. Caesar, just over forty, became a candidate against two old and respected senators, Quintus Catulus and Servilius Isauricus. Sulla had placed the election in the hands of the pontifical college itself, but Titus Labienus had it transferred to the Assembly. The contest was an orgy of bribery and added enormously to Caesar's debts, but to the general surprise he was triumphantly elected. He was also chosen as praetor for the coming year.

The law of Rullus, the impeachment of Rabirius, and the candidature for Pontifex Maximus had been open attacks by the radical chiefs upon the senatorial power. But now came an assault on its own account by the extreme left wing, the anarchists from the kennels and the clubs, in which the responsible leaders took no overt part. We may assume that they were aware of the conspiracy, and intended to win repute by checking and disarming it when it had gone a certain length. Catiline was again a candidate for the consulship, but he was now ready to take by violence what he could not get by law. He engineered in Rome and throughout Italy a great plot of the lawless, the disinherited, the bankrupt, and the desperate. At the poll it was proposed to kill Cicero, the presiding consul, and the other candidates, to carry the election of Catiline with the help of armed bands, and thereafter to introduce a millennium of debt-repudiation and public plunder. Cicero got wind of the plan. He denounced the conspirators in the Senate, Catiline being present, and on the day of the election he had his own armed bands to keep order in the Field of Mars. Insurrection broke out in Etruria, but by Cicero's vigilance the simultaneous rising in the city failed. The general levy was called out, Catiline was presently forced to show his hand and flee from Rome, after failing to murder Cicero, and the insurrection became a miniature civil war. The chief conspirators in the city were arrested, and in the beginning of the new year Catiline himself was slain in a desperate fight in the Apennine passes, and the crisis was over. The Roman accomplices were by order of the Senate strangled in prison, and the consul who had saved the state was attended to his house by shouting crowds, and hailed by Cato and Catulus as *pater patriae*.

Cicero was for the moment the most popular man in Rome, for even the mob had been scared by the orgy of blood and ruin involved in Catiline's success. He deserved the plaudits which he won, for he had made no mistakes; his secret service was perfect; he gave Catiline the necessary rope to hang himself; he had the nerve not to act prematurely, and when the moment came he struck hard. The only criticism concerns the scene in the Senate, when the summary execution was ordered of the Roman accomplices. Clearly Cicero would have been justified on putting these men to death as an administrative act on his own authority; but the doubt arose when the Senate was asked to constitute itself a court of law, and pronounce sentence without trial on men who had not been taken in armed rebellion, but were only suspects.

Caesar was in a position of peculiar difficulty. He could not assent to the proposal for summary execution without stultifying all his previous career, and notably the action he had taken a few weeks earlier in the case of Rabirius. At the same time there was no moral doubt of their guilt, the crisis was urgent with Catiline in arms beyond the walls, and to plead for leniency in the then state of popular feeling would have been almost to avow himself a sympathiser. As it was, he all but came by his death from the swords of the younger hot-bloods. In his speech, of which Sallust has preserved a full report, he pled for a sober judgment. It was unconstitutional to put a citizen to death without trial, and might be a fatal precedent. He showed that he had no confidence in the use of the senatorial prerogative, even if justified by law, which it was not; and he urged that, instead, the accused should be imprisoned for life in certain Italian towns, which would effect the practical purpose of keeping them out of mischief, and would not be in the technical sense a 'capital' sentence. The speech, embarrassed as it was, influenced opinion, and Cicero was almost half-hearted in his reply. But Cato, the tribune-elect, clinched the matter by arguing vehemently for the death penalty as an administrative act—that abrogation of formal law in the face of arms for which Marius had long ago provided the classic formula.

After Catiline's death the excitement abated, and Caesar's embarrassment was soon forgotten, the more so as Cicero let it be known that some of the secret evidence about the plot had been provided by Caesar himself. In the year 62 he was praetor, but we do not know in what court he presided. His main interest was in the intentions of Pompey, who, with the garlands of many conquests about him, was waiting on the Aegean shore for the proper moment to return, and had sent on ahead an emissary, Metellus, to spy out the land. The Catiline affair had brought the Optimates and the Populares closer together, the Senate was making eyes at the mob, and on Cato's proposal the full corn doles were restored. This must at all costs be prevented, and to Caesar it seemed that Pompey might be made the wedge to split the unnatural alliance. He proposed, therefore, that old Catulus should be called to account for his expenditure on the new Capitoline temple, that Pompey should complete it, and that the inscription should bear Pompey's name. Caesar was thus beforehand in offering oblation to the returning sun, an oblation which annoyed the Senate, gave pleasure to Pompey, and cost himself and his party nothing.

But the chief event of the year befell in his own family circle. In December in his official residence there was celebrated according to custom the annual rite of the Bona Dea, the goddess of fertility, to which only women were admitted. A young aristocrat, Clodius, brother of Catullus's 'Lesbia of the burning eyes,' had an intrigue with Pompeia, and managed to be present disguised as a music-girl. He was detected by Aurelia, who was suspicious of Pompeia, and Rome was agitated by a scandal of the first importance. Early in the new year Clodius was put on his trial for sacrilege, and Cicero, shocked to the core, was one of his chief prosecutors, thereby incurring his undying hate. The accused was acquitted owing to lavish bribery, and also, it would appear, because Caesar, the man chiefly concerned, did not press the charge. Caesar had indeed divorced Pompeia on the ground that his wife should be above even being suspected, but when called to give evidence he denied any personal knowledge of the facts. Perhaps he felt that scandalised virtue was scarcely the attitude for one on whose account Pompey had just put away his wife. Also he was not prepared to antagonise Clodius overmuch, for this strange degenerate was revealing remarkable qualities of mob leadership. He was already the chief gangster in Rome, and might be useful to one whose power over the mob was a prime political asset.

In the beginning of the year 61 Pompey landed at Brundisium, and Rome waited with anxiety for his next step. He had the chance, if he wished, to grasp the supreme power, a greater power than Sulla had ever held, for in the previous decade the fabric of the republic had rapidly disintegrated. But Pompey had no such ambition; if he had seized the autocracy, he would not have known what to do with it. To Cicero's delight he dismissed his legions and came to Rome as a private citizen; though, let it be remembered, this disbandment was rather a matter of form than of substance, for he had so loaded his veterans with bounties in his eastern campaign that he believed that he could recall them at will to his standard. He was ambitious only of personal glory, and had no far-seeing designs, his mind was not prescient or speculative, and there was a strong vein of laziness in his composition. Far more than to the reality of power he looked forward to the magnificent spectacle of his two days' triumph, when the riches of the East should be displayed before Roman eyes, and at the end, with the right Roman gesture, the new Alexander should put off his armour and return modestly like a second Cincinnatus to his home.

Pompey had been absent for five years, and he now stumbled upon a political witches' sabbath, which he was competent neither to direct nor to understand. The shouting in the streets was scarcely over before the aureole of glory deserted him. He was angry with the Senate, which had behaved cavalierly to his emissary Metellus, and had shown itself strangely unwilling to ratify his eastern settlement. His first speech was a frigid performance, which pleased, said Cicero, neither poverty nor rascaldom, nor capital, nor honesty. The Populares had treated him better, witness Caesar's action about the Capitoline temple, and he inclined towards them. Caesar was content. He might safely leave Pompey to his agents to manage, and he departed with an easy mind as propraetor to his province of Farther Spain.

The bulk of the year 61 and the early part of 60 were spent by Caesar in Andalusia and Portugal. Of his work there we know little. He fought his first little war as a commander-in-chief, a campaign against the hill tribes of Portugal and Galicia. On the civil side he dealt with the eternal problem of debt, and incidentally he himself became solvent again. He had owed something over a quarter of a million, and the bankers would have prevented him leaving Rome had not Crassus come to his aid. Now from the miserable system of confiscations and fees and the sale of captives, which was a governor's perquisite, he enriched his legions and cleared his own feet. In June 60 he was back in Rome, a candidate for the consulship.

His agents had well prepared the ground. His colleague on the popular side was one Lucceius, a rich dilettante whose function was merely to pay the bill. He had been voted a triumph for his Spanish war, but the Senate declined to permit him to stand for the consulship without a personal canvass, a dispensation which it was within its power to make. Caesar, who never let vanity stand in the way of ambition, at once gave up his triumph, laid down his *imperium*, and entered the city. His first business was to complete that reconciliation of Pompey and Crassus at which his agents had been busily working. It was not difficult, since Pompey was at variance with the Senate, who had refused among other things to allot Italian lands to his veterans, and the Equites were furious because Cato—for what seem to have been excellent reasons—had prevented a reduction of their tender for the Asian taxes. With such support Caesar's election was certain, but his colleague was not Lucceius but Bibulus, the stiffest of senatorians.

The year 60 saw a greater event than Caesar's election, for it witnessed the first alliance of dynasts. This was wholly Caesar's doing. He was now at the difficult stage in a career when a man passes from the position of party chief to that of first citizen. To his clear eyes it seemed that in Rome there were three powers. There was the mob, which was his special asset, brilliantly organised through the street clubs and caucuses by ruffians of genius like Clodius. It was a power, but he had no respect for it; when he began it was the only weapon which lay to his hand, and he had made the most of it; but he loved the degraded business of personal canvassing and mob cajolery as little as did Cato himself. In the second place there were the capitalists, of whom Crassus was the patron and Cicero the somewhat dubious voice. Politics in Rome were an expensive game, and a leader must have a treasury. Last and most important, there was the army, and this meant Pompey, for that modest Roman was not only a successful general but could at will summon back to his side many legions.

Hitherto Caesar had played the game of demagogy with immense skill and as little principle as other people. But now the governance of Rome was falling into his hand, and he must prepare to accept it. There must be some promise of continuity in a reforming administration, and for this purpose there must be a coalition of all the elements which were not, like the senatorian reactionaries, altogether hostile to change. He believed honestly that he could work with both Pompey and Crassus, for their interests did not conflict with his; they wanted especially pomp, precedence, and spectacular honours, for which he himself cared not at all. How sincere Caesar was in his desire to build up a working coalition, a practical *concordia ordinum*, is shown by his attempt to enlist Cicero's support. But Cicero since his consulship had come to regard himself as the special guardian of the ancient constitution, and he suspected the orthodoxy of his boyhood's friend.

V

The First Consulship

THERE is no warrant for believing that Caesar, when in 59 he entered upon his first consulship, had in his mind any far-reaching policy for the remaking of Rome. Hitherto he had been exercising his talents in a squalid game, building up a half-ruined party, climbing step by step the political ladder, using without much scruple whatever methods seemed to him the speediest and the best. He had not stopped to think about an ultimate goal, believing, with Cromwell, that no man goes so far as he who does not know where he is going. Now that he had reached the battlements he was still without a distant prospect. He had the consulship before him, and after that a province, and he was content to wait upon what they might bring forth. But he was already conscious of his supreme talents, conscious that he was far abler not only than his old colleagues of the half-world but than the gilded Crassus and the resplendent Pompey. He had discovered in himself the power of the administrator for putting crooked things straight and making difficult adjustments, and he desired an ampler opportunity of exercising that power. He believed, too, that he had a gift for war and for the creation of armies, and, knowing the weight of the sword in the balance, he was determined upon the enlargement of that gift. He was dimly aware that a great crisis was imminent which would decide the destiny of Rome, and he braced himself to meet it, though he could not forecast its form. Pompey and Crassus desired to be great figures, Caesar to do great deeds. The difference lay in what St. Paul calls 'the substance of things hoped for,' the ultimate orientation of the spirit.

His first task was to strengthen his ties with Pompey and Crassus. To the former he gave in marriage his adored daughter Julia—a dynastic match, which seemed to Cicero to mean the end of the republic. He settled Pompey's veterans on the land, and ratified Pompey's eastern arrangements. Following the precedent of 71 and the Gabinio-Manilian laws, he was granted an extraordinary command for five years after the close of his consulship. The Senate would have given him as his proconsular province the management of the Italian roads and forests, but this farcical proposal was rejected, and by decrees of the Assembly he was given Cisalpine and Transalpine Gaul and Illyria with four legions. In his absence Pompey would keep an eye on Italy and Rome, and for the year 58 two safe men were elected consuls, the Pompeian Gabinius and Lucius Piso, who was Caesar's father-in-law. Crassus got nothing except a reduction in the contract for the Asian taxes, but he was encouraged to hope for a second consulship and a military command, and at the moment he was wholly under Caesar's spell.

Caesar attempted at first to work with the Senate, and treated it with studied courtesy. What he asked was in the circumstances not unreasonable, and he began by introducing all his measures in the orthodox way. He made some small reforms. If the Senate was to be of any value it must be made to face its responsibilities and be open to intelligent criticism, so he arranged for an official *Hansard*, and the regular publication of its debates. He was a pioneer also in popular journalism, for he ordered the magistrates to have a summary of important news inscribed on white-washed walls in various parts of the city. Then he entered upon his main legislative programme. Apart from the bills necessary to ratify his bargain with Pompey and Crassus, his chief measures were his agrarian laws and his attempt to reform provincial administration. The first flung open the rich district of Campania to settlement and provided from the treasury, now swollen with the proceeds of Pompey's conquests, money to buy further land. The second measure, the famous Lex Julia Repetundarum, stiffened the penalties for provincial extortion, and made every member of a governor's staff equally liable with the governor himself. It provided for copies of the governor's accounts being left for inspection in the province as well as forwarded to the Roman treasury, and it prohibited specifically what was already prohibited by the common law, the leading of an army beyond the province and the making war without the mandate of Senate and people—a provision doubtless inserted to comfort tender conservative consciences.

But the Senate would have none of these measures or accept anything from Caesar. Cato tried to talk them out and had to be placed under arrest. Bibulus, the other consul, endeavoured to block them by declaring the auspices unfavourable. Caesar had no other course before him except to appeal to the Assembly and carry them by plebiscite. This was easily arranged. A tribune who attempted to veto the proceedings was brushed aside, and Bibulus was left in solitary grandeur to watch the skies. If the Senate chose to make government impossible it would be side-tracked at the cost of any informality, since the business of the state must be carried on.

But the vital event of the year was the determination of Caesar's proconsular province. Pompey had shown no jealousy of the five years' extraordinary command, for he had no reason to believe in Caesar's military gifts, and Gaul was not likely in his eyes to be the theatre of a great campaign. It was poor and barbarous and outside the ken of the civilised world. But Caesar was content. He had a liking for the people of Cisalpine Gaul, which he had already visited, and he had long been an earnest advocate of the claim of the district north of the Po to the Roman citizenship. As for Gaul beyond the mountains there seemed to be a flickering there which might soon be a flame. He was not thinking of conquests like Pompey's, but of making for himself an army and of winning a name as a defender of Rome in the field, and it looked as if there might soon be an opportunity there. Diviciacus the Aeduan chief had been in Rome two years before, and the Aedui had been specially marked for Rome's protection in their strife with the Burgundian Sequani. Now there seemed to be one of those strange stirrings, familiar in the Celtic world, among a Gallic tribe, the Helvetii, in the Swiss lowlands, who threatened to invade the Aeduan lands. Also the German Ariovistus, king of the Suebi, was a perpetual menace to Gaul. He had offered Rome his friendship, and, in order to gain time, the Senate had accepted him as an ally, but every one knew that the truce was hollow and that he was only waiting his chance to swoop westward on the Province of the Narbonne. North of the Alps there was no lack of tinder for the inevitable spark.

Caesar, sick of the wrangling in the Senate and Forum, full of the pioneer's passion for new lands, and eager for a life of action,

had one task to accomplish before he set his face to the wilds.
He must make easy the work of Pompey and Crassus by getting
rid of the chief mischief-makers.   Cato, on account of his sur-
passing virtue, was solemnly entrusted by plebiscite with a special
mission to arrange the affairs of Cyprus, and departed unwillingly,
taking with him a bookish nephew, one Marcus Brutus.   Cicero
was a more difficult case.   For him Caesar had a sincere affection;
he had tried to induce him to join the triumvirate; and, when
he failed, he had proposed to take him with him on his staff to
Gaul, an offer which an ex-consul and the leader of the bar could
scarcely accept.   But he must at all costs be got out of Rome,
and Caesar's jackal, Clodius, was used for the purpose.   Clodius,
after getting himself adopted into a plebeian family, was elected
tribune for the year 58, and his first act was to bring a bill before
the Assembly punishing with exile any one who had condemned
a Roman citizen to death without an appeal to the people—a
measure directly aimed at Cicero.   That honest man was filled
with disquiet, for by means of his clubs and his gangsters Clodius
was certain to carry his measure.   From Crassus he could expect
nothing, and his senatorian friends were apathetic or powerless.
Pompey, when Cicero flung himself at his feet, referred him to
Caesar.   Caesar repeated his offer of a post on his staff, but did
nothing more.   He would not call off his hound if Cicero could
not be induced to leave Rome by gentler means.   So he kept
his legions near the walls till the end of March, and not till he
heard that the disconsolate philosopher had turned his melancholy steps towards Brundisium did he hurry north along the
Flaminian Way.

VI

THE CONQUEST OF GAUL

HE had need for haste, for out of Gaul had come ominous news. The Helvetii were moving; in a few days they would assemble opposite Geneva, a multitude nearly four hundred thousand strong, with the purpose of crossing the Rhone, sweeping through the Roman Province, and seizing lands in the west in the vale of the Charente, where the cornfields of the Province would be at their mercy. Travelling twenty miles a day Caesar crossed the Alps, and in a week was at Geneva. It was to be nine years before he trod his native soil again.

Gaul at the time contained three great tribal conglomerations. In the south-west the Aquitani held the country between the Garonne and the Pyrenees; the Celtae occupied the Mediterranean and Atlantic seaboards, the lowlands of Switzerland and the upper Rhine, and the uplands of central France; while, in the north and north-east, the Belgae ruled from the Aisne to the Channel, and from the Seine to the Rhine. The Province itself and some parts of the interior had acquired a tincture of Roman civilisation, but elsewhere the Gauls were a primitive people, farmers and pastoralists and hunters, hardy and frugal, a big-boned, loose-limbed folk with flaxen hair and a ruddy colour, fine horsemen and stout foot-soldiers. Their mode of government varied between monarchy, oligarchy, and a rudimentary democracy, but their chief loyalty was tribal. A tribe might be a member of a confederacy, but it cherished a fierce individuality and independence.

To Rome, though she had fought its people more than once, Gaul was largely an unknown land, and being unknown it was feared. At any hour out of those northern swamps and forests might come a new torrent which no second Marius could stem. Gaul and Parthia were the danger-points of the Roman frontier. Moreover Ariovistus and his Germans, though they were for the moment quiescent, were an imminent thunder-cloud. Caesar realised that Gaul was the coming storm-centre, and that his proconsulship might begin with petty wars, but was certain to develop problems of the first gravity. He desired to make an army which would be his chief weapon in the uncertainties of the future; he desired the same kind of prestige as Pompey had won; he was as confident as Napoleon in his star, and he was conscious of his supereminent talents. But he was above all things an opportunist and was content to let his policy be shaped by events. His first duty was the defence of Italy. He knew little of the land he was bound for, and realised that he must be explorer as well as soldier; the passages in his *Commentaries* where he describes the nature of the country and the habits of the people show how keen was his scientific interest. Above all he welcomed a life of action under the open sky, for his health was beginning to suffer from the stuffy *coulisses* of Roman politics, and he faced joyfully the unplumbed chances of the years before him, for he had never feared the unknown.

He was beginning his serious military career at the age of forty-four, much the same age as Cromwell's when he took the field. But every Roman had a smattering of military knowledge, the technique of war was still elementary, and for twenty years Caesar had been practised in commanding and influencing men. He already possessed that eye for country, that coolness in a crisis, and that speed and boldness in decision which no staff college can give. The Roman army, since the Marian reforms, was an effective fighting force. Its strength lay in its non-commissioned officers, in its iron discipline and marching powers, in its superior equipment in the way of small arms and artillery, and in its superb auxiliary services, for the Roman soldier was the best trench-digger and bridge-builder in the world. Caesar had slingers from the Balearic Isles, and archers from Numidia and Crete, and cavalry from Spain, but he intended to recruit most of his horse in Gaul itself. He began with the three legions in Cisalpine Gaul, where he presently enrolled two more, and one, the famous Tenth, in the Province [1]—a force of some 20,000 men. He enlisted no infantry beyond the Alps, and all his conquering legions were drawn from the mixed population of Pied-

---

[1] Caesar was probably the first man to number his legions, thereby giving them identity and a continuity of tradition.

mont and the Lombard plain. They were a stocky type, a foot shorter than the average Gaul, but stalwart in nerve, muscle, and discipline.

The eight years of the Gallic campaigns will repay the attentive study of all who are interested in the art of war. Here we can only glance at the main movements. The first task was the migrating Helvetii. They hoped to cross the Rhone below Geneva and march through Savoy, but Caesar destroyed the existing bridge, fortified the left bank of the river, and compelled them to try the passes of the Jura. With the help of the Aeduan chief Dumnorix, the rival of Diviciacus, they had secured an unimpeded passage through the territory of the Sequani. While their long train was winding among the mountains, Caesar hurried back to Cisalpine Gaul for his new legions, recrossed the Alps by way of Mont Genèvre, hastened through Dauphiny, and came up with the Helvetii as they were crossing the Saone. There he cut off their rearguard, and headed them north into the Burgundian plain. He found himself in difficulty over supplies, and Dumnorix, who commanded his Aeduan cavalry, was not to be trusted. After fifteen days' pursuit he forced the Helvetii to give battle near the Aeduan capital Bibracte (Mont Beuvray, near Autun), and after a long and desperate day completely routed them. He was fighting against odds of two to one, and his troops were still untempered. The remnant of the Helvetii were sent back to their old home, and he turned to the graver menace of Ariovistus.

Caesar's lightning speed, which had routed the Helvetii, proved also the undoing of the German chieftain. Ariovistus was then in upper Alsace. The victory of Bibracte had swung over the doubting Gallic tribes to the Roman side, and they were eager to fling off the superiority which he had imposed on them. Caesar began with diplomacy, asking only that further German immigration west of the Rhine should cease, but he received a haughty reply, and the news that a fresh army of Suebi was mustering on the east bank of the river. He delayed no longer, but marched straight for Vesontio (Besançon), the capital of the Sequani, which he made his base. He had some trouble with his troops, especially with the unwarlike military tribunes, who were awed by the legendary prowess of the Germans, and he restored confidence by one of those speeches which he knew how to direct straight to men's hearts. ' If no one else follows me,' he said, 'I go on with the Tenth legion alone, and I make it my bodyguard.'

He marched through the Gap of Belfort and found Ariovistus on the Rhine near Mülhausen. Some days were wasted in idle negotiations, during which the treachery of the Germans became clear. Then Ariovistus marched his army westward along the foot-hills of the Vosges, with the obvious intention of cutting the Roman line of supply. Six days later Caesar forced him to give battle, by threatening him in flank and rear. The engagement of September 18th was fought on the plan of Austerlitz, the weak Roman right forming a hinge on which the rest of the army swung to break the enemy's right and centre. Caesar's left was for some time in a critical position, and was saved by young Publius Crassus, the son of Marcus, the commander of the cavalry, who flung in his reserves at the critical moment. The enemy was cut to pieces, Ariovistus fled across the Rhine, and for several centuries the German overflooding of Gaul was stayed.

In the autumn of 58 Caesar withdrew his troops into winter quarters in the country of the Sequani, and, leaving Titus Labienus in command, returned to Cisalpine Gaul. He had technically broken the provisions of his own Julian law by leading his army beyond his province, and to winter it outside Roman territory was a still more daring innovation. His formal justification was that he had the express instructions of the Senate to protect the Aedui, and that this was the only way of doing it; his real defence was the compulsion of facts. He had come to realise the weakness of Gaul, split up among a hundred jealous tribes ; if he could bring it under Roman sway he would not only make the frontier secure, but would add to the empire a race which he greatly admired, and which, he believed, would be an invaluable possession for the future. His dream was shaping itself of a new kind of empire, the strength of which would lie not in its wealth and its relics of an older civilisation but in the quality of its people. In the free air of the north he felt his body invigorated and his mind clarified, and he was now convinced beyond a peradventure of his genius for war. That winter he perfected his plans for the conquest of all Gaul.

In the spring of 57 he set out on his great errand. Central and southern Gaul were his, but the fierce people of the north, the Belgae, were unconquered, and he had word that they were mustering to drive out the Romans. He had enrolled two new legions in Lombardy, which gave him a total of eight—perhaps 40,000 men. From Besançon he marched into Champagne, where he made the Remi, who dwelt around Rheims and Châlons, a Roman nucleus like the Aedui further south. He found two of the chief Belgic tribes, the Suessiones (dwelling around Soissons) and the Bellovaci (around Beauvais), drawn up on the heights north of the Aisne. He crossed the river in the neighbourhood of Berry-au-bac, and built an entrenched camp as his advanced base. The enemy found this position impregnable, and, being in difficulties about supplies, began to retreat. They were pursued by Labienus and the cavalry, who punished them severely. Caesar swung westward and took order with the Bellovaci and the Suessiones, capturing the chief town of the latter. Then he marched north against the heart of the Belgic confederacy, the strong nation of the Nervii, who dwelt in the woody flats along the Scheldt and the Sambre, that land which was destined to be the cockpit of later history. Here he encountered an enemy worthy of his steel. The Nervii at some point between Charleroi and Namur surprised the Romans, and there ensued a soldier's battle like Malplaquet, fought not very far from the scene of Marlborough's victory. Caesar himself was compelled to fight in the ranks to maintain the spirit of his troops, till the arrival of his brigade of Guards, the Tenth legion, turned the tide. The Nervii were all but annihilated, the Belgic confederacy was dissolved, and the campaign was won. They were of all the enemies he encountered the one whom he most admired, and his sober prose kindles almost to a sober poetry when he describes their unavailing courage.

The news of this decisive battle created a profound sensation in Rome. The Senate, after Caesar's despatch had been read, decreed a public thanksgiving of fifteen days—Pompey had only had ten days for Mithridates. Affairs in the capital were in a

curious position. Clodius, Caesar's party manager, had kept the
Populares active by every kind of fantastic law and criminal
outrage. But popular feeling was turning against that demagogue,
and Caesar was beginning to see the need for calling off his
hound. He was always prepared to make use of blackguards;
he did not like the pious rogue, and preferred his ruffians to be
naked and unashamed; but he never permitted the rascality
of an agent to go beyond the bounds of policy. He made no
objection to the recall of Cicero as a concession to the respectable
classes, and that homesick exile was given a great popular reception when he returned in September. Pompey had found a
jackal of his own, the tribune Milo, who was ready to stand up
to Clodius, and it was very necessary to keep Pompey in good
humour. Cicero, grateful to his laggard patron, carried a proposal in the Senate to give Pompey for five years complete control
of the Roman corn supply and the supervision of all ports and
markets in the empire, and Caesar's agents readily agreed.
Something had to be done for Pompey to prevent him growing
jealous of the repute which Caesar was winning so fast. But
Pompey was not satisfied. He saw that he was now only a
figure-head; he wanted real power once more, and that meant
an army and an independent command; and he did not see how
he could get it without alienating those conservatives who were
now sedulously cultivating him, and who were whispering in his
ear that he was the only hope of the republic.

In the year 56 the Gallic operations languished. Caesar paid
a visit to his other province of Illyria, leaving it to his lieutenants
to deal with the Aquitani in the south-west, and the maritime
tribes of the Atlantic coast. Labienus on the Moselle kept an
eye on the Germans, and Publius Crassus had a short and
brilliant campaign against the Aquitani. But the Veneti in
southern Brittany gave more trouble, and a fleet had to be collected and partly built on the Loire, with which Decimus Brutus,
during a long summer's day while the legions looked on from the
mainland cliffs, won one of the most curious naval battles in history.
Caesar behaved to the conquered tribes with what may seem
extreme brutality, for he put the chiefs to death and sold the rest
of the males as slaves. His defence, which he states frankly, was

E

that they had broken the law as to the inviolability of envoys, and that, in order to protect his future supplies, it was necessary to read them a sharp lesson. Then he turned east along the Channel coast and subdued the Morini and the Menapii, Belgic tribes who had been allies of the Veneti and who dwelt in the Pas de Calais and Flanders. From the shore he saw the distant cliffs of the ' white land,' and his explorer's interest was awakened in the strange island of the north from which the secret religion of the Gauls drew its inspiration.

If in that year the Gallic war had few notable incidents, it was otherwise with the political game in Rome. Authority seemed to have gone both from the senatorian conservatives and from the great capitalists, and a younger set, without morals or policy, people like Mark Antony and Curio and Caelius, were casting their lines in the troubled waters. Catullus, the genius of the decadence, was abusing Pompey and Caesar in the lofty conservative vein which is only possible for an aspiring scion of the middle classes. Pompey was finding his life intolerable from the mischievous pranks of Clodius on the one side and the pedantic denunciations of Cato on the other. Caesar, watching the political game from north of the Po, saw that things were nearing a crisis, and that that crisis must be averted if he was to complete his work in Gaul. Domitius Ahenobarbus, a rich and stubborn senatorian, was candidate for next year's consulship, and he made no secret of his intention to demand Caesar's recall. Cicero, too, in the beginning of April proposed in the Senate that Caesar's Campanian land policy should be put down for discussion in the following month. Unless immediate action were taken the arrangement of 59 would crumble.

Caesar acted promptly. He invited Pompey and Crassus to meet him in the middle of April at Luca (Lucca) in the extreme south of his province. Thither they duly came, attended by a host of senators and political aspirants, and there the triumvirate was re-established, since the three, if they were but agreed, were omnipotent. Caesar offered liberal terms—far too liberal if he had consulted his own interests; but he was eager to have the matter settled and to get on with his work in the north, he liked Pompey, and he was determined to do nothing to hurt his beloved Julia. Pompey and Crassus were to be next year's consuls, and thereafter to have the governorships of Spain and Syria respectively for a term of five years. Pompey might stay in Rome and administer Spain by lieutenants, but Crassus was to be permitted to realise the dream of his life and lead from his province an army to the conquest of Parthia. Caesar was to be confirmed in his proconsulship of Gaul for a second space of five years—that is to the beginning of 49.

The terms were gladly and gratefully accepted, for they relieved Pompey from an impossible position and they gave Crassus all that he had ever dreamed. Somehow Clodius was put on the leash, and Cicero's support was not long in doubt. In June in the Senate the latter made one of the best of all his speeches in defence of the Luca arrangements, and he praised Caesar's Gallic exploits with insight and eloquence. The conquest of Gaul, he said, was not the mere annexation of a province, but the dispersion of the one menace to the empire. The Alps had been piled by Heaven as a rampart for Italy, but now they might sink to earth, since Italy had nothing to fear. There is something more in the speech than forensic rhetoric ; there is a real admiration for Caesar's greatness. Cicero had been snubbed and ignored by arrogant senatorians and left in the lurch by Pompey, and he turned to his boyhood's friend who had always treated him kindly. ' Since those who have no power,' he wrote to Atticus, ' will have none of my love, let me take care that those who have the power shall love me.' Caesar met him half-way. He took his brother Quintus as one of his general officers, corresponded with him regularly on literary matters, read and praised his bad verses, and lent him money. For the moment Cicero was an ardent Caesarian, convinced, as he said, by his judgment, his sense of duty and the promptings of his heart. ' I burn with love for him.'

The Luca conference gave Rome a brief interlude of peace. In the year 55, Caesar, to complete his conquests, had to look to the Rhine frontier. Two powerful German tribes, the Usipetes and the Tencteri, had been forced by the Suebi to cross to the west bank of the river, and were now a dangerous element on the edge of Gaul, since these bold mercenaries were being courted by all the Gallic malcontents. He determined to crush this coalition so sternly that it would never again revive. He marched against the newcomers and ordered them back. They prevaricated and argued, and some of their horse made a treacherous attack on a body of Roman cavalry ; with this as his justification Caesar detained their chiefs, who had come to confer, and launched his legions against the leaderless hordes ; there was a great massacre and few recrossed the Rhine. It is a ghastly tale, the ugliest episode of the Gallic wars, and it was unsparingly condemned in the Senate by Cato and by more reasonable men than Cato. But Caesar, merciful both by temperament and policy, seems to have had no doubt about the justice of his action. The German peril was not to be trifled with, and the German demand for westward expansion could only be answered ' by sharp pens and bloody ink.' Then he proceeded to deal with the Sugambri, a tribe east of the Rhine ; they had been giving trouble to the Ubii, who were allies of Rome. His purpose was to teach the powerful Suebi that if they threatened Gaul he could assuredly threaten Germany. He bridged the Rhine at a point between Coblenz and Andernach, a marvellous feat of engineering, and remained eighteen days on German soil, while the Sugambri fled to the dark forests of the interior.

The rest of the summer was occupied with the first expedition to Britain. On August 26 he sailed from Portus Itius (between Calais and Boulogne, perhaps Wissant), and found himself early next morning off the coast west of Dover. The tide carried him down channel, and the landing was made on the low shores of Romney marsh. It was not seriously opposed, but the unfamiliar tides played havoc with his ships. While they were being repaired, an attack of the natives was beaten off and the local tribes sued for peace. After taking hostages he put to sea again, and reached Gaul in safety. It had been only a reconnaissance, but the second expedition was a more serious affair. All winter ships were being built, and on the 20th day of the following July —after some trouble with his Gallic horse, in which the Aeduan Dumnorix was killed—Caesar sailed again, with five legions and a considerable body of cavalry. He landed on the beach at Deal, entrenched a camp, and marched into the interior. He found himself opposed by a strange people, who tattooed their bodies with a blue dye, and were uncommonly skilful in their use of war chariots. Their king was one Cassivelaunus (Cadwallon), whose capital was near St. Albans. Caesar crossed the Thames, and after some desultory fighting forced the king to submit. But it was impossible to winter his legions there, and the conquest of the country was clearly a large undertaking with little hope of profit. After taking the usual hostages and fixing a tribute which was certainly never paid, Caesar returned to Deal and recrossed the Channel. His purpose had been partly scientific— to see for himself a mysterious land and people ; partly military, for to Britain could be traced some of the threads of Gallic unrest; and largely political. The crossing of the Channel, like the bridging of the Rhine, was the kind of feat that fired the imagination of Rome, and gave to its performer a mystic aura of invincibility.

When he returned from Britain in the autumn of 54, Caesar may well have regarded the conquest of Gaul as a thing accomplished. He had carried the Roman arms to every corner of the land, and even beyond the Rhine and the narrow seas. He had been merciless when mercy seemed to him short-sighted, as in the case of the Veneti and the German invaders, but his general policy had been one of conciliation. He had made partisans of many of the Gallic leaders, and he had provided a profession for warlike youth by forming a new Fifth legion, the 'Lark,' entirely from Gauls. As for the situation in Rome, he was spending the immense sums he had won from his proconsul's perquisites in lending money to needy citizens and in erecting superb public buildings as gifts to the people. Pompey and Crassus were attached to him by strong ties of self-interest, and Cicero had become a friend and a panegyrist instead of a critic. He looked forward to five years more in Gaul in which he could make the province a loyal daughter of Rome, and then to a second consulship when he could realise the ideas which were slowly growing up in his mind as to the future shaping of the empire.

These happy forecasts were rudely shattered. He had still to face the inevitable reaction. During three desperate years he had to reconquer Gaul, and then find himself forced unwillingly to conquer the world.

VII

THE REVOLT OF GAUL

THE trouble began during the winter of 54, and, as was to be expected, among the Belgae. That winter Caesar tarried in the north, for the harvest had been bad and supplies were difficult, and he was compelled to distribute his army over a wide extent of country. His own headquarters were at Amiens ; one legion, under Fabius, was among the Morini north of the Scheldt, one under Quintus Cicero among the Nervii at Charleroi, and one under Labienus among the Treveri near Sedan. One, consisting of Gallic recruits but strengthened by five veteran cohorts, was among the Eburones at Aduatuca, in the neighbourhood of Liège. Around him in the Amiens and Beauvais district he had three under Trebonius, Plancus, and the quaestor Marcus Crassus, whose younger brother Publius had now gone to Syria with his father.

The winter had scarcely begun and Caesar was still at Amiens when the plot which had been maturing during his absence in Britain revealed itself at Aduatuca. In command there were two officers, Sabinus and Aurunculeius Cotta, of whom the former was the senior. Ambiorix, the chief of the Eburones, attacked the entrenched camp, and, being beaten off, asked for a parley. Protesting that he had been driven against his desire into hostilities, he told a circumstantial tale of how all Gaul, with German support, was rising against the Romans, and urged the commanders to join hands at once with Caesar and Labienus, guaranteeing that they would not be attacked on the road. Caesar was a hundred and fifty miles off, and the nearest legion, Quintus Cicero's at Charleroi, was forty-five miles away. Sabinus, with only 6000 men, most of them half-trained, fell into the trap. He set out at dawn, and found himself surrounded by the enemy. He and Cotta were slain, and a mere handful escaped to Labienus.

Ambiorix, swollen with victory, now persuaded the Nervii

to attack Quintus Cicero. Cicero was in bad health, and the attack came as a complete surprise to him, but he was of different metal from Sabinus. He sent messengers to Caesar to report the situation, beat off the assault, and, in response to Ambiorix's overtures, declared that Romans made no terms with an enemy in arms. Then began a desperate siege. All the stores and baggage were burned by the enemy's fireballs, and presently nine men out of ten of the little force were dead or wounded. Meantime no word came from Caesar, and it was doubtful if any had reached him, for messenger after messenger was caught by the enemy and tortured to death under the Romans' eyes.

But one got through. At last a javelin was found stuck in one of the towers, with a message in Greek, ' Be of good courage, help is at hand '; it had been flung by one of Caesar's Gallic horsemen. Very soon the besieged saw clouds of smoke on the horizon, and knew that the Nervii villages were burning, and that Caesar was near. When the solitary messenger from Cicero reached Amiens, Caesar at once sent word to Crassus to come and take his place, to Fabius to join him on the road, and to Labienus to move to Cicero's aid if he could. Then by forced marches he covered the eighty miles to Charleroi. He had only two legions, for Labienus was himself in straits and could not join him. Ambiorix, with his 60,000 men, advanced to crush the 8000 of the relieving force, but Caesar refused to be drawn into a precipitate battle. He entrenched a small camp which was an invitation to the enemy's attack ; the attack duly came, the Gauls were admitted almost inside the ramparts, and then like a thunder-clap came the unexpected counter-stroke, and Ambiorix's horde was driven panic-stricken into the marshes. Caesar did not pursue them, but marched on to Charleroi without the loss of a single man. There he congratulated Cicero and his gallant remnant on their new Thermopylae, and there he heard the tragic tale of Aduatuca. The news of the relief spread like wildfire, and Labienus was freed from the threats of Indutiomarus and the Treveri.

Caesar spent an anxious winter among his troops, with the legions of Quintus Cicero and Crassus concentrated round Amiens. He had many conferences with the Gallic chiefs, and from these it was clear that a new and dangerous spirit was

abroad.   The slaughter of the cohorts at Aduatuca had inflamed
racial pride, and everywhere in the province there was a mutter-
ing of unrest.   Labienus, indeed, held his own among the Treveri,
and Indutiomarus was slain, but though the flame died down the
ashes smouldered.   Caesar raised two new legions in Cisalpine
Gaul, and borrowed a third from Pompey, who had no need of
troops, since he refused to go near his province of Spain.   When
the campaigning season opened in 53 he led punitive expeditions
against malcontent tribes like the Nervii and the Menapii;
crossed the Rhine again to overawe the Suebi, and made an
example of the Eburones, though Ambiorix succeeded in escaping
into the fastnesses of the Ardennes.   In the autumn he quartered
most of his legions further south in the neighbourhood of Sens
and Langres, and returned to Cisalpine Gaul to keep an eye
upon Rome.

   He had no sooner crossed the Alps than revolution broke out,
and a far more formidable enemy appeared than Ambiorix or
Indutiomarus.   The fiery cross was sent round, secret meetings
were held everywhere, and a consciousness of nationality, a sense
that now was the last chance for regaining their lost freedom,
inspired many even of those Gauls who had appeared to be
devotees of Rome.   This popular movement for a time brought
about unity among the fissiparous tribes, and it found its leader
in Vercingetorix.   He was a young Arvernian noble, whose
father had once attempted to make himself king of Gaul.   To
ancestral prestige he added high military talent, and a character
which both charmed and impressed all who met him.   That
winter he was busy among the villages of Auvergne, and his
emissaries visited all the neighbouring tribes, till by the new year
he had a vast mass of tinder waiting for the spark.

   The spark came with an attack by the Cornutes upon the
Roman commissaries at Orleans.   Vercingetorix from his headquarters at Gergovia, the mountain town south-east of the Puy
de Dôme, sent out his summons for revolt.   He had a plan with
which he believed he could conquer.   He could dispose of great
clouds of cavalry, and the Gallic horse, who had been the mounted
arm of the Romans, had during the recent troubles melted away.
He would never attack the unshakable legions, but he would cut
off their supplies and with his cavalry shepherd them to starvation

and disaster. Above all he would deprive them of Caesar's leading. A belt of revolution would prevent their commander-in-chief from reaching them on the upper Seine, and he believed that he was the match of Quintus Cicero and Labienus.

The news reached Caesar in early February in Cisalpine Gaul. The situation was desperate. Affairs in Rome urgently demanded his attention, for his party there seemed to be crumbling, but in Gaul it looked as if the labour of seven years had come to naught. The trouble now was not in the north and east, but in the centre and the south, which he thought had been finally pacified. The very Province itself was in danger. Of all the tribes he could count only on the Remi, the Lingones, and the Aedui, and he did not know how long he could be sure of the Aedui. He crossed the Alps without drawing rein, and in the Province his difficulties began. How was he to rejoin his legions? If he sent for them they would have to cut their way south without their general; if he tried to reach them he ran an imminent risk of capture. All the rebel country lay between him and his army.

The one hope lay in boldness, and his boldness was like a flame. He arranged for the defence of the Province, and then in deep snow raced through the passes of the Cevennes, which no man before had travelled in winter. He was carrying fire and sword over the Auvergne plateau when the enemy still thought of him as south of the Alps. Vercingetorix hastened to meet him, which was what Caesar desired. He had drawn the rebel army on a false scent. Leaving Decimus Brutus to hold it, he returned to Vienne on the Rhone, picked up some waiting cavalry, galloped up the Saone valley through the doubtful Aedui, and early in March joined his legions at Langres. While Vercingetorix was still entangled with Decimus Brutus, Caesar had concentrated ten legions in his rear at Agedincum on the Yonne. He had won the first round.

The events of the months that followed, the most hazardous and the most brilliant in Caesar's military career, must be briefly summarised. Vercingetorix was forced by public opinion to be false to his own wise strategic creed, and was compelled to defend the city of Avaricum (Bourges). He cut off Caesar's supplies and reduced his army to scarecrows, but the Roman fortitude did not weaken. Avaricum was carried by assault after four weeks' siege, and the fate of its people was a terrible warning. Then Vercingetorix flung himself into Gergovia with a large army, and Caesar sat down to a blockade—a difficult task, for Labienus was away on the Seine with four legions and the besiegers had only some 25,000 men. Moreover Caesar had to leave the siege to punish the Aedui, who were sending a large contingent to the enemy. He tried to take Gergovia by assault, and was repulsed with heavy loss—his first blunder and his first defeat. He could not induce Vercingetorix to give battle, and meantime his supplies were being systematically cut off by the Gallic horse. The Aedui were in open revolt, Labienus was in difficulties further north, and the Province was in dire danger. Caesar bowed to the compulsion of facts, raised the siege of Gergovia, and crossed the Loire into Aeduan territory. There he found supplies, effected a junction with Labienus, and received a contingent of German cavalry which he had sent for from the Ubii. He turned south-east into the country of the Sequani, his plan being apparently to secure there a base of operations which would enable him to defend the Province and keep open his communications with Italy, and from which he could begin again the conquest of Gaul.

Vercingetorix played into his hand. In a great assembly at Bibracte he had been made high chief of all Gaul, and his elevation seems to have weakened his caution. He attacked Caesar on the march, and was so roughly handled that he decided that he could not face the Romans in the field, so he flung himself into the mountain citadel of Alesia (Mont Auxois) above the little river Brenne, where he hoped to repeat the success of Gergovia. Around the hill Caesar drew elaborate siege-works and beat off all the sallies of the besieged. The messengers of Vercingetorix summoned aid from every corner of Gaul, the national spirit burned fiercely, and a relieving force of no less than a quarter of a million infantry and 8000 horse assembled. Caesar with his 50,000 foot and his German cavalry was now enclosed between Vercingetorix and the hordes of his new auxiliaries ; the besieger had become also the besieged. The full tale of that miraculous long-drawn fight—the greatest of Caesar's battles and one of the greatest in history—must be read in Caesar's own narrative. In the end the relieving force was

decisively beaten, Alesia surrendered, and the Gallic revolt was
over.

Vercingetorix in defeat rose to heroic stature. He offered
his life for his countrymen, for, as he said, he had been fighting
for Gaul and not for himself; splendidly accoutred he appeared
before Caesar, stripped off his arms, and laid them silently at his
feet. The victor for reasons of policy showed mercy to the broken
Aedui and Arverni, but he had none for Vercingetorix. He was
sent to Rome as a prisoner, six years later he adorned his
conqueror's triumph, and then he was put to death in a dungeon
of the Capitol. No Roman, not even Caesar, knew the meaning
of chivalry. Of Vercingetorix we may say that he was the first,
and not the least, of that succession of Celtic paladins to whom
the freedom of their people has been a burning faith. He was,
after Pompey, the greatest soldier that Caesar ever faced in
the field, and no lost cause could boast a nobler or more tragical
hero.

At last Gaul was not only conquered but pacified, and never
again did she seriously threaten Rome. Indeed she was destined
to remain the last repository of the Roman tradition, and its
mellow afterglow had not wholly gone from her skies when it
was replaced by the dawn of the Renaissance. At this point
in his chronicle Caesar lays down his pen. He wintered among
the Aedui, and next year was engaged in small operations to
consolidate his power. His main task now was to organise the
new province, and, though it was probably not formally annexed
to Rome till his dictatorship, he was already organising its
government and assessing its tribute. He was also winning his
way into the hearts of many of the leading Gauls, so that in the
later crisis of his fortunes they stood unflinchingly by his side.

The campaigns in Gaul are Caesar's chief title to what has
never been denied him, a place in the inner circle of the world's
captains. He was in the first place a superb trainer of troops.
He raised at least five new legions, and he so handled them that
they soon ranked as veterans. Again, he was a great leader of
men, having that rare gift of so diffusing his personality that
every soldier felt himself under his watchful eye and a sharer in
his friendship. Strategically he had an infallible eye for country,

a geographical instinct as sure as Napoleon's. He had that power of simplification which belongs only to genius, and he never wasted his strength in divergent operations, but struck unerringly at the vital point. A desperate crisis only increased his coolness and the precision of his thought. He understood the minds of men, and played unerringly on the psychology of both his own soldiers and the enemy's; indeed he made the enemy do half his work for him; and he had a kind of boyish gusto which infected his troops with his own daring and speed. He had able marshals, like Labienus and Quintus Cicero and Publius Crassus, but he was always the controlling spirit. He was essentially humane—'mitis clemensque natura,' Cicero wrote—but he was implacable when policy required it. Nor must it be forgotten that in his generalship, as in that of all great captains, there was a profound statesmanship. He never forgot that success in the field was only a means to an end, and that his purpose was not to defeat an army but to conquer and placate a nation.

VIII

THE RUBICON

THE years of the revolt in Gaul saw the gradual breakdown of the Luca settlement and the dissolution of the triumvirate. While Caesar was fighting for his life against odds every despatch from Rome brought news of the worsening of his political prospects, and, adroit party chief as he was, he could not at that distance and in the midst of so many urgent tasks control successfully the party game.   In the autumn of 54 Julia died, his only child and Pompey's wife, and she was soon followed by his mother, Aurelia.   Julia's infant son did not long survive her, and so the family tie between the two dynasts was broken. Pompey was proving himself wholly unable to control the anarchy in the capital.   'We have lost,' Cicero wrote despairingly, 'not only the blood and sap, but even the outward hue and complexion of the commonwealth as it used to be.'   That disillusioned man could only solace his enforced leisure by writing political philosophy in which he portrayed his ideal republic.   His chief consolation was his friendship with Caesar, who found posts for every friend he recommended, and entrusted him with the spending of great sums on his new public buildings.   For the moment he ranked with Oppius and Balbus as one of Caesar's agents.

Next year the triumvirate suffered a further shock, for Crassus perished in his Parthian campaign.   The ambitions of the luckless millionaire ended miserably among the Mesopotamian sands, and his bloody head was flung on to the stage at the Parthian court, where a company of strolling players were performing the *Bacchae* of Euripides.   The East had triumphed over the West, and the quaestor Gaius Cassius had much ado to lead the remnant of the beaten army back to Syria.   On Crassus Caesar could always reckon, but Pompey alone was an easy mark for the intrigues of the Optimates, and he began to drift rapidly away from his ally.   He refused Caesar's offer of the hand of his great-niece Octavia, and chose instead a daughter of Metellus Scipio, one of the most rigid of the senatorians. The year closed with a political pandemonium, in which it was impossible to hold the consular elections. Daily there was bloodshed in the streets, and Cicero was nearly killed on the Sacred Way.

In January 52 Clodius, the bravo of the Populares, was slain in a brawl on the Appian Way by Milo, the bravo of the Optimates and a recent candidate for the consulship. This brought matters to a head, for some kind of order must be restored. Pompey, on the motion of Bibulus and Cato, was made sole consul for the year; that is, a virtual dictator. He had now ranged himself definitely on the side of the Optimates, and that year saw the end of the triumvirate; for, though he still professed to be in alliance with Caesar, all his measures were cunningly directed against Caesar's interests, while Caesar, busy with the Gallic revolt, could reply only by providing feasts and shows for the populace. In the blackguard Clodius he had lost his most audacious and resourceful henchman. One of Pompey's laws provided that no consul or praetor could proceed to his province till five years after holding office. He approved a bill introduced by the tribunes and carried by plebiscite, permitting Caesar to stand for the consulship while absent from Rome, but this concession seemed to be abrogated by a further law which confirmed the old rule about a personal canvass. Caesar's proconsular office formally terminated on March 1, 49, but since he was entitled to his *imperium* until the arrival of his successor, it would really continue till the end of that year. Unless he were elected consul for 48 he would become a private citizen, and as such would certainly be impeached and probably killed; but he could not lay down his *imperium* without becoming a private person, and he could not retain it if he left his province; therefore he must be allowed to be a candidate while still with his army. Such had been the Luca arrangement, and now Pompey seemed to be trying to whittle it away. The plot against Caesar was revealing itself.

Next year, 51, Caesar, his task accomplished, published his *Commentaries* on the Gallic war. His purpose was twofold: to give a succinct soldierly narrative of the great struggle and to interest the Roman people in their new dominion; and to show

that the campaign had been forced upon him by dire necessity
and that he had only acted in accordance with the spirit of the
constitution.   The book was primarily an electioneering pamphlet,
the most brilliant known to history.   The consuls in this year,
Sulpicius Rufus and Marcus Marcellus, were both senatorians;
the first, one of the few attractive figures of the time, might be
trusted to act fairly, but Marcellus was a violent partisan, and,
like Cato, made no secret of his intention to have Caesar recalled.
The cabal was now plain for all to see, and Pompey had gone
over body and soul to the conservatives.   One incident showed
how the wind blew.   Caesar had always maintained that the
Transpadanes, the dwellers north of the Po, were Roman burgesses
as of right, but a town-councillor of Novum Comum came to
Rome, and Marcellus had him flogged (Pompey not objecting)
for pretending to the Roman citizenship—a glaring insult to the
proconsul of Gaul.

In the year 50 the plot spread fast.   One consul, Aemilius
Paullus, was a Caesarian, and all but one of the tribunes.   One
of the latter, Curio, now came to the front.   He had been a
bitter critic of Caesar in the past, but Caesar had won him over
by paying his numerous debts, and he became his principal agent,
more respectable than Clodius and more effective because less
freakish.   The nature of the attack had declared itself, and
Caesar, back now in Cisalpine Gaul, could watch the various
moves.   His provincial command must in any case cease by
January 1, 48.   He had the right to expect that his successor
would be one of the consuls for 49, who would only relieve him
in 48, by which time he himself would be consul.   He had also
been given the right of standing for the consulship *in absentia*.
But Pompey's law, enjoining an interval of five years between
the consulship and a proconsulship, enabled the Senate to
appoint to a province for 48 any one of consular rank.   Caesar
therefore would be actually relieved of his province and his
army on March 1, 49, the formal date of the close of his command.
That is to say, an agreement solemnly entered into had been
upset by subsequent enactments.

On every ground of equity Caesar had cause to complain.
Curio made the most of the grievance.   While Aemilius Paullus
delayed the debate in the Senate, he harassed Pompey with

incessant jibes and accusations and vetoes in the Assembly, pointing out that this new precisian about the constitution had himself broken every article of it, and had been simultaneously consul and proconsul. He proposed, no doubt at Caesar's instigation, that both Pompey and Caesar should lay down their provinces—to which Pompey could not assent. It was now clear to everybody that the contest was being narrowed to a personal issue—no longer radicals and conservatives, Populares and Optimates, but Caesar and Pompey. In June the Senate decided that each should give up one legion for the Parthian war, and Pompey accordingly requested Caesar to return him the legion lent in 53. Caesar at once complied, but no more was heard of Parthia, and the two legions were detained by Pompey in Italy. He had begun to mass his forces.

The breach came early in 49. Both consuls were senatorians, but among the tribunes was Mark Antony, one of Caesar's lieutenants in Gaul. On the first day of the year, Curio, the ex-tribune, appeared in the Senate with a letter from Caesar, of which the consuls tried to prevent the reading. Caesar had already from beyond the Alps sent proposals for peace, and now he declared his final terms. They were moderation itself. He offered to give up Transalpine Gaul and eight of his legions if he were allowed to retain Cisalpine Gaul and Illyria with two—an arrangement which was only to last till he entered upon his second consulship. Further, he declared that he was ready to lay down his command if Pompey would do likewise. He asked not more but less than he had been granted at Luca. It was the last hope of peace, and Cicero, who had just returned after a strenuous year as governor of Cilicia, thought—and he claimed to speak for the majority—that the terms should be accepted. But Pompey's slow and irresolute soul had been stiffened into obstinacy, and he would have none of them. He let his supporters know that the moment for action had come. The Senate decreed that Caesar must give up his province by March 1 of that year on pain of being proclaimed a public enemy. The Caesarian tribunes vetoed the resolution, but on January 7 the Senate declared a state of war, enjoining the consuls to see that the republic took no hurt. A general levy was ordered, and the treasury was put at Pompey's disposal. Mark Antony and

Quintus Cassius escaped from Rome in the disguise of peasants and fled towards Caesar's camp at Ravenna.

While the tribunes were speeding along the Flaminian Way Caesar had come to a decision. His enemies had taken the initiative in opening the flood-gates of civil war. He himself had respected the law which Pompey had scorned, but the moment had come when all laws had little meaning. He had already sent across the Alps for the rest of his troops, and on January 10, as soon as the news arrived from Rome, he called together the soldiers of the Thirteenth legion, and unfolded to these young men of north Italy, whose cause he had always championed, the nature of the crisis and the reward which was preparing for the conqueror of Gaul. Their enthusiasm convinced him of the loyalty of his army. That afternoon he sent off secretly an advance party to seize the Italian border-town of Ariminum (Rimini)—his first act of revolution. He attended the local games and dined quietly with his staff, and then after dinner slipped off with a small retinue and crossed the little brook, called the Rubicon, which was the Italian frontier. We may reject the legends which grew up later about his hesitations and doubts on the brink of the stream and his relapse into antique superstition; such was not the nature of the man, and in any case he had taken the irrevocable step hours before when he sent off his advance guard to Ariminum. But Asinius Pollio may well have heard him, as he crossed, murmur the tag from Menander, ' Let the die be cast.'

There is no record of Caesar's thoughts during these last fateful days, but it is permissible to guess at them. He was most deeply anxious for peace. On this point the evidence is overwhelming, both from his deeds and from the admissions of his opponents. He had gone to the extremest lengths in concession, and had been willing to put himself well within the danger of his enemies. He knew the weakness of his own position. The complex party machine which he had built up in Rome had no meaning in civil war. What availed it that he had the urban rabble on his side if to all the substantial classes his name was anathema? The old nobility, the bureaucracy, the capitalists looked upon him as a menace to the state and to their own

F

fortunes, and many hated him with the vindictiveness which the dull always show towards a genius beyond their comprehension. Even among honest folk his name stank because of the tools he had been forced to use. Pompey had seven legions in Spain and the better part of ten in Italy, he had the authority for a general levy, and he had all the financial resources of the state, including the rich provinces of the East. Caesar himself was poorer than when nine years before he had gone to Gaul, for he had spent the fruits of his victories on his largesses in Rome. He had, it was true, nine veteran legions, of magnificent fighting quality, but they were now reduced in numbers and wearied with long campaigns. Could he count on their loyalty if he embarked on a struggle with the embattled forces of that commonwealth of which they had hitherto been the servants? They longed for peace, all Italy longed for peace, and the man who forced on war would incur a universal odium. What matter that this man had been shamelessly treated! Plain people would look only at the fact that he was defying the established government of the republic.

In the face of such handicaps Caesar was forced to his decision in the first place on personal grounds. He was literally fighting for his life. If he submitted he was a doomed man. When later he walked among the dead at Pharsalus, he was heard by Pollio to murmur to himself, 'This is what they brought me to. If I had dismissed my armies, I, Caesar, would have been condemned as a felon.' But with such a character personal fear plays only a little part; more grave was the ruin of a career and the downfall of the ambitions of a lifetime. By the labours of thirty years he had made for himself a dominant position in the state, and this was now in jeopardy. He had begun by playing the obvious game for its obvious prizes, careless what weapon he used, but as he moved upward his motives had changed. Certain attachments he had always cherished, the sentimental attachments of his kin and his party, but slowly he had acquired deeper and prouder loyalties. Unless everything were to go by the board, he must be prepared to 'put it to the touch to win or lose it all,' to make the supreme effort of courage and to stand alone.

Gradually the conviction must have forced itself on his mind that there was no way but revolution. Senatorial government was now in itself a revolutionary thing, for it played fast and loose with the law and disregarded utterly the spirit of the constitution. This slovenly lawlessness could only be checked by a nobler and wiser kind. Pedants still prated about the preservation of the republic, but there was no republic to preserve. With his clear insight Caesar looked upon the life of Rome and saw its rottenness. The old regime had gone beyond hope of recall, and for a Periclean democracy the first conditions were wanting. He knew the Optimates, for he belonged to them by birth; he knew the bourgeoisie, for he had been at various times its bogey and its darling; he knew the mob, for he was still its leader. In no class was there any sound tradition of civic liberty and decency, and the ancient constitution which formally survived was a mere parody of government. He was not yet confident as to the right course for the future, but he was very clear that there must be a wholesale demolition of rubbish and a rebuilding from the foundations.

But the creed towards which he was feeling his way was not negative only. If Rome was moribund, her domains had still the stuff of life. In his wars he had learned something of their people, and he believed that there was material there for the making of a great nation. The East he did not know, but he could speak at first hand for the West—for Italy, for Spain, for the land beyond the Po, for the wide spaces of the North. He had now a conception of a different type of empire—an empire of vigorous local life and culture, self-governing under some new and more generous polity, not merely a territory of Rome, but Roman in a truer sense than the city by the Tiber.

There things were still on the lap of the gods. In the meantime there was the urgent crisis before him, the duty of following his star, of bringing order into chaos by the force of his genius and in the last resort by his sword. If the future depended upon one man, that man would not be found wanting. It was a true instinct which led later ages to regard the crossing of the Rubicon as a decisive moment in the history of mankind.

IX

THE CONQUEST OF THE WORLD

IN four years Caesar battered down the walls of the old Rome and began the building of the new, and in these years, incidentally, he conquered the world. He moved about the globe like a fire, habitually daring extreme occasions, taking the one chance in a thousand and succeeding, careless of life and fortune, conducting himself like one who believes that he has a divine mission and that the gods will not recall him till it is fulfilled. His work may well seem to reach the extreme compass of what is possible for a mortal spirit. But he could not have achieved it unless the fabric he assailed had been rotten and the men he fought only relics and simulacra. He is the one living man among a medley of phantoms.

At dawn on January 13 Caesar occupied Ariminum. He straightway sent Mark Antony across the Apennines to occupy Arretium (Arezzo) and so protect his flank, while he marched south along the Adriatic, taking the little coast towns. A message from Pompey induced him to make another effort for peace; he wrote begging for an interview, and proposed that they should both disarm, that Pompey should proceed to Spain, and that he himself should give up his *imperium* and go to Rome to stand for the consulship. For some weeks he hoped and toiled for conciliation, but Labienus, his chief lieutenant, had gone over to Pompey and had filled his mind with tales of the weakness of Caesar's command, and Pompey hardened his heart.

Caesar's aim was to manœuvre his opponent into a corner where he could force upon him a personal meeting, for he believed that if he could break through the cordon of senatorian advisers he could make Pompey see reason. But Caesar's speed had been too successful, for it scared his enemies out of reason into panic. He was the 'man from the north,' with behind him all the prestige of that dim land from which in past times conquerors had marched to the gates of Rome. Pompey might have a greater weight of numbers, but Caesar had the spearhead. Moreover, they knew in their hearts that Caesar had been tricked and insulted and had many accounts to settle. So every road running south and east from Rome was thronged with fleeing politicians and all the classes whose consciences were bad and who had much to lose; they did not even tarry to empty the state coffers. Among them went Cicero, much out of temper and with no illusions left about Pompey and the senatorians.

Presently Pompey recovered his wits. He may have meant at first to make a stand at Brundisium and challenge Caesar's small force. But he did not trust his troops, and he found his new levies hard to mobilise in the winter weather. He went first to Capua, and then to Luceria in Apulia, which was on the road to Brundisium. At Corfinium, eighty miles to the north-west, Domitius Ahenobarbus was left to collect an army. But Caesar was upon him, and on February 20 he took the place, sent back Domitius to his master, and enlisted the senatorian levies under his own standard. He still hoped to bring Pompey to book in Italy, and force him and the Senate to conclude a reasonable peace. He took no man prisoner, and dismissed every Pompeian who fell into his hands with friendly messages. 'My method of conquest,' so ran his published declaration, 'shall be a new one; I will fortify myself with compassion and generosity.'

Pompey, who had now been joined by the whole senatorial debating society, and by all the rich and timid who saw even in this broken reed the only support for their fortunes, was in no mood either to stand or to treat. He had decided to leave Italy and to fight in the East, which was his old campaigning ground. His vanity had been so deeply wounded that he was ready for war to the uttermost. A fleet was collected at Brundisium, and, when Caesar arrived there on March 9, part of the Pompeian army had already sailed. Caesar tried to blockade the remainder and again sought an interview with Pompey, but with the loss of two ships Pompey made his escape and there were no transports in which to follow him.

Italy was now in Caesar's hands, for in two months his deadly swiftness had broken up or immobilised ten legions. But Italy lay between two fires, great armies in Epirus in the East and in Spain in the West. Caesar hastened to Rome to patch up some kind of interim government. He implored the senators who had stayed at home to help him to restore order and to carry on the administration. He strove to allay the fears of the well-to-do and made an arrangement about debts which disappointed his more impecunious supporters. He took possession of what funds remained in the treasury, and left Lepidus, the praetor, as the chief officer of government in the city, and Mark Antony, the tribune, in command of the Italian troops. This latter was an unfortunate appointment, for it was by his association with Antony that Caesar's reputation has been most seriously smirched. Gross in habit, a savage in appetites, almost illiterate (he wrote vile Latin), without the rudiments of statesmanship, he had no gifts as a leader except the 'Caesariana celeritas,' which in his case was often misdirected; and there is good reason to suspect at various times his loyalty to his master.

Then, having decided that if one is between two fires it is well to begin by quenching the nearer, Caesar started early in April for Spain. 'I go,' he said, 'to meet an army without a general, and shall return thence to meet a general without an army.'

The key-point of Massilia (Marseilles), defended by Domitius Ahenobarbus who had been released at Corfinium, declared for Pompey, and Caesar left its reduction to Decimus Brutus with a hastily prepared fleet. Then he crossed the Pyrenees to deal with the army of Spain. He found it north of the Ebro at Ilerda (Lerida) on the river Segre—seven legions, to meet which he had six, and a strong force of Gallic cavalry. His aim was to fight a bloodless campaign, since he was fighting against Romans, and to manœuvre the enemy into a position where he would be compelled to surrender. In forty days he succeeded, by taking risks which would have been insane except for a general who had a veteran army in which he could implicitly trust. By diverting the Segre he forced the Pompeians to move south to the Ebro, overtook them on the march, drove them into a hopeless position from which they were compelled to retreat towards Ilerda, hung on their heels, brought them to a halt, surrounded them, and left them no alternative but surrender. He asked only that they should disband, and he gave them food and their arrears of pay. Hither Spain was now in his hands, and Farther Spain, under

Varro the antiquary, presently made its submission. Early in September he was at Massilia, which had yielded to Decimus Brutus. Only in Africa was there any set-back, where Curio had been beaten by Juba the Numidian king, and slain.

Caesar had now under his control all of Italy, Spain, Gaul, Sardinia, and Sicily, and the food supply of the capital was thus assured. He had been made dictator in order to hold the consular elections, a post which he filled for eleven days, till he was duly nominated to his second consulship. After seeing that the full citizenship was granted at last to the inhabitants of Transpadane Gaul, he turned his face eastward, and by the close of December was ready to embark at Brundisium. A lesser man would have been content to control the West and remain in Italy on the defensive, but Caesar saw that this would mean a splitting up of the empire, and he was not minded to let any part of the Roman domains slip from the hands of the master of Rome. His duty was to seek out and beat his enemy before he did further mischief.

Meantime Pompey, with his retinue of patricians and capitalists, was comfortably entrenched on the Illyrian coast at Dyrrhachium (Durazzo). He had got himself an army, and the twin points in his policy were the control of the sea and of the vast recruiting grounds of the East. He had a magnificent fleet under Bibulus, and Caesar could scarcely lay his hand even on transports. He did not believe that his enemy could follow him, and his intention was to return and reconquer Italy in the spring. The sea gave him the strategical initiative, and he had all the advantages in numbers and equipment. His obvious course was to take the offensive, but, confused by the divided voices of his entourage, he remained supine. Caesar, with as many troops as he could find shipping for, escaped the watching Bibulus, and on January 5, 48, landed a hundred miles south of Dyrrhachium and pushed northward to Apollonia. He was clinging to an unfriendly coast, with a dubious hope of supplies and precarious communications.

What followed is one of the most audacious episodes in military history, in which Caesar suffered the second defeat of his career. He fortified a camp on the south side of the river Apsus, while

Pompey sat on the opposite bank. Mark Antony brought over the rest of his legions, and managed to land them at Lissus, well to the north of Dyrrhachium. Caesar by a flank march joined him before Pompey could intercept him, and the latter fell back on Dyrrhachium. Caesar established himself to the east of the town, and by a line of circumvallation penned in Pompey between himself and the sea. But twenty thousand men could not imprison fifty thousand, and Pompey, by a sudden assault at a weak point of the enclosing lines, inflicted upon his opponent a severe defeat. Caesar is said to have declared that his antagonist could have won the campaign at this point if he had known how to follow up an advantage.

Retreating to Apollonia, Caesar waited to see what the enemy proposed to do. The right course for Pompey was to make forthwith for Italy, which would have fallen helpless into his hands; in that event Caesar intended to march round the head of the Adriatic and fight from the base of Cisalpine Gaul. Or he might join his father-in-law, Metellus Scipio, who was bringing reinforcements from Syria, and whom Caesar had sent off two legions under Domitius to intercept. Pompey chose the latter course and turned east along the Egnatian Way to meet Metellus. Domitius brought off his legions just in time, and joined Caesar in the north-west corner of the plain of Thessaly. Pompey, united with Metellus, turned southward, intending to wear down Caesar's small army by manœuvring and to use his powerful cavalry to cut off its supplies. But Labienus's talk about the poor quality of Caesar's men had done its work, the young bloods of the aristocracy insisted on putting an immediate end to their detested enemy, so at Pharsalus Pompey at last offered battle.

Pharsalus, one of the decisive actions of the world, has no great tactical interest. It was a victory of veterans of uniform type and training against a motley levy, of resolved genius against irresolute talent. Pompey's plan was to outflank Caesar's right—his shieldless side—with his 7000 cavalry, but Caesar anticipated it, and placed a fourth line of six cohorts there in special reserve. There, too, he placed his small but efficient body of horse, and the unconquerable Tenth legion. After addressing his men he ordered the charge. The two centres were at once interlocked, and when the Pompeian cavalry swung to the outflanking movement they were met by Caesar's infantry reserve, who used their javelins as stabbing spears and routed the horsemen. This decided the issue. Caesar flung in his fourth-line supports; the enemy broke, fled to his camp, which was soon stormed, and surrendered in masses. Pompey himself galloped to Larissa and thence to the coast. He had lost 15,000 killed and wounded and 24,000 prisoners. At Mytilene he took ship for Egypt, and was murdered as he landed at Pelusium, a melancholy end for a just man who had stumbled upon a destiny too great for him. The time was now the late summer.

Caesar followed hot-foot on the trail, for it was not his way to leave a task half-done. At Alexandria he heard the news of Pompey's death, and discovered that he had stepped into a nest of hornets. The children of Ptolemy Auletes were fighting for the throne, and he found himself involved in a squalid strife of eunuchs and parasites with little more than 3000 legionaries behind him. Once again, as at Dyrrhachium, he was clinging desperately to a hostile shore without supports. The conqueror of Pompey was besieged all winter in Alexandria, and it was not till the end of March 47 that he was relieved by the young Mithridates of Pergamos, and Cleopatra and her younger brother were placed together on the throne. To that winter belong many strange tales. He had an affair with Cleopatra and delayed in Egypt three months after the arrival of Mithridates, though the affairs of the whole world clamoured for his attention. He is said to have sailed with her far up the Nile, and to have dreamed of penetrating to its mystic sources between the hills Mophi and Crophi. That may well be true, for he was always an ardent geographer and avid of new lands; over a man, too, who for eleven years had led the life of the camp, the wit and beauty of that supreme enchantress may have cast a spell. She had a son during the year whom she fathered upon him, and whom Augustus afterwards put to death as an impostor. Caesar's friends disbelieved the tale of Caesarion's paternity, and later ages are free to decide as they please.

But the delay, whether due to Cleopatra or to the necessity of settling Egyptian affairs, gave the embers of opposition time to blow to a flame, and there was mischief afoot in Rome, in North Africa, and in Spain. Caesar left Egypt in June, marched north through Syria, and in a swift and brilliant campaign crushed the insurrection of Pharnaces, the son of the great Mithridates. Then at last he set out for home after an absence of twenty months. At every point in his journey he settled local problems on a basis over which he had long pondered. When he landed in Italy, he met the disillusioned Cicero, whom he sent off to his books with friendly encouragements. In Rome he spent three arduous months. He had been made dictator, and so had the whole administration on his shoulders, and Mark Antony had let things go wildly wrong. Caesar devised a practical solution of the urgent question of debtors and creditors, and quelled a mutiny among his troops by addressing them as 'citizens' instead of as 'fellow soldiers.' Then in the middle of December he set out for Africa, for there the senatorian remnant had massed for a last stand. He went by way of Sicily, where in his eagerness to be gone he pitched his tent within reach of the sea spray.

On the first day of the year 46 he landed in Africa to begin what was to be the most difficult campaign of the civil war. A third time he had flung himself into an unfriendly country with inadequate forces, and, since these forces were mostly new recruits, he had first of all to train them. He was fighting against desperate men, inspired by Labienus, the ablest of his old marshals, and against the craft of their Numidian allies. It was not till early April that he received the rest of his army and was able to offer battle. He invested the town of Thapsus, and the enemy, in an attempt to relieve it, was drawn into a field action. That day Caesar seems to have had an attack of his old ailment, epilepsy, and after the enemy was broken the fight passed out of his control. The Pompeians had shown extreme brutality, his legionaries had many scores to settle, and he was unable to prevent that which he had always laboured to prevent, a butchery of Romans. He moved on to Utica, where Cato was in command. Cato had no power either to stay the rout of fugitives from Thapsus or to defend the place; he did his best to arrange for the embarkation of the garrison for Spain, and then, after reading in the *Phaedo* of Plato, fell upon his sword. So died one who had lost his way in the world, and had retired inside the narrow fortalice of his own self-esteem.

Numidia was added to the Roman domains, and placed under Sallust the historian, and in July Caesar was back in the capital. There he had to go through the wearisome business of celebrating grandiose triumphs, and to take up the heavy burden of the still chaotic government. 'We are slaves to him,' Cicero wrote with startling acumen, 'and he himself to the times.' What he did in Rome during the next six months we shall see later; one thing was the reform of the calendar to make it conform with the solar year, and this meant that the year 46 had to be extended to four hundred and forty-five days. In the intercalary period he fought his last battle. Pompey's son Gnaeus and Labienus had raised the standard of revolt in Spain, and they must be dealt with before the empire could have rest. It was an enterprise in which even the Roman conservatives wished him well. They had no desire to come under the tyranny of a savage like the young Pompey; as Gaius Cassius said, if they were to have a master they preferred the 'old and gentle one.' The campaign, conducted by both sides with intense bitterness, lay in the valley of the Guadalquivir around Cordova and southward to the foot-hills of the Sierra Nevada. At Munda, on March 17, 45, came the deciding battle, the sternest of all Caesar's actions except Alesia. It was not till evening, after a long day of silent and desperate bloodshed, that the Pompeians broke. No quarter was asked or given, Labienus and the young Pompey perished, and the bodies of the slain invested the little town like a rampart. His great-nephew, a boy of eighteen, Octavius by name, accompanied Caesar, and on that day first acquired his hatred of the blundering folly of war.

There was peace now on earth, though in the Far East the thunder-cloud of Parthia was still dark. All that summer was spent in arranging the affairs of Spain and Gaul, and Caesar did not recross the Alps till September. Meanwhile in Rome plebiscites and senatus-consults heaped fresh honours on the conqueror, and men held their breath to see what the master of the world would do with his winnings.

X

FACTS AND VISIONS

In the six months left to Caesar of life two major tasks filled his thoughts. Crassus had bequeathed him the Parthian problem as a bitter legacy, and the defeat of Carrhae must be avenged before Rome could be securely mistress of the world. This was more than a mere incident of frontier defence, for he wished to make the East as Roman as the West, and to revive under the Roman eagles the glory of its ancient culture. He had dreams of rebuilding its famous cities and of planting new colonies on the Euxine and the Aegean. Moreover, for his imperial reconstruction he needed money, and the East was still the world's treasure-house. His enemies whispered that he meant to move the centre of power out of Italy, and that not Rome, but Alexandria or Ilium, would be the future imperial capital.

Honours were showered on him, beyond prudence, if not beyond reason. He was so indisputably the master of the world that his friends laboured to devise emblems of his mastery, while his foes were extravagant in their honorific proposals in order that the recipient might be held up to ridicule. Caesar early made two of his purposes clear. He did not mean to perpetuate the military dictatorship, and he began to disband his legions; he desired to establish the rule of one man, so he treated the Senate as no more than an advisory council of state. For the rest, he accepted what was pressed upon him with ironical complaisance, for he held that no titles could increase or detract from the reality of his power. Consul, dictator, censor, *pater patriae*, Imperator for life—these distinctions added nothing to one who was in fact monarch.

It would have been well for him had he been more fastidious about such baubles, for names may have a terrible potency. There were some, friends and foes, who would have had him called king, and no doubt the title would have been useful in his coming campaign in the East. He declined it, for he realised

that kingship was no exact description of the place he had won
for himself, and that in Roman minds it was cumbered with
heavy prejudice; but he refused without conviction, and thereby
planted many seeds of suspicion. Rome saw an oriental bias
in a mind which was always truly Roman.

What seems to us the more extravagant honour, the approach
to deification, really mattered less—his image carried in the
solemn procession of the gods, his statue in the temple of Quirinus
with the inscription *Deo Invicto*, the new gild of the Luperci
Juliani. The idea of the man-god was familiar to the East and
not unknown in Rome, for quasi-divine honours had been paid
to Scipio Africanus. The ancient state was also a church, and a
saviour of the state attracted naturally a religious veneration.
Posidonius had made room in his teaching for the deification of
rulers, and Posidonius was the fashionable philosopher of the
Roman intellectuals, while the cosmopolitan populace saw
nothing in the conception to alarm them. Caesar, sceptic and
realist, shrugged his shoulders and let popular folly have its way.
But he may have seen in it something which might be of use to
the empire of which he dreamed. The Greek city-states had
failed because they had no ultimate mystical point of unity; they
had been too rational, and the rational always invites argument.
If the world needed a single ruler, it might be well if that Imperator were also made *divus*, by the foresight of the wise as well
as by the superstition of the vulgar.

The urgent task which confronted him had to be faced alone.
He appointed the occupants of the regular offices—too cavalierly
perhaps, for they had little meaning for him in that strenuous
hour of reconstruction. He had a multitude of devoted henchmen, but no cabinet, no colleagues whom he could lean upon for
counsel. Fourteen years of unremitting toil had worn out his
body, though they had not lowered the vitality of his mind. His
health was broken, and his fits of epilepsy were becoming too
frequent. Yet, as happens sometimes to a man in middle life
who finds himself after long absence back in a familiar world,
there was a curious return of youthful interests, as if he longed to
resume before it was too late some of the pleasures which he had
so long forsworn for ambition. He dined out much, and talked
freely; too freely, for his heavy preoccupations made him forget

his old tactical discretion. He lived carefully, and an innocent vanity seems to have revived in him. He liked the permission granted him to wear everywhere his laurel wreath, for it concealed his growing baldness, and he was proud of his high red leather boots, which were a tradition of the ancient Alban kings. He had taken to literature again, and amused himself with pamphlets on grammar and style, of which he was a fastidious critic, preferring the dry Attic manner to the more Corinthian rhythms of Cicero; and he published a reply, which Cicero praised, to the numerous eulogies of Cato. Cleopatra had come to Rome with a vast oriental retinue, desiring to share the throne of the master of the world, and Roman gossip made Caesar once again her devout lover. It is more likely that the Queen of Egypt's presence was less of a delight than an embarrassment; for such pleasures he was too busy and too weary.

For in the last months of his life he was engaged on no less a task than the remaking of the world. For years he had been pondering the matter, as Napoleon in his Eastern campaign pondered the reconstruction of France, and it was now his business to put into concrete shape the scheme which he had devised among the African sands and the Illyrian glens and by the reedy watercourses of Gaul. It is not easy to decipher the blurred palimpsest which is all that remains to us, but some of the original script may still be read.

On one point he was adamant—the old constitution had gone for ever. To revive the substance of the republic, as Cicero wished, was beyond the power of man, and to have restored its forms would have been a piece of foolish antiquarianism and a plain dereliction of duty. Caesar was no iconoclast, but he was a little impatient of the trivial, and did not see the value of an occasional condescension to human weakness. The Senate, the ancient rock of offence, was largely increased in numbers; he may have intended to make it a council representative of the whole empire, but for the moment, while he treated it with respect, he kept it powerless. The Optimates were quietly set aside, though he seems to have had in mind the building up of a new patriciate, based upon the historic houses. But the cardinal matter was the creation of a system under which the sovereign power should be in the hands of a single man, for it seemed to him that no other plan could save the world from anarchy. He was such a man, and, having no son of his body, he looked to his great-nephew to continue his work, for an elective principate was impossible in the then confusion of things. The old Roman *imperium* seemed the natural means by which the new supreme power could be grafted on the state. He aimed at a civil commonwealth, but it was proof of the difficulties of the task that the word which best described the new sovereign was one associated with military command.

Having determined the central power he turned to the details of government. He began the codification of the laws which Hadrian was to complete, notably the praetorian edicts embodying that *jus gentium* which was valid for all free citizens of the empire. He dealt drastically with the scourge of usury, and extricated many honest men from the toils of debt; protected Italian agriculture; extended the bounds of land settlement; suppressed extravagant luxury; abolished the farming of the provincial taxes; in a word, put into effect all that was valuable in the policy of the earlier democrats, while, by the introduction of a means test for recipients, he lessened the evils of the corn dole. He had dreams of restoring the family discipline of an earlier Rome, and there is evidence that, like Augustus, he wished to revive the ancient cults of the Italian soil—'Pan and old Silvanus and the sister nymphs'—for he had a tenderness for all deep-rooted simplicities. He sought, too, to develop the material resources of his domain, not only to rebuild Carthage and Corinth and drive a ship-canal through the Isthmus, but to drain the Pontine marshes, construct a great port at Ostia, carry roads through the Apennines, and make Rome a city worthy of her fame.

Many of these projects might have been fathered by any aedile of genius. The largeness of Caesar's grasp is to be seen rather in his fundamental policy of empire. His first principle was decentralisation. Rome was to be now only the greatest among many great and autonomous cities. He passed a local government act for Italy which was the beginning of a municipal system, one of the best of Rome's creations, and he proposed to apply its principles throughout the empire, so that the Roman citizenship should be free to all who were worthy of it. The

Imperator should nominate the provincial governors and thereby take responsibility for their competence and honesty. The empire was to be rebuilt on a basis of reason and humanity, and, while local idiosyncrasies were to be preserved, the binding nexus would be Roman law and Roman civilisation. He was well aware that government by the consent of the governed was not so much a moral as a physical necessity, and he believed that only by giving to the parts order, peace, and a decent liberty could that consent be won. For sound administration he must have an expert civil service. Already in Gaul he had trained a great staff of competent personal assistants, and now he laid the foundations of that imperial bureaucracy which for four centuries was one of the buttresses of Roman rule.

Such was Caesar's scheme of empire, inspired by the two principles of the ultimate sovereignty of one man and of wide local liberties, and on it the later edifice was built. Instead of a city and a host of servile provinces there was to be a universal Roman nation, in which the conquered should feel that they ranked with the conquerors, and might exclaim in the words of Themistocles, 'We had been undone had we not been undone.' It is easy to see its defects. There was no certainty of continuance in the repository of the sovereign power. The army, if the sovereign were not a great soldier, might interfere malignly in the conduct of affairs. But it seems idle to criticise it on the ground that it lacked representative institutions. Had these been confined to Rome the old oligarchy would have returned, and with vast distances and slow and difficult transport any world-wide system was strictly impossible. Caesar had to make such bread as his indifferent grain permitted. Nevertheless, he offered his world a new evangel. For the first time in government prejudice was replaced by science and tradition by reason. He made the rule of law prevail, and gave the plain man a new order and a new hope.

His achievement—if we must attempt to summarise it—was first that he was a 'swallower of formulas,' a destroyer of dead creeds and decayed institutions. On the constructive side he gave his country a further lease of life by infusing into her veins the fresh blood of the peoples she had conquered. From the provinces were to come in future days many famous Romans—

Virgil from his own Transpadanes; Lucan and Seneca and Martial; the great emperors and soldiers of Spanish, African, Gallic, and Dacian stock; the princes of the Christian church who transmuted the cities of Cecrops and Romulus into a City of God. Again, he gave civilisation a life of five further centuries before the dark curtain descended. The empire fell in the end because of the pressure of the barbarians on its frontiers, and because of the ruin of the middle classes within by insensate burdens, and the degradation of the proletariat into a light-witted pauper rabble. These are the causes which at all times are the ruin of great nations—*de nostro tempore fabula narratur.* Caesar by his conquests staved off the descent of the outland hordes, while by his internal reforms he kept the danger from the urban mob within bounds, and safeguarded productive industry in town and country.

He gave the world a long breathing-space, and thereby ensured that the legacy of both Greece and Rome should be so inwoven with the fabric of men's minds that it could never perish. He taught no new way of life, no religion; he had no comfort for the weary and the sick at heart; he was a child of this world, content to work with the material he found and reduce it to order and decency. But he made it certain that the spiritual revelation for which mankind hungered would not be lost in the discords of a brutish anarchy. His standards were human, but the highest to which humanity can attain, and his work may well be regarded as the greatest recorded effort of the human genius.

The man who achieved it—and herein lies Caesar's unique fascination—was no leaden superman, no heavy-handed egotist, but one with all the charms and graces. The burden of the globe on his shoulders did not impede his lightness of step. War and administration never made him a narrow specialist. His culture was as wide as that of any man of his day; he loved art and poetry and music and philosophy, and would turn gladly to them in the midst of his most critical labours. He was the best talker in Rome and the most gracious of companions. There was no mysticism or superstition in his clear mind, but he was not without certain endearing sentimentalities. He was

G

tolerant of other men's prejudices and respected their private
sanctities. Combined in him in the highest degree were the
realism of the man of action, the sensitiveness of the artist, and the
imagination of the creative dreamer—a union not, I think, to
be paralleled elsewhere.

But the spell of his intellect was matched by the spiritual
radiance which emanated from him to light and warm his world.
He could be harsh with the terrible politic cruelty of a society
based upon slavery, but no one could doubt the depth of his
affections and the general benignity of his character. He had
no petty vanity; the *Commentaries* is the most unegotistic book
ever written. This man, whose courage in every circumstance
of life was like a clear flame, had a womanish gentleness and the
most delicate courtesy. He never failed a friend, though his
friends often failed him. He was relentless enough in the cause
of policy, but he could not cherish a grudge and he was incapable
of hate; his dislike of Cato was rather the repugnance of a
profound intellect to a muddy and shallow one. In Cicero's
words, he forgot nothing except injuries. When Catullus abused
him he asked him to dinner, and when an enemy fell into his
power he dismissed him with compliments. The meanness and
the savagery which are born of fear were utterly alien to his soul.
The most penetrating and comprehensive of human minds and
the bravest of mortal hearts were joined in him with what is best
described in a phrase of Mark Antony's which Dio Cassius
reports, an 'inbred goodness.'

His dreams were to be fulfilled, but his immediate work
failed, as it was bound to fail, for he was a man of genius and not
a demigod. The pioneer is rarely the exploiter, and the man
who destroys an old edifice and marks out the lines of a new one
does not often live to see the walls rise. Caesar made the empire
by preparing the ground for it, but, like King David, he had to
leave the building to another. He had aroused too many deep
antagonisms to be permitted to complete his task. He was too
much above his contemporaries, too far in advance of his age,
too solitary in his greatness. Moreover, the world had not yet
learned its lesson and the forces of strife were not yet spent.
Years were still to follow of anarchy and misery till Rome in

utter weariness could accept Caesar's evangel, and a different type of worker could finish his work, the slow, patient 'trimmer' who interwove so cunningly the new with the old that men accepted novelties as common sense. The future was with his great-nephew Octavius, the son of the country banker, now a pleasant modest youth of eighteen. It was given to Augustus to bring into being what Julius dreamed.

During the last months of 45 it was plain that clouds were massing on the horizon. Caesar had pardoned his enemies, but they did not forgive him, and the remnants of the old senatorian faction looked on at his doings in impotent hate. Honest conservatives regarded the new monarchy as an impious breach with a sacred past, and ambitious men like Gaius Cassius felt themselves shamed and overshadowed by Caesar's lonely greatness. The wise youth, Marcus Brutus, Cato's nephew and Servilia's son, had become wiser than ever, and had won great repute, in spite of his notorious avarice, as a repository of the antique virtues. Even Caesar respected him, for he seemed to have a *gravitas* uncommon in that age. Brutus was rapidly becoming intoxicated by the flattery of his friends and by his own brand of rhetoric. Some, too, of Caesar's old companions in arms, like Decimus Brutus and Trebonius, were growing estranged. A general can count more securely on the loyalty of the rank and file than upon that of his marshals, for these are apt to think that his fame has been of their making, and to be jealous of any pre-eminence which they do not share. Moreover, there was widely diffused in Roman society an uneasiness about what the future might hold, and fear about the Parthian campaign. Men saw moving from the East the spectre of an oriental monarchy in place of the Rome which they knew and loved.

Caesar was aware of these hidden fires, but he refused to deviate one step from his course. He would have no bodyguard, and walked unattended and unarmed in the streets, for it was better, he said, to die like a free man than to live like a tyrant. When his friends warned him of conspiracies he smilingly put them by. The honourable fatalism, which is necessary for any great achievement, was now, as always, his philosophy; the gods would not send for him until his task was finished, for only on that presumption could life be lived. But it is clear that in these

last months he thought often of death. Sometimes a great
weariness overcame him, and he was heard to say that he had
been long enough in the world.   On the night before his end the
conversation turned on the best kind of death, and he said
abruptly, as if he had long pondered the matter, 'a sudden one.'
But he would not change his habits or take any precautions, for
such would have been beneath his Roman pride.   Perhaps, too,
in a mind so prescient there lay another reason.   He may have
come to realise that the task he had set himself could not be
completed by his hands, but that its success would be assured if
it were sealed with his blood.   'For where a testament is, there
must also of necessity be the death of the testator.'

XI

THE END

ON the 19th of March 44, Caesar was to leave for the East on his Parthian campaign. On the Ides, the 15th, a meeting of the Senate was called to make the final arrangements, and this was the occasion which the conspirators selected for their deed. A month before at the Wolf-festival, the Lupercalia, Caesar had been offered a crown by Antony, and when he had put it aside there had been shouts of 'Hail, O King!' although the main plaudits were for the rejection. What had to be done must be done at once, for the Roman people were plainly in a divided mood. It was resolved that the Senate's meeting was the proper occasion, since the whole body of senators would thus be compromised, and the murder would have the colour of a ceremonial act of justice. On the night of the 14th the conspirators dined with Cassius. Some proposed that Antony and Lepidus also should die, but Marcus Brutus objected that this would spoil the sacrificial character of the deed. Cicero was not admitted to their confidence, being regarded as too old, too garrulous, and too timid. Caesar supped with Lepidus, and at the board sat his old marshal, Decimus Brutus, now one of the leaders of the plot.

The morning of the Ides was fair spring weather. It was the festival of an ancient Italian deity, Anna Perenna, and the Field of Mars was thronged with the commonalty of the city, dancing, and drinking in rude huts of boughs. Caesar had a return of his old fever; his wife, Calpurnia, had slept badly and had dreamed ill-omened dreams; the auspices, too, were unfavourable, though he had never set much store by auspices; so he sent Antony to postpone the Senate's meeting. The conspirators, with daggers in their writing-cases, were at the rendezvous at daybreak in the colonnade of Pompey's Curia, and in case of need Decimus Brutus had a troop of gladiators stationed in the adjoining theatre, where a performance was going on. But no Caesar appeared, and presently came Antony with news of the adjournment. The gang were in despair and despatched one of Caesar's former lieutenants to his house to plead with him to change his mind. The mission was successful. Caesar shook off his lassitude, ordered his litter, and just before noon arrived at the Curia.

Trebonius detained Antony in conversation in the porch, for Antony's bull strength was formidable. The dictator entered the house—a little haughty and abstracted, as if his mind were on higher things than the senatorian ritual. A paper had been put into his hands by some one in the crowd, which contained the details of the plot, but he did not glance at it. The senators rose, as he advanced and sat himself in his gilded chair. A petition was presented, and the conspirators clustered around him as if to press its acceptance, kissing his breast and seizing his hands. Annoyed by their importunity he attempted to rise, when one of them pulled the toga from his shoulders. This was the preconcerted signal, and Casca from behind wounded him slightly in the throat. He turned and caught his assailant's arm, and in an instant the whole pack were upon him, like hounds pulling down a deer. He was struck in the side, in the thigh, in the face, and his assailants stabbed each other in their blind fury. He covered his head with his gown in a vain effort of defence, but his frail body was soon overpowered, and he fell dead with twenty-three wounds at the base of Pompey's statue.

The deed was done, and Brutus, raising aloft a dripping dagger, cried out to the ashen Cicero that liberty was restored. He began a prepared speech, but there was no one to listen, for the senators had fled. The murderers, still shrieking and babbling in their excitement, rushed out of doors, and one of them lifted up a cap of freedom on a spear and called on the people to revere the symbol. But the streets were empty. The revellers of the Anna Perenna festival had fled to their homes, the booths were closed, the theatre audience had scattered, and the gladiators of Decimus Brutus were looting far and wide. The ominous silence brought some sobriety into disordered minds. Where was Antony? Lepidus and his legion were not far off. Rome seemed to take their deed less as a liberation than as an outrage. They ran stumbling to the Capitol for refuge.

Presently came three faithful slaves, who carried the dead

body to Caesar's house, and, as the litter passed, men and women peeped out of their shuttered dwellings, and there was much wailing and lamentation. A little later Brutus and Cassius descended to the Forum to harangue the people, but they found that the listeners received their appeals in silence, so they hurried back to their sanctuary. As the March dusk fell Cicero visited the refugees and did his best to hearten them. He told them that all Rome rejoiced at the tyrant's death, but they had seen the faces in the streets, and disbelieved him. They begged him to go to Antony and call upon him to defend the republic, but he declined, for he knew better than to put his hand in the wolf's mouth.

Meantime, in the home on the Palatine, Calpurnia was washing the wounds of her dead husband, and Antony was grimly barricaded in his house, and Lepidus sat in the Forum with his avenging legion. In the Capitol the liberators continued their feverish council, every man of them twittering with nerves, now expanding in sudden outbursts of rhetoric and self-admiration, now shaken with terror and crying that all was lost. . . . They feared for themselves, but they believed that they had done with Caesar, not knowing that their folly had perfected his task and made his dreams immortal.

BIBLIOGRAPHICAL NOTE

ANCIENT

THE chief authorities are the *Orationes* and *Epistolae* of Cicero, the seven books of Caesar's own *Commentarii de Bello Gallico*, and the three books of his *Commentarii de Bello Civili*; the eighth book *de Bello Gallico* and the *de Bello Alexandrino*, probably written by his lieutenant Aulus Hirtius; and the *de Bello Africano* and the *de Bello Hispaniensi*, the work of unknown officers. The *Catilina* of Sallust contains one of Caesar's speeches, and there are references to him in several of the lyrics of Catullus and in some of the fragments of Varro. These, together with the Julian laws contained in the *Corpus Juris Civilis* and the Berlin *Corpus Inscriptionum Latinarum*, are all we have in the way of contemporary sources.

The books by Asinius Pollio and by the Caesarians Oppius and Balbus have disappeared, but their contents were undoubtedly used by later writers. The classic Roman history of Livy (who was born in 59 B.C. and was therefore almost a contemporary) has come down to us in an imperfect form, and the eight books dealing with the Civil War survive only in a summary. Livy was of the old republican school, and we may assume that his opinions were repeated by subsequent biographers. These obviously incorporate great masses of floating tradition about Caesar, and it is impossible to say what is fact and what is legend. The *Pharsalia* of Lucan (A.D. 39-65) is the work of a strong anti-Caesarian, and a glorification of Cato. Suetonius (*c*. A.D. 100), in his chapter on Julius in his *de Vita Caesarum*, shows the same spirit in a more moderate form, and he was followed by Plutarch (*c*. A.D. 45-127). It is likely that both Suetonius and Plutarch were much influenced by Livy. Appian (*c*. A.D. 138) in his Ῥωμαικά, is a more objective writer, but he is hasty and careless. A sounder historian is Dio Cassius (*c*. A.D. 155-235), who attempts some independent valuation of Caesar's character, and writes in a cool detached tone, but he too is demonstrably inaccurate. To these non-contemporary writers who worked on material which is now lost to us there may be added the fragments of Nicolaus of Damascus (in Müller's *Fragm. Hist. Graecorum*) who lived under Augustus, the occasional gossip of Aulus Gellius, and the two books of the *Historia Romana* of Velleius Paterculus, who was praetor under Tiberius.

MODERN

The chief general works on the period are Drumann, *Geschichte Roms* (1834-44: new ed. by Gröbe, 1906); Duruy, *Histoire Romaine*

(1881); Mommsen, *Römische Geschichte* (1854-56: Eng. trans., 1894); and Guglielmo Ferrero, *Grandezza e decadenza di Roma* (1902: Eng. trans., 1907). Of these writers Drumann is the safest guide. Mommsen is a historical genius of the first order who has made Roman history live again for the world, but he carries his admiration of Caesar to the point of idolatry, and he is over-fond of drawing inexact parallels with modern conditions. Ferrero has remarkable narrative skill, but he is apt to let his imagination run riot, and his ingenuity is often perverse. A work more limited in scope but admirably judicious and careful is Rice Holmes's *The Roman Republic and the Founder of the Empire* (1923). Excellent, too, is the treatment in the *Cambridge Ancient History*, vol. ix.

The best life of Caesar is that of Warde Fowler (1891). Froude's *Caesar* (1879) is like Mommsen's *History*, the work of a man of genius who weakens an argument, which I believe to be substantially sound, by overstating it. The *Histoire de Jules César* (1865-66) of Napoleon iii. contains the results of archaeological research in France up to the date of its publication. All three books are the work of strong admirers. E. G. Sihler's *Annals of Caesar* (1911) is a useful critical analysis of the evidence. A recent biography on popular lines is Matthias Gelzer's *Caesar der Politiker und Staatsmann* (1921). The case of the moderate conservatives like Cicero will be found in Strachan-Davidson's *Cicero* (1894), and the essay on ' Cicero's Case against Caesar ' in vol. v. of the edition of Cicero's *Letters* by Tyrrell and Purser (1897).

Various episodes of the life have been the subject of special monographs. The most important is Eduard Meyer's *Caesars Monarchie und das Principat des Pompejus* (second ed., 1919), which also contains a valuable account of the authorities ancient and modern. The quarrel with the Senate which led to the civil war—a vital point in Caesar's career—has been exhaustively discussed by Mommsen in his *Die Rechtsfrage zwischen Caesar und dem Senat* (1857), and by later writers like Guiraud and Holzapfel. The campaigns have been treated by experts—Napoleon i. (*Précis des guerres de César*, 1836), Napoleon iii. (*op. cit.*), Colonel Stoffel (*Hist. de Jules César—Guerre Civile*, 1887, and *Guerre de César et d'Arioviste*, 1890), and by the Duc d'Aumale in a celebrated article in the *Revue des Deux Mondes*, May 1858. But so far as the Gallic Wars are concerned everything is superseded by Rice Holmes's encyclopaedic *Caesar's Conquest of Gaul* (second ed., 1911). We still await a synoptic study of Caesar's military genius, such as Captain Liddell Hart has given us for Scipio Africanus.

The busts of Caesar will be found fully treated of in Bernouilli's *Römische Iconographie*. For the Roman machine of government in Caesar's day the reader may consult A. H. J. Greenidge's *Roman Public Life* (1901) and Sir H. Stuart Jones's chapter on ' Administration ' in *The Legacy of Rome* (1923). Roman private life is dealt with compendiously in Marquardt's great *Privatleben der Römer*, and most attractively in Boissier's *Cicéron et ses amis* (1865: Eng. trans., 1897), and Warde Fowler's *Social Life at Rome in the Age of Cicero* (1908). For the background of political and ethical thought during the period, reference may be made to P. Wendland's *Die hellenistisch-römisch Kultur* (1907), Warde Fowler's *Roman Ideas of Deity* (1914), E. Bevan's *Stoics and Sceptics* (1913), and Professor Barker's essay on ' The Conception of Empire ' in *The Legacy of Rome*.

No proper understanding of Caesar is possible without some knowledge of the work of Augustus, a figure second in importance only to Julius. For this the reader may be referred to Mommsen, *Provinces of the Roman Empire* (1884: Eng. trans., 1886); W. T. Arnold, *Roman Provincial Administration* (1906); Stuart Jones, *The Roman Empire* (1908); and Rice Holmes, *The Architect of the Roman Empire* (1928-31).

III
THE MASSACRE OF GLENCOE

ALICIAE
FILIOLAE
DILECTISSIMAE

I

The Fort of Inverlochy

THE Governor's room in the fort was a cheerless place on that afternoon of late December. It was barely furnished; a couple of travelling-chests, a big deal table crowded with papers, one or two chairs of local make with seats of untanned hide, and a camp bed in a corner. On the floor were skins of deer, and on one wall a stand of arms. The peat fire was burning badly, as it always did in a north-west wind, and the blue smoke from it clouded without warming the air. The small windows were plastered with drifting snow. The man who sat writing at the table stopped to listen to the gale, which howled outside and deadened the tramp of the sentry's feet. He shivered, and turned up the collar of his military greatcoat.

Colonel John Hill was an old man, well on in the sixties, with a lean tired face and washed-out eyes. He held himself erect, but rheumatism crippled his movements. That spring he had been sick for three months with fever and ague, and, though his health had improved in the summer, the wet autumn had brought a relapse and he had felt strangely inert and vigourless. Moreover, at no time in his long career had he been so cumbered with perplexities. He had got little out of life, and now the burden of it was becoming too heavy for him. Long ago he had lost all ambition and asked only for peace and a modest comfort, but these blessings were still denied him.

He took from a file a copy of the letter he had written to Lord Tarbat eight months before—Tarbat had always been his friend. 'I find illwishers grow upon me,' he read, 'and some great men. They say I am old, and would, I think, have me to reduce all the Highlands myself, which, if I could do, there would be as little need for them as there is for this garrison. I would his Majesty would give me any other place where I could be serviceable to him, and let some emulators take this, and then I might be quiet.' That plaint reminded him of the Psalms of David, and he muttered a verse or two to himself. He had always been a religious man.

The weather matched his mood. He let his pen drop, sank his chin into his greatcoat, and permitted his mind to run over his past vicissitudes and present distractions. For forty years and more he had been a soldier. Long ago in Cromwell's day he had served under George Monk in Fitch's regiment, and had come from Ruthven to command in this very fort of Inverlochy which Monk had built to bridle the wild Highlandmen. He had been young then and had loved the service, and the great Duke of Albemarle was a leader he had been proud to follow. He himself had been popular with the natives, and had hunted and fished with the chiefs; many a gift of salmon and venison had reached him from the hills; he had proclaimed Richard Cromwell in the market-place in the presence of Lochiel and Glengarry, and when King Charles came back to his own he had surrendered Inverlochy to Lochiel in all friendliness. He was a soldier, and knew no politics.

Since then he had heard the drum in various quarters of the world, but he had always cherished happy memories of Scotland. He had corresponded with the old laird of Culloden and with his son Duncan, the present laird, and he had now Duncan's brother John as his major. When the Revolution came he had been Constable of Belfast Castle and had made a stout stand against the Irish rebels; but for him, he believed the victory of the Boyne would not have been achieved. His reward had been to be sent to Scotland in June 1690, to take over the Inverlochy garrison which General Hugh Mackay had revived on Monk's plan.

There had been trouble from the first. Mackay, whose temper had not been improved by Killiecrankie, was captious, vain and irritable, with none of Monk's calm supremacy. The Jacobite commander-in-chief, Thomas Buchan, had indeed been soundly beaten by Sir Thomas Livingstone at Cromdale, and had since been vainly attempting what Mackay called the 'chicane' of war in Aberdeenshire, but it had been feared that any day he might come west to trouble Lochaber. Hill had felt himself called to too arduous a service. Scotland was a bleak place for a man who was in failing health and growing old. He considered that he deserved more comfortable rewards. The knighthood which was his due still tarried. He wanted a pension. He wanted a good regiment, and had only got an amalgam of the weak remnants of Kenmure's and Glencairn's. Above all, he wanted to be paid monies due to him. All his life he had been spending out of his own pocket on the public service: on providing a minister's stipend in the days of Cromwell; on garrisoning Belfast; and now on finding Inverlochy in the bare necessaries of life and defence.

His one pride was this fort of his, for of the policy which it exemplified he had been the chief begetter, and it carried the memories of his far-away youth. It had been re-christened Fort William, and the new works had been erected in eleven days. Mackay had found fault with the old site in the angle of the river Nevis, on the plea that it could be commanded from higher ground—as if the clans had much artillery! But he had made a solid business of the defence—fosse, wall twenty feet high palisaded around, *glacis* and *chemin couvert*. The chief trouble had been the barracks inside for the garrison of more than a thousand men, for no wood could be got in that countryside of scrub birch and hazel, and the Government were unconscionably slow in sending timber from Leith and the Clyde. Every week he had to write to Melville or Tarbat or Livingstone pleading for supplies.

It was not Mackay's blame. Before he left the Scottish command he had written to the Duke of Hamilton—Hill had seen the letter—declaring that the Inverlochy fort was 'the most important of the kingdom at present, and that which will at length make such as would sell their credit or service at such a dear rate to the King of no greater use, nor more necessary to him, than a Lothian or Fife laird,' and urging that 'it be by no means neglected though other things should be postponed.' But supplies still came laggardly. The garrison was short of ammunition, ill-clad and ill-shod; it was provisioned from Argyll and Kintyre, but food was constantly running low, and the men's rations were often only meal and water and a tot of *aqua vitae*. Small wonder that their temper was getting ugly.

There had been other troubles, some of them happily past. The first garrison had been four companies of the Angus regiment, four of Argyll's, and nine of the laird of Grant's. The Angus men, and especially their chaplain, did not like the place, and they had been sent to Flanders; Hill had regretted it, for they were good soldiers. After that he had been left with Grant's and Argyll's, and now they were all Argyll's. These last were Highlanders, and he was a little doubtful whether hawks could be trusted to pick out hawks' eyes. Angus's whiggamores were a troublesome folk, but more dependable. Then there was the question of a deputy-governor and lieutenant-colonel for the garrison. He refused to have a Highlander, and in the end got a certain James Hamilton, a Lowlander with good connections —a competent man, but a difficult subordinate, for he was in private correspondence with Sir John Dalrymple, the Secretary for Scotland, and Livingstone, who had succeeded Mackay as commander-in-chief, wrote to him more often than to the Governor.

Lastly, there was the eternal anxiety about communications. There were three routes to Inverlochy: one by sea from the south, and two by land. Of the land routes, that from Inverness had to pass through Glengarry's country, and that from Atholl through Badenoch was commanded by Keppoch, and in any case was not open till the middle of June. The only safe communication was by water. But the Government showed no sense of the importance of the sea route, they sent too few frigates and kept up no regular system of supply. Yet Lochaber was a powder magazine, a turn of fortune's wheel on the Continent and French ships of war would be off its coast, Buchan and the other Jacobite leaders were still at large. Hill never sent out his patrols into Brae Lochaber or west into the Rough Bounds without a fear lest they should bring back news that the fiery cross had gone round and that the heather was ablaze.

He disliked politics, but he had perforce to take a hand in them, and a fine confusion they presented to a simple fighting man. At the head of all was William, a great king and a fine soldier whom Hill revered; but how could one who had just finished a stiff campaign in Ireland, and was now engaged in a life-and-death struggle in Flanders, spare time for the affairs of this distant northern land? Yet William had recognised the merits of the Inverlochy scheme; a namesake of Hill's own, a captain of Leven's, had seen him at Chester on the matter nineteen months ago, and the King had peremptorily ordered the Council to supply everything needed for the work. That was well enough, but the King's vicegerents in Scotland had no such clearness of purpose. To a plain soldier like himself they seemed to be concerned more about their personal aggrandisement than about the peace of the realm, and to rate the settlement of their Kirk higher than the pacification of Scotland. He was a devout man, but he had no patience with their religious bickerings. The fortunes of the land were on a razor's edge, and those lawyer folk would not see it. They squabbled about their family interests, when a single reverse to British arms on the Continent might stir the Highlands and send down on the Lowlands a spate of desperate men.

There was Melville, with his big head and ashen face and mean presence, who thought more of advancing his son Leven's career than of soldierly measures of defence. A Presbyterian of the old rock and no doubt an honest man, but a slow and tortuous one. There was Tarbat, handsome and genial, but slippery like all of the Mackenzie blood. And now there was the Master of Stair, another lawyer, who was said to hold the chief place in the King's confidence. Hill had never met him, but he had heard much about the Dalrymples. His mother was said to have been a witch, and the old Viscount, his father, was reputed the craftiest brain in the kingdom. Sir John, now Master of Stair, was one of the new Secretaries of State; he was hated by the Presbyterians for having been King's advocate under James, and by the Jacobites for having shamelessly turned his coat. No man had ever in his hearing said a good word for Sir John, but all had spoken with solemnity of his devilish subtlety and cold relentlessness of purpose. But even if these civilians meant honestly, they were hampered by utter ignorance of the Highlander. Tarbat was different; he knew his own race, and Hill had found him the easiest to work with. The others were Lowlanders, knowing less of the Gael than Hill knew of the Kamchatkans, but with an ancestral hatred and distrust of all who wore tartan. There were indeed two Highlanders who had the knowledge, but they were scarcely men to ride the ford with. There was Argyll, who

H

had offered to serve against his own father and for whom none had a kind word.   And there was Breadalbane.

The last was the personage who for the past twelve months had been giving Hill his most anxious thoughts.   He had known him of old, and trusted him not at all.   No one living had had a stranger career, for this Highland chief had made himself great and rich by a combination of the methods of attorney and cateran.   As Sir John Campbell of Glenorchy he had lent money to the bankrupt Earl of Caithness, and foreclosed on his title and estates; he had fought a battle at Wick to establish his claim; being deprived of the title he had won as mortgagee, he had got a new patent as Earl of Breadalbane; he had extended his territory from Loch Awe to Loch Tay by beggaring his neighbours; he had been deep in every Jacobite plot, and yet he had some inexplicable secret influence at William's court.   Next to Argyll he was the most powerful man in the Highlands, but he was less disliked than Argyll, for he had a certain surface geniality.   His avarice was notorious, but he could be friendly when it cost him nothing.   Mackay had hated him, and Mackay for all his megrims was an acute judge of character.

Breadalbane had no love for Inverlochy, for he had a scheme of his own—that the Government should make it worth the while of the chiefs to submit and live at peace.   This was a popular policy among the Scottish statesmen of Highland blood, for each wanted to be chosen as intermediary, since doubtless there would be pickings in the business.   There was sense in the proposal, Hill thought, if it were adopted side by side with his own and Mackay's scheme of forts and garrisons.   Some of the money allotted might be used to buy up the disputed feudal superiorities which were a sore point with the clans; Argyll, for example, had certain claims to superiority over Macdonald lands, and there could be no peace till that thorn was plucked out.   Hill himself had been inclined to make the attempt when he first came to Scotland, the efforts of Campbell of Cawdor having failed, and he had spent some weary weeks travelling the Highlands without success.   The sum named was too small, only £2000, and the proffered peerages found no acceptors.   Hill's reason assented to the plan, but his instincts were against it, and he feared its maleficent extension.   The time had not yet come to trust the

Highlanders; a just and firm policy was the immediate need. A wise man like Duncan Forbes of Culloden saw this, and he was as good a Highlander as Breadalbane, who wanted to turn the clans into a standing army in Government pay.

Eight months ago the financial scheme had been revived. There had been some curious by-play about the business at which he could only guess, for the chiefs themselves had been sounded as to the best negotiator. None would accept Argyll; Glengarry had wanted Atholl; but Lochiel had been strong for his cousin Breadalbane, and Breadalbane had been chosen. There had been a moment in the previous spring when the Government had leaned to severity, and he had been ordered by the Council forthwith to summon and disarm the clans and compel an oath of submission at the point of the sword. The order had been insane and he had protested, but he had duly issued the summons, and found that the 'middle sort of people' everywhere were ready to submit. Lochiel, Keppoch, Clanranald, the Macleans and the MacIntoshes, the men of Appin and Glencoe, all seemed to be in a yielding humour; only Sleat and Glengarry were refractory, and the latter had set about fortifying his house.

But presently he heard that the order was rescinded, and that Breadalbane was busy with his diplomacy. In the last days of June there was a conference at his castle of Achallader, which looked over Loch Tulla from under the shadow of the Glenlyon hills. Many of the chiefs were present, and the Jacobite leaders, Buchan and Barclay, and there a truce was signed to last till October 1. During that period there were to be no acts of hostility by either side on land or sea. There were also certain secret articles which provided that the truce was only to hold if James approved, and if there was no general rising, and that, if it fell through, Breadalbane was to rise for James with a thousand men.

Hill had got wind of the secret clauses and had duly sent them to Sir Thomas Livingstone, his official chief, while the Council received another copy from a nephew of Buchan. The result had been a furious row with Breadalbane, who was sore also at the failure of his bribery scheme. With that he had made no headway. The chiefs would not submit to be patronised by one whom they considered no better than themselves, and they distrusted his promises, believing that the London gold would never get beyond the vaults of Kilchurn. Hill's conscience in the matter was clear. Much as he disliked Breadalbane, he had done his best to help him, and had laboured to persuade Keppoch and Lochiel. But meantime the Government had followed up the Achallader truce. On the 27th of August 1691, there was issued at Edinburgh a proclamation pardoning and indemnifying all who had been in arms against the Government, provided that, before the first day of January 1692, they took the oath of allegiance before a sheriff or sheriff-depute.

Hill had not been fully convinced of the wisdom of the step. To ask within a period of five months the disavowal of the politics of a lifetime was to ask a good deal. He would have preferred to let Jacobitism as a sentiment die slowly away, but to keep a strict check on its armed manifestations. But his duty was to obey, and at any rate the Government seemed to have got a new vigour. Recalcitrants were to be firmly dealt with, and the regiments of Leven and of Buchan's Whig brother John were ordered to be ready for action.

At first he had been hopeful. In May there had been, as he had reported, a very genuine desire on the part of the clans to come in, except for a few hot-heads. The Appin and Glencoe men had been willing to go to Inveraray, and take the oath before Argyll, their feudal superior, a marvellous concession for two most turbulent septs. Achtriachtan, one of the cadet gentry of Glencoe, and the tacksman of Inverrigan had made their submission and been given his protection early in November. The Government had been discreet, and had been faithful to the 'gentle methods' which he had recommended. He had had trouble with Stewart of Appin, who had imprisoned one of his soldiers, and he had been compelled to arrest him and a son of Glencoe and bring them to Inverlochy, but they had been released on the Queen's special order.

But as the months passed he had been growing anxious. The honour of the Highlander had been touched, and no man would take the lead in renouncing ancient loyalties, especially as there were constant rumours of French fleets on the sea and of King James returning to his own. He had expected trouble with Sleat and the contumacious Glengarry, but the whole Highlands seemed to be recusant. It was now almost the end of December and few clans had come in. Lochiel, Glengarry, Keppoch, Appin had not sworn, and only a day or two remained. . . . That morning he had had word that Lochiel was starting for Inveraray. It was like the crooked Highland mind to deem it more honourable to postpone to the last moment an inevitable step.

Hill rose and walked to the window on the side away from the wind. The snow had stopped drifting, and the last gleam of daylight revealed beyond the rampart a shoulder of hill, a strip of leaden loch, and a low sullen sky. He shivered. There were months yet of winter before him, and his ague would assuredly return. What a God-forgotten country, and what a cruel fate for an old man to be marooned among these wilds! He thought of his daughters in London whom he never saw; he should be in the bosom of a family at his age, with a knighthood and a pension and a sinecure, instead of dwelling cold in the wilderness. . . .

And then—for the man's mind was just—he was a little ashamed of his humour. After all, he had position and respect, a roof to cover him and food to eat, which was more than could be said of some of James's men who had embraced beggary for a scruple. It was more than could be said of most of the clans, who every winter were on the verge of starvation. All round him the common folk looked white and peaked. To send soldiers, who had a bellyful of meat under their belts, against such scarecrows was scarcely decent. . . . To his surprise, as he looked over the darkening narrows of Loch Linnhe, he found himself a partisan of the Highlanders.

The truth was that he liked them, as Mackay had liked them. Mackay had always said that they were the best natural material for soldiers on earth, and he agreed with him. That made them a peril to the State, but some day it might make them a shining buckler. They had done famously at Killiecrankie, and at the worst they had been true to their salt. Moreover, they were friendly folk and well-mannered, and when they spoke English at all they spoke it intelligibly, and not like Angus's whiggamores, whom he had found wholly incomprehensible. They were noble companions in the chase or over a friendly bottle. For some of

them, like Lochiel, he had a warm affection. Besides, he felt
himself called on to be their protector, for had he not known
them for nearly forty years? His policy was Monk's rather than
Mackay's; Monk had believed in a firm policing hand and with
it patience, while Mackay had wanted to set a date for surrender
and after that 'to rouse them out of the nation as the bane thereof.'
He did not like that kind of language, though by it Mackay only
meant burning their houses and crops; it was too like Breadalbane's talk of 'mauling' them, which he suspected had a more
sinister implication than Mackay's. The worst enemy of the
Highlander might be other Highlanders.

Suppose their recalcitrance continued beyond the appointed
day. Then there would be ugly work, since the troops would
be loosed among the winter hills. There would be beyond
question barbarities, and he was less afraid of Leven's and
Buchan's Lowlanders than of his own men of Argyll's. In his
recent letters there had been talk of extirpation, an ominous
word. He comforted himself by reflecting that a great clan, like
the Camerons or the Macdonalds, could not be extirpated; there
would be some bitter fighting, and then, when the lesson had been
learned, there would be peace.

Yes, but what of the lesser septs? The Appin Stewarts?
They would not be an easy folk to shepherd, for they had the
sea and the sea islands for a refuge. The Glencoe men? . . .
He pulled himself up sharply, for he realised that Glencoe was
precisely the kind of case he dreaded.

The clan there was a branch of the Macdonalds, but cut off
in a long chasm of a glen from their kinsmen. They were a small
people, less than a quarter of the clans of Maclean or Sleat or
Glengarry or Lochiel, less than half of Appin or Keppoch. But
they could muster fifty fighting men in the field, and they were
natural warriors. They had been at Killiecrankie and afterwards with Buchan and Cannon; they were Catholics, and
staunch Jacobites, and ill regarded by Government. They were
cattle thieves like the rest, and unhappily their raids took them
into the domains of potent and revengeful people like Argyll and
Breadalbane. Argyll hated them because, like Appin, they
formed a salient that jutted into his own territory. Breadalbane
had all manner of ancient grudges against them, and in the June

conference at Achallader he had had high words with their chief
MacIan over an alleged theft of cows, and had threatened to do
him a mischief—Hill had this direct from the chief's son.

He had long known MacIan—as a young man he had given
Monk no trouble—and had liked him for his high spirit and good
nature; no Highlander was better spoken of for fidelity to his
word and courage in battle than that gigantic old man. He had
liked, too, the second son, Alasdair, one of Buchan's captains,
who for some time had been his prisoner at Inverlochy. He
could not think happily of that little clan at the mercy of
callous Lowland lawyers like Stair and ruthless intriguers like
Breadalbane. Achtriachtan and Inverrigan had made their
peace, but there was no word of any movement by the other
MacIans. The fools, the pitiful fools, when the sword of
Damocles hung above their heads!

Anxiety had driven out of Hill's mind his own grievances.
This was a miserable business just when the Highlands were
settling down. For months he had been writing to Livingstone
and the Council that the whole district was peaceable and civil.
Peaceable and civil—these had been his very words. Except for
a little raiding in the Rough Bounds the land had been at ease.
Yet in a month's time it might be in the throes of a bloody war.
The best news he could get would be that every chief in Lochaber
was posting to Inveraray or Inverness. Especially those stubborn
fools of Glencoe, who were certain to be the first burnt-offering.

From his window he had a view of a corner of the barrack
square, and the road from the main entrance. There seemed
to be the stir of some arrival. In the gathering darkness he had
a glimpse of a man dismounting from horseback. It could not
be one of his patrols, for no patrols had gone out that day in the
wild weather. It could not be his deputy Hamilton returning,
for he was not expected back from the south yet awhile. He
moved from the window as an orderly entered with a lamp, and
behind him his major, Culloden's brother.

The latter's weather-beaten face was puckered in a grin.
'Who do you think is here, sir?' he asked. 'A penitent seeking
mercy. No less than Glencoe himself!'

'Glencoe!' Hill cried. 'Bring him here instanter. The
very man I have had in my mind all afternoon.'

Major Forbes ushered in a remarkable figure of a man. He was very tall, nearly six and a half feet, but so broadly made that his massiveness rather than his height was what first caught the eye. He had the dark wild eyes of Clan Donald, and a fierce nose like the beak of a galley. His white hair fell almost to his shoulders, and two great moustachios like buck's horns gave him the air of a Norse sea-king. His age was nearer seventy than sixty, but he held himself like a youth. In his bonnet was a bunch of faded heather, the Macdonald badge. He had trews of the dark tartan, and huge riding-boots of untanned leather, his broad belt carried a dirk and a brace of pistols, and at his side swung a long sword. He wore a fine buff coat, instead of the doublet of bull's hide for which he was famous. Hill knew the tale of that coat—it had been part of the plunder of Edinglassie and had been often referred to in the processes of forfeiture against Dundee's followers. . . . He had not seen the man for thirty years. The Governor of Inverlochy reflected ruefully that age had dealt more kindly with this turbulent chieftain than with a docile servant of the law like himself.

The old man held up his right hand in salutation.

'It is MacIan,' he said. 'He has come to take the Government's oath.'

'You have been too long about it,' Hill replied drily, for his anxiety had made him irritable. 'Why do you come here? You should be at Inveraray.'

'You are the Governor of Inverlochy.'

'I am a soldier, and the law ordains that the oath must be taken before a civil officer.' He picked up a paper from the table. 'These are the words of his Majesty's proclamation:—

"*The persons who have been in arms before the time foresaid, and shall plead and take benefit of this our gracious indemnity, shall swear and sign the oath of allegiance to us by themselves, or the sheriff clerk subscribing for such as cannot write, and that before famous witnesses, betwixt and the first day of January next to come, in presence of the Lords of our Privy Council—or the sheriff—or their deputes—of the respective shires where any of the said persons live.*" The words are explicit. Only a civil officer can swear you.'

Hill spoke tartly, for this was an old grievance of his. He had often urged that the Governor of Inverlochy should have the powers of a civil magistrate, as he had had in Monk's day.

'Three months back you received Achtriachtan,' the old man protested.

'I received Achtriachtan into the King's peace, and gave him a written protection, but I warned him that he had not fulfilled the law, and must go to Inveraray to complete his submission. You knew that, MacIan, you and your clan. In May last you were willing to go to Argyll at Inveraray, you and your cousins of Appin.'

'That was in May,' was the answer. 'Since then I am not liking the name of Campbell. I was at Achallader in June and had ill words from the fox of Breadalbane.' He spoke good English, with the soft lilting accent of the Gael.

Hill laughed. 'I have been informed of that. My lord Breadalbane had somewhat against you in the matter of cattle-lifting.'

MacIan drew himself up.

'There was talk of that, but it was a lawful act of war. After the death of the Graham, Coll of Keppoch and we of Glencoe, returning to our homes, drove a booty from Glenlyon who was an enemy of our King. Was that a greater fault than the killing of the red soldiers at Killiecrankie, for which your Government offers pardon?'

'That was not the first cause of offence given to my lord Breadalbane?'

MacIan's gravity broke into a smile.

'Maybe no. Glencoe has never loved Glenorchy—or Glenlyon, since Mad Colin hung thirty-six braw men of ours on the Meggernie braes. Maybe it is true that cattle beasts from Glenorchy have sometimes found themselves in Coire Gabhail, and that there has been some dirking of Campbells by MacIans. Gentlefolk will always be bickering if they live too near, and be gartering their hose tighter when the nights grow dark. But the MacIans have never wronged their neighbours as Breadalbane has, or by a coward's law pleas and dirty parchments stripped them of the lands they heired from their fathers.'

'No. I never credited your clan with a taste for parchments. . . . But let us talk sense, for this is a grave business.

You are within the danger of the law for your doings in the late rebellion. You have incurred the undying hatred of the most powerful folk in the Highlands, Argyll and Breadalbane. The King in his mercy offers you a way of peace. What do you do? First you come to the wrong place—to Inverlochy—to me, who can do nothing for you.'

'I am a soldier, and would make my submission to a soldier.'

'A plague upon your punctilios. I tell you, though I were Schomberg 'or Talmash I would be powerless. The law says a civil officer. . . . Secondly, you put it off till the last moment. In two days it will be the New Year and the period of mercy will have closed. Was that not blind folly, with the menace of an offended Government hanging over you, and your good friends of Glenlyon and Glenorchy waiting for their revenge?'

The old man's face was troubled.

'I did only as others did. How many have sworn? Lochiel is but now gone to Inveraray.'

'So you know that? But Lochiel is in a different case from you. He is the head of a big clan, and Argyll has always been his friend. Glengarry has not sworn, but he has a strong castle and is ill to come at. You are a little people, and you have no friends near by, and the great folk love you as a shepherd loves a fox, and you are so situate that Glencoe can be inclosed like a nut between the crackers.'

The other's eyes grew more troubled, but his voice was proud.

'As one fighting man to another so I speak to you, Colonel, and I will tell you the naked truth. I could not take my oath to your Government.' (Hill noticed that he said 'Government' and never 'King'—for him there could be but the one king.) 'Not till I was assured that a certain hope had gone. You say truly that we of Glencoe are a small people, but we have had no traitors among us since the daughter of MacHenry first brought the glen to Clan Donald. The men of Ian Abrach draw their blood from Ian Og Fraoch, the son of that Angus Og who sheltered King Robert in his castle of Dunaverty in the south. Our race and our religion make us true to the lawful line of kings, and though we were to be swept from the earth we could not forswear that allegiance save by our King's order.'

'That order is come?'

'Such is the word brought to me.'

'Well, you are in the devil's own predicament. Loyalty is a high virtue, MacIan, though yours is a thought perverse. We were friends in youth and I would fain help you. I cannot receive you into the King's peace. You must get you to Inveraray, and you have two days to do it in. In this foul weather you may be hard put to it and be late for the fair. Have you any well-wishers there?'

'I have many ill-wishers, and the chief of them is MacCailein Mor himself.'

'Argyll is not in the town at present, which is the better for you. Sir Colin Campbell is the sheriff-depute.'

'Ardkinglas, though a Campbell, is an honest man,' said the chief.

'I am happy to agree with you. He is also my friend, and I will write him a letter. Go straight to Ardkinglas and do not meddle with Duncanson the procurator-fiscal, for he has no good-will to any of your name.'

Hill sat down at the table and took up his pen, reading aloud each sentence as he wrote it. He begged Ardkinglas to receive this 'lost sheep' who had misread his Majesty's proclamation and sought peace in the wrong quarter. Though MacIan were a day or two late—for the weather in Lochaber was severe—let a point be stretched and his submission be received. He subscribed himself his friend and well-wisher and colleague in the great task of peace-making.

As he sanded the ink he observed that MacIan had set his bonnet on his head and was rebuttoning his buff coat as if for instant departure. The chief took the letter, placed it in an inner pocket, and offered his hand. 'May God and the saints have you in keeping,' he said. 'In two hours I must be beyond Loch Leven.'

'Not so,' said Hill. 'Prayer and provender never yet hindered a man. You will sup with me—I have something better than the salted mart, for the last frigate brought certain Lowland delicacies—and you will sleep here. The wind is veering, and I think there will be no more snow.'

He was wrong. At three in the morning when, by the light of a waning moon, MacIan mounted his shelty and, attended by his four running footmen, turned his face down Loch Linnhe, the wind still set icily from the north-west, and snow was again falling. Hill, who in a greatcoat and nightcap saw him off, watched the little party disappear in the brume. 'If he does not perish in a drift,' he muttered to himself, 'he will be a week late. God send that Ardkinglas be merciful!'

II

INVERARAY AND EDINBURGH

MacIan and his gillies took the road down Loch Linnhe in a thick downfall of snow. The drifts were small, for the full force of the wind was cut off by the Ardgour hills. It was still black darkness when they reached the narrows of Loch Leven, and found on the beach the boat by which they had crossed the previous afternoon. Here, too, there was some shelter from the storm, and they made the passage without difficulty. Three miles on the left a light twinkled. That came from MacIan's own house of Carnoch at the foot of Glencoe, where his kin waited anxiously to hear the result of his errand. One of the gillies was sent off with a message, but he himself had no time to waste. The quickest route to the south, had it been summertime, was up the Laroch stream, between Ben Vair, the 'Mountain of Lightnings,' and his own Meall Mor, and so by Glen Creran to Connel Ferry, but in this weather a fox or a deer could not have made that journey. He turned to the right and took the shore road through Appin.

Dawn came upon them near Duror, a dawn of furious winds and solid driving snow. Happily it was a fine snow with sleet in it, and so it did not greatly clog the path, but the force of the gale was enough to lift a man off his feet. The running gillies, bent double, their bonnets dragged over their brows, their wet kilts plastered about their thighs, and their bare legs purple with the cold, felt it less than the chief on his shelty. He brought the folds of his plaid twice round his throat, but even so, and for all his years of hardihood, he felt numbed and crippled by the savagery of the heavens. Not a wild thing, bird or beast, was stirring—they knew better; but he himself dare not seek shelter, though the warm chimney-corner of Ardsheal awaited him a mile off. For he knew that he was riding on a mission of life and death. He tried to comfort his heart by reminding himself that the great Montrose had travelled this very road at the same time of year before that fight at Inverlochy when he set the heather above the gale. But Montrose had had open weather for his march, and the gale seemed now for good to have overtopped the heather.[1]

They made slow progress, and midday found them no further than Appin Kirk. At the inn of Creagan they had a dram of hot whisky and a bite of bread and cheese. But the wind there was so fierce that the ferryman dare not trust his coble on the water, and they were compelled to go round by the head of Loch Creran, a circuit of several miles. MacIan's hope was to be beyond Loch Etive before nightfall—maybe even to reach the inn at Taynuilt under Cruachan. But with the afternoon the wind grew stronger and the snowfall more resolute, and it was almost dark when he reached Barcaldine, where the road turned south through Benderloch to the sea.

Whether he had desired it or not he had to halt at Barcaldine, for the road passed close to the castle, and half a dozen fellows in the Campbell tartan ran out to bar it. They recognised the old man, and their faces were not kind. MacIan knew the place too well, the keep, built long ago by Duncan of the Seven Castles, which commanded the shore road from Appin to Lorn. He cursed the fate that had brought him within its pale, for the Campbells of Barcaldine were near kin to Breadalbane, and one of them had been the companion of that fox when he carried war into Caithness.

As he had feared, the garrison was of Glenorchy men. Its commander was a Captain Drummond, one of Breadalbane's Tayside neighbours, and the troops were of Argyll's regiment. MacIan presented Hill's letter, but at first Drummond would not read it. He had all the Lowland ill manners, so hateful to the Gael, who would use an enemy like a gentleman till he dirked him. The old man was treated half as spy and half as prisoner, given bare quarters and coarse food, and held under constant surveillance. He spent a night of anxiety and discomfort, but in the morning Drummond had relented. After all, he dare not offend Hill, for he and his men were under orders for the Inverlochy garrison. MacIan had something of a breakfast and was told that he might continue his journey, but it was not till the

---

[1] The heather is the Macdonald badge; the gale, or bog-myrtle, the Campbell.

afternoon that his gillies were dug out from a noisome cellar, his shelty recovered, and a start made.

Twenty-four precious hours had been lost. Late that night

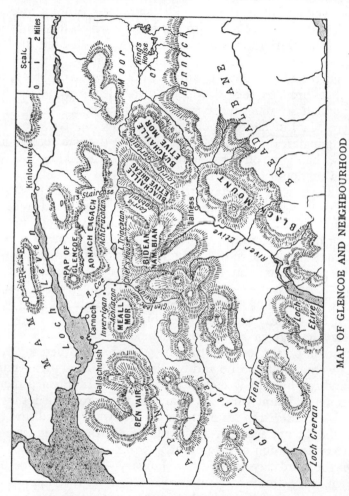

MAP OF GLENCOE AND NEIGHBOURHOOD

the party reached Taynuilt, and as he got to bed MacIan heard a clock strike midnight. The New Year had begun and the time of probation was officially past.

Next day, in a second snowstorm, they struggled up the Pass of Brander beside a swollen river, and came to Loch Awe,

scourged by a thousand blasts from the gullies of Cruachan.
Never had he known such a blizzard. Five or six miles an hour
were nothing to his long-limbed gillies, but now in an hour they
could cover less than a mile. The snow was drifting too, and
often they had to take to the rough hillside which the winds had
swept bare. Darkness was on them before they had left the loch,
and they spent the night in an empty sheiling. By the next
morning, the second day of January, the storm had abated, and
early that forenoon they dropped down Glen Aray to the little
burgh which lay snug in the trench of its sea-loch.

Here MacIan had staggering news. He was two days late,
and Ardkinglas, the sheriff-depute, was not there to receive him.
Sir Colin had gone on a Hogmanay visit to kinsfolk, he was told,
and had no doubt been storm-stayed.

For three wretched days the old man abode in Inveraray.
Hill's letter was protection enough and had been received
respectfully by the sheriff's office, but the burgh was not a healthy
place for his tartan, and, with half the people still festive from the
Hogmanay revels, there would be a certainty of brawls if it were
seen in the streets. So he and his men found quarters in an
obscure hostelry, and stayed indoors all day, while MacIan
morning and evening visited the sheriff's house to get news of the
laggard Sir Colin. He was miserably anxious, for he saw that
his delay had given a supreme chance to his enemies. If the
sheriff stood on the letter of the law, as he was entitled to do, his
estates were forfeit and he and his clan were broken men—name-
less, landless, like the wretched Macgregors. Ill-omened memories came to haunt him. A spaewife had prophesied that he
would be murdered in his own house. He was resolved that that
house should not see him again till he returned to it with the
Government pardon in his pocket.

On the third day—the fifth of January—Sir Colin came back
to town, rosy from his travels. He was a just man, whose
patriotism was for all the Highlands and not merely for his clan,
and he earnestly desired peace. He read Hill's letter and read
it again, and knit his brows. For he was in a quandary. MacIan
had missed his chance, and the law should take its course; he
had no power to extend the period laid down in the King's
proclamation. But if he refused to receive him, MacIan's life

would be forfeit, for he was aware of the hounds waiting to be unleashed, and he had an honest man's tenderness for one whom he knew to be an honest foe.

'What makes you so dooms behindhand?' he asked, and was told the storm and the detention at Barcaldine—not to mention the initial mistake of the bootless errand to Inverlochy.

'Well, you're in a fine creel. I see nothing for it but that I should decline to give you the oath. The thing's clean beyond my power.'

The old man, knowing that here was no enemy, but a perplexed friend, humbled his pride and begged for mercy. He even wept, he whose eyes were not used to tears. Let him be permitted to take the oath, he said, and every man of his clan would do the like; if any refused, he would be sent to prison or impressed for the Flanders wars. Sir Colin was moved, and finally persuaded.

'Come back the morn,' he said, 'and I'll see what can be done for you.'

When MacIan returned on the 6th of January, the sheriff-depute had made up his mind. 'I'll swear you,' he said, 'but, mind, I cannot guarantee that the thing is in order. Our sheriff-clerk is in Edinburgh, and I will send the certificate to him, and get him to take the opinion of the Council on the matter. Not that I think they will quarrel with what I have done, for no more than me do they want further dispeace in the Highlands. Likewise I will write a letter to Colonel Hill, asking him to give you and yours full interim protection. That is the best I can do for you, MacIan, but I think it will suffice. It is not likely that the Council will question my judgment. You can sleep sound in your bed in yon fearsome black glen of yours.'

That afternoon in better weather the chief departed thankfully from the town of Inveraray, which seemed to his mountain eyes part miracle and part prison. He had no fear for his safety. The Campbell word was law now in the land, and in Argyll Sir Colin was the second greatest Campbell.

After his departure Ardkinglas, according to his promise, wrote to his namesake Colin Campbell, the sheriff-clerk of Argyll, now in Edinburgh, enclosing the certificate of MacIan's submission and asking that it should be declared by the Council to be in order. He also wrote to the Governor of Inverlochy com-

I

mending Glencoe to his protection, but for some reason omitted to send off the letter for three days. But one important missive he despatched at once by a special messenger. He sent an account of the whole business to his chief Argyll in London.

The further history of the certificate of MacIan's oath is obscure. The Scottish Privy Council in that month of January was not greatly interested in the pacification of the clans; to it, and to William, a more urgent matter was the coming General Assembly of the Kirk and what might be the policy of the Presbyterian hot-heads. The certificate duly reached the hands of the sheriff-clerk in Edinburgh, who took it to the clerks of the Council, Sir Gilbert Elliot, the founder of the Minto family, and Mr. David Moncrieff. They naturally refused to receive it, since the time limit had expired. Thereupon the sheriff-clerk, along with Mr. John Campbell, a Writer to the Signet, took the opinion of a lord of Session, Lord Aberuchill, also a Campbell. There seems to have been no question of clan bias, for these Campbells may be presumed to have been anxious to do Ardkinglas's will. Aberuchill, who was a member of the Privy Council, put the matter before several of his colleagues, one of whom was the new Lord Stair, the father of Sir John Dalrymple. They gave it as their view that the certificate could not be accepted without a special warrant from the King, and accordingly it was scored through and cancelled.

The matter was never brought before the Council as a whole, though such had been Ardkinglas's intention, for there was no need of that if good legal opinion held that the Council had no power to extend the time. We need not suspect malign Dalrymple influence, for the decision was on the face of it sound law; the Proclamation of August 27 permitted the oath to be taken before the Lords of the Council as well as before the sheriffs, but gave neither of these parties any power to vary its conditions.

It is more difficult to explain why the matter was not referred to London and the King's pleasure taken. The probable reason was that before this could be done—for the wheels of Scottish justice moved slow—word came that the fate of MacIan had already been decided. For the next stage of the drama we must turn to the South.

III

KENSINGTON

I

A CHIEF actor must now be introduced on the stage. The day is the 11th of January in the year 1692. The scene is the palace of Kensington, which William had bought from Lord Nottingham and made his chief dwelling, because he found Whitehall bad for his asthma and Hampton Court too remote from London.

A man sat in a warm wainscoted room with a table of papers before him. He congratulated himself that in this wintry weather his business with the King gave him quarters in the palace, so that he was not compelled to jog twice a day along the miry footpad-haunted roads which linked Kensington village with the capital. Now and then he cast a glance from the window at the new Dutch garden in which workmen were busy, and thought that he might well borrow a hint from it for his own Galloway home of Castle Kennedy. But chiefly he kept his eyes on his papers, for he had much troublesome business on hand.

The occupant of the chair was a handsome full-bodied man in his forty-fourth year. Sir John Dalrymple, now Master of Stair, was a figure not easily forgotten. The face framed in the huge perruque was immensely intelligent. The eyes under the broad brow were cool, wary and commanding. The lips were full but compressed, there was humour at the corners of the mouth, and the heavy jowl had a jovial, almost porcine, air. Yet the impression left upon the spectator was not that of geniality, but of a mocking competence, an almost arrogant self-complacency. And something more—something subtle and tortuous, a warning that this man would not be easily fathomed, and might be an uncertain colleague and a precarious friend. The seventeenth-century chroniclers were fond of finding 'aliquid insigne' in their characters' faces—Sir Philip Warwick found it

in the Duke of Hamilton's, and Clarendon in the younger Vane's.
This something extraordinary was beyond doubt in the mobile
countenance of the man in the chair.

He came of a strange family. His father, Sir James, the first
Viscount Stair, had raised himself from a small Ayrshire lairdship
to the peerage, the repute of the greatest Scots lawyer of the day,
and a share in the inner councils of the King. He had been
many things in his time—soldier, professor, advocate, lord of
Session; he had quarrelled first with Lauderdale and then with
Claverhouse; though no fanatic he had tried to protect the
Covenanters, and had been for some years an exile in Holland
before he returned with William. He had written on religion
and on the law—on the latter so profoundly that he still ranks
as the great institutional jurist of his country. His ability all
men admitted, but few trusted him and fewer liked him. There
was something uncanny about him and his race; he had a
masterful wife whose piety did not save her from charges of
dabbling in forbidden arts; fate seemed to brood over the house
of Stair as it shadowed the house of Atreus, and a daughter and
a grandson were the centre of tragic tales.

The son's life had been not less chequered than the father's.
He had been more than once in prison, and had often gone in
danger of his head. He had been Claverhouse's bitter enemy,
yet he had become James's Lord Advocate, and had been responsible for the prosecution of James Renwick, the last martyr
of the Covenant. He had taken the chief part in offering the
crown of Scotland to William, and had had the difficult task
of managing William's business in the first Scottish parliaments.
Now, with the King often abroad at the wars, he was the virtual
ruler of Scotland, for his colleague in the north, Johnston of
Wariston, was a trivial being. He had as few friends as his
father, and far more avowed enemies, since the Jacobites hated
him as a turncoat, and the extreme Presbyterians as a trimmer
and a Laodicean. He admitted the second charge, for if there
was one thing he detested it was a high-flying religion. As to the
first, his defence was that he had served James only to prepare
the way for the inevitable revolution, since he had always been
William's man. He flattered himself that he had been a consistent Whig.

The man was not all of one piece. He had a human side known to his few intimates. In private life he was notably good-natured, and his conversation was full-flavoured and merry. Sometimes in debate his dignity would break down, and he would scold an opponent like a fishwife. But the figure he presented in public affairs was clean-cut, impregnable, and highly unsympathetic, for alone of Scottish statesmen he had a policy, and the determination to enforce it. Let us try to set down the ideas at the back of his head.

He had his father's legal mind, but he was several stages further off than his father from the turbid old Scots world of fevered beliefs and unprofitable loyalties. He was emphatically the man of a new age, with something of the same outlook as Somers and Halifax. He sought order and reason and civilisation, and he hated all that he believed to stand in the way of these blessings. They were his faith, though he was sceptical about most things.

For a sentimental Jacobitism he had only scorn, and of religious fanaticism he was wholly intolerant. He honestly desired that Scotland should settle down into reputable ways, when her citizens should be secure in life and goods, and could advance from their present grinding poverty to the prosperity which he believed to be within their compass. He remembered too bitterly what had happened before the Revolution to wish to see that anarchy perpetuated.

Also, for he was a statesman with a wide vision, he saw the needle-point upon which Britain stood. A little laxness here, a blunder there, would shiver the brittle framework of peace. Jacobitism was still a cave of Adullam to which might resort the multitudinous forces of discontent. Quiet at home was the first essential, for William, of whom he was the loyal servant, was fighting a desperate battle—how desperate was only known to a man like him who had lived with the King in his Flanders camps. He was opposing with weak allies the greatest monarch and the most formidable confederation in the world. He had to face Luxemburg, the little, harsh-featured hunchback who was the foremost military genius of the day, the greatest general produced by the house of Montmorency; a brilliant second in Boufflers; and a sagacious war minister in Louvois. Ireland was for the moment quiescent, but the continental campaign of 1691 had been a failure, with the loss of Mons and the defeat at Leuse, and the omens were not bright for the new year. It was his business to see that no folly at home crippled the force of the British stroke beyond the Channel.

The Master of Stair was a Lowlander with most of the merits and every defect of that stalwart breed. The virtues which he respected were order, sobriety, prudence, industry; he had no taste for the romantic glories and little patience with them. His blood was cool and his imagination strictly disciplined. Not only was he a Lowlander, but he was a son of that south-west region of Scotland where the Lowland qualities of individualism and independence were found in their most truculent form. Small as his liking had been for the Covenant, he had tried to protect the Covenanters, realising that, though in a temporally perverted form, they had the virtues which might make the kind of citizens he desired to see. Therefore he was utterly impatient with those who preferred a romantic whimsy to common sense, and with all the sentimental rodomontade for which his old enemy Claverhouse had died. If Scotland was ever to become a civilised land it must get rid of this lumber of the Middle Ages.

Above all, he was intolerant of the Highlands. It shocked his orderly mind that one half of Scotland should be as barbarous as the wilds of America. He had to the full the Lowland hatred and fear of those northern mists from which time and again had come banditti to trouble the peace of Scotland. The Highlands were the home of a clan system which was half autocratic and half communal, and in both respects hateful to a Whig. They were the last refuge of Jacobitism. The life was barbarous and brutal, and the King's writ ran limpingly. There lay the danger-point, and if the peril was to be crushed it must be done at once, for the present police force, Leven's and Argyll's regiments, would soon be required in Flanders. He had never crossed the Highland line, but he had met Highlanders, and he liked them little—Glengarry, Lochiel, Appin and the rest of them, huge, flamboyant, witless bravos.

Fortunately there were some few Highlanders who were on the side of common sense. Tarbat was one; he had no great love for Tarbat, but at any rate he talked the language of educated men and he knew on which side his bread was buttered. Argyll, too; a trumpery creature, but his interests were now solid for the Government. Breadalbane—and at the thought of Breadalbane the Master lay back in his chair and pondered. This was the hardest nut of all to crack, and the most important in the platter.

The man was in town. He had come up at Christmas to report. He had been at the palace that very morning. Breadalbane's face rose before Dalrymple, for in his sleeping and waking hours it was a constant enigma to him; and well it might be, for the face as it looks at us from the canvas of Sir John Medina seems to have been formed to conceal the soul behind it. It has the gravity of a Roman senator and the proud stateliness of a Spanish hidalgo; the mouth is steadfast and not unkindly, the eyes under the heavy lids have a sober dignity. Dalrymple flattered himself that he had no illusions about Breadalbane. He knew his past in all its shamelessness, a past of money-lending, blackmail, oppression, chicanery, and, when the need arose, of violence and murder. He knew that to the core he was avaricious and selfish, with no higher thought than his money-bags and his rent-rolls. He was aware that he had been deep in many treasons, and even now was suspected on good evidence of having intrigued in the summer on James's behalf with the Highland chiefs. He knew that he was the most comprehensively distrusted man in all Scotland.

But there was much to be said on the other side. No one denied his remarkable abilities. After Argyll he could bring more men into the field than any Highland grandee. And, like Dalrymple, he wanted peace. It stood to reason that he did, for his great domains, which stretched from Loch Awe to the haughs of Tay, were especially at the mercy of disorder. Behind him were the savage clans of Lochaber who loathed the name of Campbell, and had a readier access to his lands than they had to Argyll's. A settlement of the Highlands would enable him to reap in comfort what he had sown through fifty disreputable years. William could offer him more than James, for if the Stuarts returned it would be Glengarry and Sleat and Clanranald who would be in favour, not Breadalbane, however much he might have contributed to that return.

Besides, he had a policy. Breadalbane knew his countrymen and had no doubt about the proper course. He had done his best with the scheme of bribing the clans, but that had failed. He had not opposed the King's proclamation of August. But he had been very clear about what the next step should be, if submission did not follow. The next proclamation must be written with a sharp pen and bloody ink. 'Mauling' was his phrase: the recalcitrants must be so handsomely mauled that their will to resist would be crushed for ever. All the rebels, if possible, but if not, a selected few like Keppoch and Glencoe as an example. He had argued his case brilliantly, and Dalrymple had been convinced, for this man knew the nature of the Gael.

Yet as he lay back in his chair he was not quite at ease on the point. After all, the man had been one of the leaders of the Highland host which ten years ago had descended upon his own westlands. It was odd company for a Whig to find himself in. He had staked a good deal on Breadalbane and his nicely calculated honesty. He had written him letters which might some day be brought up against him. That day a Highland policy must be determined on, and he was still in two minds. There was a long *dossier* on the subject, and he must refresh his memory about the past. From a drawer in the table he took a bundle of papers, for he was a careful man and made his secretary copy every letter of importance to which he put his name.

II

Eight months ago he had been sanguine that the King's law could be brought to the Highlands without further bloodshed. He hated war—it was not his business, and he did not understand it, and he most earnestly desired a peaceful settlement. He had flung himself heart and soul into Tarbat's scheme of bribing the chiefs, and, because Breadalbane seemed the best agent, he had laid himself out to conciliate Breadalbane. How many letters had he not indited to him last summer from those comfortless Flanders camps! On June 25 he had written to encourage him in his negotiations. 'If they will be mad, before Lammas they will repent it, for the army will be allowed to go into the Highlands, which some thirst so much for, and the

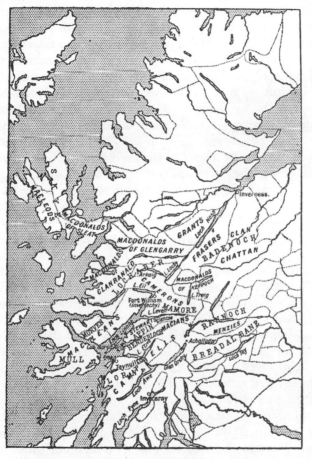

MAP OF THE WESTERN CLANS

frigates will attack them; but I have so much confidence of your character and capacity to let them see the ground they stand on, that I think these suppositions are vain.' A month later he had begged Breadalbane to get the clans to meet him in Edinburgh, and in the meantime he had been warning

Livingstone that no acts of hostility should be committed against the Highlanders.

On September 28 from Loo he had encouraged Breadalbane to persevere in the good work, and urged that nothing should be done to exacerbate Highland feeling by undue suspicion. 'The best cure of all these matters is, that the chieftains do it (take the oath) as quickly as can be, which will take off the trials or suspicions against the rest.' Two days later he told him that he had spoken to the King about the money required, which would be forthcoming when needed, and reiterated his belief in his honesty, which so many were doubting. 'The best evidence of sincerity,' he had written, 'is the bringing the matter quickly to a conclusion. . . . I hope your lordship shall not only keep them (the clans) from giving any offence, but bring them to take the allegiance which they ought to do very cheerfully, for their lives and fortunes they have from their Majesties.'

The Master raised his head and considered. His conscience was clear. Never had man been more earnest in the cause of peace.

He turned the pages of the file and was reminded how in early December his hopes had begun to wane. There was a brief letter to Hamilton, Hill's second-in-command at Inverlochy, warning him that the garrison might soon have to take the field on a punitive expedition, 'for the winter-time is the only season in which we are sure the Highlanders cannot escape us, nor carry their wives, bairns and cattle to the mountains.' The bribery plan had failed, and the clans showed no signs of obeying the King's proclamation of August. He was back in London then, and closer in touch with home affairs, and it looked as if nothing remained but a winter expedition. There must be no delaying after the day of grace, January 1, was past, for the regiments of Leven and Argyll would soon be due for Flanders.

To Breadalbane he wrote on December 2 that he thought that Clan Donald should be rooted out, and his 'doited cousin' Lochiel. As for the rumours about Breadalbane's own conduct, he had discussed them with the King, who treated them as trifles. . . . He had not quite given up hope, for next day he wrote again to Breadalbane with the news that Tarbat had had letters from Glengarry, and had seen William, who had gone carefully into the proposed payments to the different chiefs. 'By the next I expect to hear either that these people are come to your hand, or else your scheme for mauling them, for it will not delay . . . I am not changed as to the expediency of doing things by the easiest means and at leisure, but the madness of these people and their ungratefulness to you makes me plainly see that there is no reckoning on them, but *delenda est Carthago*. Yet. who have accepted, and do take the oath, will be safe, but deserve no kindness. . . . Therefore look on and you shall be satisfied of your revenge.'

The Master re-read the last letter, and with it another of the same date to Hamilton at Inverlochy. To the latter he had written: 'Let me hear from you with the first whether you think that this is the proper season to maul them in the cold long nights, and what force will be necessary,' and he added that he had written to the same purpose to Colonel Hill. Since the clans were apparently not coming in, it was very necessary to strike hard as soon as the new year began. Argyll's regiment was at Inverlochy, Leven's was at Inverness, and Buchan's (John the rubicund Whig, not his brother Thomas the sallow, saturnine Jacobite) was under notice to join it. What was in his mind was a brief vigorous campaign of mauling —'letters of fire and sword' in the old Scots phrase—the burning of hovels and stores, the driving away of cattle, and, when they resisted, the slaughter of men. It would be directed chiefly against Glengarry and his Macdonalds—'That's the only popish clan in the kingdom, and it will be popular to take severe courses with them.' This had always been Breadalbane's advice, and Breadalbane knew his countrymen.

There came a gap in the correspondence during the Christmas and New Year season, since Tarbat and Argyll and Breadalbane were all in London. For the first week of January 1692 the old plan stood. Here was his letter of the 7th to Livingstone, the Scottish commander-in-chief, informing him that the orders would go out next day. It should be a short and sharp business. These were his words: 'You know in general that those troops posted at Inverness and Inverlochy will be ordered to take in the house of Invergarry, and to destroy entirely the county of Lochaber, Lochiel's lands, Keppoch's, Glengarry's, Appin and Glencoe. If there be any opposition the troops (that is Leven's and Buchan's regiments) will need to join; if not, they may act separately, which will make the work the shorter. I assure you their power shall be full enough, and I hope the soldiers will not trouble the Government with prisoners. The slighting the offered mercy, and depending still upon foreign assistance, will justify all the severity which can be used against those who can neither be obliged nor trusted. . . . It's true, it's a rigid season for the soldiers to work, but it's the only time they cannot escape you, for human constitutions cannot endure to be now long out of houses. A few days will do all that's at present either necessary or possible.'

The Master with his quill underlined these sentences. They seemed to him sound common sense. He was a convert to Breadalbane's view, the need of blood and iron. But in moderation. He had always prided himself upon being a moderate and humane man. A sharp lesson, after ample warning, would save much suffering in the future, and might bring to reason the chiefs who were now gambling with the lives of their wretched peoples. His policy was not extirpation—you could not extirpate the Macdonalds and the Camerons in a few days — but punishment.

A good policy, but now, alas! impossible. For the very next day had come news that the clans, after procrastinating to the last moment, had taken the oath. Lochiel and Appin had sworn at Inveraray—Glencoe too, so Hill reported; and Keppoch at Inverness; only Glengarry stood out. The whole plan of the punitive campaign had miscarried; all that remained was to deal with Glengarry and his fortified castle, and a troublesome little expedition like that would have no solemnising effect upon the Highland mind. On the 9th he wrote to Livingstone: 'For my part I could have wished the Macdonalds had not divided, and I am sorry that Keppoch and MacIan of Glencoe are safe. . . . I would be as tender of blood or severities as any man, if I did not see the reputation of the Government in question upon slighted mercy, and the security of the nation in danger by those who have been obstinate to that degree that, if we believe them rational, we must think they depend upon such assurances of help that we can never oblige them even to their own advantages from this Government, and therefore it must make sure of them.'

The Master restored the bundle of papers to its drawer, and turned to the letter he had begun to write. He had seen the King and was sending his instructions to Livingstone about the expedition against the few recalcitrants. The Macleans in Mull, about whom there was some doubt, would be left to Argyll. Sleat, who was also doubtful, was to be dealt with. Glengarry, about whom there was no doubt, was to be attacked and Invergarry taken. William's inclinations were mild. Rebel chiefs were to be given quarter, and the commonalty, if they took the oath, were to be assured in their lives and property. In the covering letter to Livingstone the Master was emphasising this mercifulness. 'I am most concerned,' he wrote, 'for the poor commonalty. I do well know, if nothing be done to disable them, they will join with their lairds and chieftains whenever these appear. . . . I think they should have some ease and feel the advantage of having the King their master . . .'
He broke off to reflect upon his deep dissatisfaction with the whole business. There had been a general taking of the oath, but it had been insolently and defiantly put off till the eleventh hour. Glengarry might be punished, but that gave no security for peace, since nothing would have been done to change the Highland mind, no swift dramatic judgment, such as Breadalbane had always pled for, which would awe those barbarous but impressionable souls. . . .

A servant announced that the Earl of Argyll desired to see him. Argyll might throw more light upon the business. The Master had no belief in Argyll, either in his brains or in his character; his prominent shifting eyes were an advertisement of his instability to all the world. But Argyll had means of getting news which never entered the official flying packets.

He resumed his letter to Livingstone with a fateful sentence. 'Just now my lord Argyll tells me that Glencoe hath not taken

the oath, at which I rejoice. It's a good work of charity to be
exact in rooting out that damnable sept—the worst in all the
Highlands.' Ardkinglas's despatch to his chief had brought the
news that, though MacIan had sworn, it had been six days too
late. He was still within the law's danger.

III

During the next few days there were many consultations
between the Master, Argyll and Breadalbane, and several inter-
views with the King. On the 16th William signed additional
instructions to Livingstone, which concluded thus: 'If McKean
of Glencoe, and that tribe, can be well separated from the rest,
it will be a proper vindication of the public justice to extirpate
that sept of thieves.'

That day the Master wrote to Livingstone telling him that
the King would only receive recalcitrants now 'on mercy,' a
reference to Glengarry; but 'for a just example of vengeance I
entreat this thieving tribe in Glencoe to be rooted out in earnest.'
To Hill he wrote on the same day in the same terms, but with an
ominous addition. 'The Earls of Argyll and Breadalbane have
promised they shall have no retreat in their bounds. The passes
to Rannoch would be secured, and the hazard certified to the
laird of Weem to retreat them. In that case Argyll's detachment, with a party that may be posted in Island Stalker, must
cut them off.' On the 30th he told Livingstone: 'I am glad
that Glencoe did not come in within the time prescribed. I
hope what's done may be in earnest, since the rest are not in a
condition to draw together to help. I think to herry their
cattle or burn their houses is but to render them desperate,
lawless men, to rob their neighbours; but I believe you will be
satisfied it were a great advantage to the nation that thieving
tribes were rooted out and cut off. It must be quietly done,
otherwise they will make shift for both the men and their cattle.'
To Hill, also on the 30th, he wrote: 'When anything concerning
Glencoe is resolved, let it be secret and sudden.' And on the
23rd Livingstone had written to Hamilton telling him that he
and the Inverlochy garrison would be judged according to how
they handled Glencoe. The Court, he added, rejoiced that

MacIan had not taken the oath in time, 'so that the thieving nest might be entirely rooted out.'

Argyll's news had given the Master a new policy. He now saw a chance for a dramatic stroke which would carry terror to every rebellious heart. In Scotland commissions of fire and sword had been frequent shot for the rusty blunderbuss of criminal justice, and as a learned lawyer he knew all about them. To 'destroy by fire and sword' was the common style of proclamation against 'intercommuned rebels.' That treatment had long ago been meted out to the Macgregor clan. In 1640 Argyll, the famous Marquis, had been given such a commission against the Atholl and Ogilvy lands. The words had a specific meaning, and to 'extirpate' did not mean to exterminate, but at the worst only to make a clan landless and chiefless. The attack was usually made by day and in summer, and involved burning of crops and houses and driving of cattle, but as a rule little loss of life. This was how the Master intended the Macleans to be handled by Argyll, and Glengarry by the Inverlochy and Inverness garrisons.

But as regards the MacIans he meant extermination. He wanted a spectacular punishment, and this seemed a chance for it. It would need an army to exterminate great clans like Glengarry's and Lochiel's, dwelling over a wide stretch of country; even Keppoch, with open boundaries, would be hard to manage. But the MacIans in their ravine of Glencoe were a simpler matter. If the passes at either end were netted not a soul need escape.

How came this savage notion to dominate the mind of a politic and not inhumane statesman? The answer must be that he got it from Breadalbane and Argyll—but principally from Breadalbane. He wanted an exemplary sacrifice, and Breadalbane showed him where to find it. The Master himself knew less about Glencoe than he knew about the passes of the Alps. He disliked the clan because he had been told that they had been among the chief obstacles to the bribing policy of the previous summer, and that they were bitter Jacobites and notorious caterans even beyond the average Highlander. Breadalbane told him these things. He also pointed out that the physical nature of Glencoe made the place a trap which could be set and watched by a handful of troops. No need to trouble about Leven's and Buchan's regiments. He painted the MacIans as a blot upon the Highlands, a mere rabble of vermin, a disconsidered sept of Clan Donald whom even the other Jacobite clans would not study to avenge. His hatred and his local knowledge made his arguments weighty, and when he showed how he and Argyll could block the bolt-holes the Master was convinced. If we need further evidence for Breadalbane's part, we may note the fact that the executants of the tragedy were mostly his creatures, and that an evil conscience brought his steward to Glencoe after the massacre to try to buy the silence of the survivors.

The Master has come down to history with a heavy weight of blood-guilt upon him, and, even if Breadalbane's crime was the more heinous, it is hard to say that his condemnation is undeserved. He chose to depart from the standards of the civilisation which he preached, partly because he allowed a consideration of policy to over-ride the human decencies, partly because he regarded the Highlands, and especially the MacIans, as something less than human. It should be observed that barbarous cruelty, the slaying of young and old, man and woman and child, is not the only charge, for the scheme involved treachery, though he may have had no inkling of the deeps to which that treachery was to descend. A man of his intelligence cannot have been ignorant that treachery was inevitable if his instructions were carried out to do the thing 'quietly' and to be 'secret and sudden.' He knew that the MacIans were living in fancied security, believing that Ardkinglas's acceptance of their oath had satisfied the law. Any sudden assault would be upon trusting and unsuspecting men. Having willed the end, he had willed also the unholy means.

How shall we apportion William's share? I find it impossible to believe that he was not a consenting party to the plan of wholesale murder. He knew nothing of the Scots practice of 'fire and sword,' and the mild interpretation given to the word 'extirpate'; to him it must have borne its literal meaning. The main instructions he countersigned at the top as well as at the bottom, as if to give them special authority, which weakens Burnet's plea that he signed the document without reading it.

It is clear from the correspondence that he went minutely into the business of the payments to the chiefs, and that the Master of Stair communicated to him every step he took. He heard that MacIan had taken the oath, though late; he knew that Glengarry, who had not sworn at all, was to be mercifully treated; but he approved of the extermination of the little clan of Glencoe as a politic expedient. The fact that he did not punish the principal malefactors when the truth became known is another proof that he felt that he was deeply implicated, for he was a man who was always honest with himself. Technically he carried the chief responsibility, for the measure was a military act, and Hamilton and Livingstone were not responsible to the Secretary for Scotland but to the King.

There is much to be said in extenuation. He knew nothing of the Highlands, and regarded Glencoe as a mere robbers' den. He was engaged in a life-and-death struggle, and had small leisure to inform himself about what he considered the uncouth barbarians of the north. He had no love for Scotland, and respected no Scotsmen but Carstares and the Dalrymples, and he may well have thought the blotting out of a few hundreds of its people to be no very serious matter. He was a great man, but neither humane nor gracious.

The burden of the scheme framed at Kensington in the latter half of January must rest upon three men, Breadalbane, the Master, and the King. The first has the heaviest share, the last the lightest. The guilt varies with the degree of knowledge, and the intimacy of the relationship between the wronged and the wronger. In William it was a crime against humanity in general, in the Master of Stair against his fellow Scots, and in Breadalbane against those who shared with him the blood and traditions of the Gael.

K

IV

GLENCOE

GLENCOE is a gash like a sword-cut among the loftiest and wildest of the Highland hills. At the western end of the Moor of Rannoch stand the sentinel Shepherds of Etive, and from their corries streams combine to form the infant Etive, which flows south-west to the sea-loch of that name, with on its left bank the *massif* of the Black Mount. North of the Shepherds the waters drain westward, and presently descend into a deep-cut glen, which stretches to Loch Leven. The northern wall is the long ridge of Aonach Eagach, the 'Notched Hill'; its south the two Shepherds, the Buachaille Etive Mor and the Buachaille Etive Bheag; and then, going westward, the great bulk of Bidean nam Bian, the highest mountain in Argyll, till the ridge bends northward and sinks to the sea at Meall Mor.

The natural outlets are at the west, or sea end, towards Ballachulish, and in the east to the inn of Kingshouse, whence the traveller can make his way to Rannoch and Lochaber, or south to Glenorchy and the Breadalbane country. In the nine miles of its length the glen has few entries on its flanks. There is no gap in the northern wall of Aonach Eagach save the old military road, which climbs by the Devil's Staircase towards Kinlochleven and Mamore. On the south side, beginning from the east, there is the pass called the Lairig Gartain, leading between the two Shepherds to Glen Etive. After that there are only chimneys for the cragsman, till, on the north-west side of Bidean nam Bian, the two glens of Fionn and Bhuidhe provide difficult routes to Glen Etive and Glen Creran. In all the Highlands there is no other such well-defended sanctuary.

Down in the valley bottom the river Coe, after leaving the bleak moorlands of its birth, runs in deep linns between buttresses of crag, till, midway in its course, it expands into the shallow and boggy Loch Triachtan. On the shelf north of the loch stood at that time the village of Achtriachtan, with the house of one of the cadet gentry of the clan. Thence it flows through natural woodlands, receiving on its left its main tributary from the corries of Bidean nam Bian. Just north of the point of junction stood another village, Achnacon, and a little further down the hamlet and farm of Inverrigan. The sea is now in sight, and among dunes and woodlands, some natural and some planted, stood the house of Carnoch, the principal house in the glen and the residence of the chief. The clan, apart from outlying shepherds' bothies and the high sheilings of the summertime, lived around Carnoch, and in the three clachans of Achtriachtan, Inverrigan and Achnacon.

The marvels of the glen have been the theme of much prose and verse. Looking down it from the east in wild weather it can appear like some prison-house of the *Inferno*, but from the same standpoint, when the sun is sinking beyond Ardgour and the peaks are rose and gold above its purple abyss, it may seem a gateway to happy enchantments. The quartzite and schist formation, seamed by broad belts of porphyry, has contorted the rocks into fantastic shapes, which are grim or fairy-like according to the light and the weather. I know no landscape so capricious in its moods. I have sat on a crag of Aonach Dubh and peered down through driving snow into what seemed to be a hyperborean hell; and I have looked up the glen on a June evening, when the hills drowsed in a haze like sloeberry bloom and the clear streams crooned among flowers and grasses, so that the place seemed, in Neil Munro's words, one of the 'blessed corries, so endowed since the days when the gods dwelt in them without tartan or spear, in the years of peace that had no beginning.'

The savagery was only in the hills, for Glencoe itself was a fruitful and habitable place. There were juicy pastures by the stream and on the shelves of the two Shepherds, where black cattle could feed, and sheep and goats, and the ewe-milkers were busy on the summer mornings. It was sheltered from the north and east winds, and its winters were mild. Loch Leven and Loch Linnhe gave its people herrings and salmon, and the Coe was famous for its sea-trout. Oats and bear did well in the lower haughs. The hills were the haunt of the red deer, and the hazel coverts of roebuck, and the ancient royal Forest of Dalness was part of MacIan's territory and tenanted by a clansman. It is clear that Glencoe had a name not for bleakness but for snugness and comfort. 'This countrie is verie profitable, fertill,' wrote the seventeenth-century topographer, 'plenteous of corne, milk, butter, cheese and abundance of fish.' 'A beautiful valley,' wrote the author of the *Memoirs of Locheill,* and the eighteenth-century report was 'a glen so narrow, so warm, so fertile . . . a place of great plenty and security.' It was a 'garden enclosed' as contrasted with the stony uplands of Knoydart or Mamore.

The life of the little clan that dwelt there was not the idyllic thing which some enthusiasts would have us picture it, but no more was it the naked barbarism of current Lowland belief. The MacIans had their own type of civilisation, their own economy, religion and laws. They were of the old faith, though it is not likely that a priest came often to celebrate mass in Glencoe. They were reported among their neighbours to be 'very resolute, hardy, and stout, and to have the least vanity of any of the septs of Clan Donald.' The society was patriarchal, the chief being the protector of his people, and also the judge, in which duty he had behind him a great mass of ancient traditional law. No fault was ever found with MacIan on these scores. Their economy was rudimentary but by no means barbarous. They grew their own corn, which sufficed except in a season of dearth. In summer and autumn hunting gave them ample store of game and fish. For the winter, cattle were salted down and salmon kippered. The herring gabbarts from the Clyde brought them Lowland manufactured goods to be exchanged for their fish and skins. The surplus of the black cattle was sent south in droves to the Lowland fairs. A certain amount of money circulated, and luxuries were not unknown; there was a smattering of education, and many could talk English and a little French.

Normally their life was peaceful, but now and then the crops would fail, the cattle could get no winter fodder, and after the ancient fashion the young men would go out to drive a prey from the lands of ancestral enemies. Behind all these raids, whether in Argyll or Breadalbane or further afield, there was always, it should be remembered, a sense of getting back that of which they had been unlawfully deprived. Sometimes, too, there was a matter of personal revenge, reprisals when there was no hope of otherwise obtaining justice. It has been truly said that the inefficiency of the Government was largely to blame for the lawlessness of the Highlands. In those raids and vendettas there was much blood and cruelty. Life for such folk was a hard thing; they could suffer much, and were not chary of making others suffer; but even the brutality was governed by iron rules which were never infringed. There were laws not to be broken—the sanctity of an oath, the inviolability of a guest. Their life was like that of the Homeric heroes, cruel and brutish, but controlled by certain taboos which were adamantine.

In actual comfort the society of the glen probably far exceeded that of a Lowland parish of the time. There was not the back-breaking monotonous toil on sour, ill-drained land. The chase gave the men healthy exercise. Their food was better, except in the depth of winter—full meals of flesh as contrasted with the Lowland sowens and bear-meal bannocks. Their bodies were better nourished and developed. If they had no Kirk to enforce discipline, they had a high-handed chief. The houses were no worse, and fuel was more plentiful. Occupations were more varied, there was more social freedom, and more light and colour in their lives. They were worse citizens of Scotland, and of the world, than the peasants of Penpont or Muirkirk, but in their own enclave they had a richer and more wholesome civic life.

The keynote of such a society was a sense of ancient civilisation and a pride of race, in which every member of the clan shared. The long past of Clan Donald was an intimate thing to the humblest, almost like a living memory. They could not forget that the sons of Ian Abrach descended straight from that Angus Og of Islay who was also the father of the first Lord of the Isles. Tales ran in their heads of which their own kin had been the heroes, for there was no saga of the Isles in which they could not claim a part. And not Clan Donald alone, but their own little people had made a name for valour that rang through the Highlands. Ninety years back had not certain Moray lairds brought Alasdair MacIan Og of Glencoe to Morayland on a bond of maintenance to fight in their quarrels? A Glencoe man had guided Montrose in his famous descent upon Argyll.

The life in the glen, too, had its refinements and its hours of merriment. On the summer evenings on the haughs there would be tossing the cabar, and races among the young men, and fierce games of shinty. Up in the sheiling-huts in the twilight the girls would spin, or dance to the pipes, or listen to old tales and harpers' tunes. In the winter nights, when the birch billets made the peat fires leap, and the doors were shut, there would be snug gatherings; the old men at their tobacco, the wives at the spinning-wheel, and the young folk at their songs and tales. For great verse had been left to this little clan. Then would be heard the high deeds of Finn and Oscar, Caolte and Oisin, and the tragical tale of Deirdre, and a motley of adventures that made the breath catch and the blood run quick. Some of the stories came very near to them, for not twenty miles away to Loch Etive side had come the Sons of Uisnach. Some of the songs, too, were their own. It was in the dark slit of Coire Gabhail that the fairies had whispered to the herd-girl the tune of *Crodh Chailein*, 'Colin's Cattle,' the most effective of all milking songs, and the sweetest of lullabies.

By the 8th of January MacIan was back in Glencoe, somewhat weary, but with a mind at peace. He summoned at once Achtriachtan and the tacksman of Inverrigan.

'You have letters of protection from the Governor of Inver-lochy,' he said, 'but they are not enough. You and all the males of my people must journey to Inveraray to take the oath, once the roads are open. Meantime I have sworn on your behalf, to see that Glencoe keeps the Government's peace. I have had kindness from Colin of Ardkinglas, and it must be repaid in strict honour. My children must bide as quiet in this glen as a hedgehog in its winter's hole. I, MacIan, have sworn it.'

He asked for news, and was told that word had come by way of Mamore that Glengarry and his clan were up, and that some of Argyll's men, under Robert of Glenlyon, had gone out against them. He frowned at the name.

'Robert of Glenlyon is a bad person to be loose in Lochaber.

Does son Alasdair know that his bonny kinsman is so near? It was an ill day for Appin when he took auld Glenlyon's widow to wife.'

For the rest of January there were snowstorms which levelled the clefts with the braes; frosts, too, which made every waterfall a stack of silver spears. But that was on the high hills; in the valley bottom the fall soon melted. Now and then came soft mild days when the pastures showed bleached and sodden, and Loch Triachtan was blue with the reflection of the skies—the weather when, according to the Gaelic saying, the badger turns in his winter sleep and dreams of spring. The people of the glen, who had had anxious minds at the New Year, turned again to their several avocations. The women made the dyes of lichen and heather and seaweed for the wool they had spun, or wove that wool into plaiding; the old men mended cobles and steadings; and the young men were on the hill all day, bringing back fat hinds, and now and then a ptarmigan, or ranging the woods for roebuck and capercailzie, or on the shores of Loch Triachtan at sunset when the wild duck gathered.

Meantime, as we have seen, there was much afoot in London, and the posts to the north carried fateful letters. Livingstone, the commander-in-chief, received the King's instructions, dated January 16, and a covering letter from the Master of Stair. The Master on the same date wrote to Hill at Inverlochy, giving the details of the plan as arranged with Breadalbane—Argyll and Breadalbane watching the southern passes, the laird of Weem cutting off all retreat into Perthshire (with a special eye to the friendly Atholl clans), and a detachment from Hill's garrison blocking escape towards the Moor of Rannoch. Forbes, Hill's major, picked up this letter in Edinburgh, and, according to his instructions from his superior, broke the seals and forwarded it to Inverlochy. On his journey thither at the end of the month—he travelled by Lorn and Appin—he fell in with some of Argyll's regiment at the ferry of Ballachulish, and learned that they were bound for quarters in Glencoe.

When he reached Inverlochy he found Hill in a sad state. He had received the King's instructions and the Master's letter, and disliked the whole business. After getting the message from

Ardkinglas he had given orders that the MacIans should be considered loyal subjects and in no way molested, and now here was a plan in train to root them out, a very different treatment to that proposed for the still rebellious Glengarry. That was bad enough, bad, he thought, as public policy, besides being a rebuff to himself. But what perturbed him more was Forbes's account of what he had seen at Ballachulish. Soldiers of the Argyll regiment, but all Breadalbane's men, and seeking lodging in Glencoe! It looked as if some hideous piece of foul play were being meditated. He had virtually been superseded, too, for Livingstone was sending instructions direct to Hamilton, his second-in-command, and it was Hamilton who was managing the affair without confiding to him the details. His humanity and professional dignity were alike outraged.

But what could he do? He could send in his papers. That would not stop the mischief, though it would ease his mind. The honest man was in a sad quandary. His conscience pricked him, but he remembered the monies due to him by the Crown, and the pension and knighthood which still tarried. He thought of his daughters and his lonely old age. So he decided to stand back, wash his hands of the whole concern, and do nothing except what his official duty demanded.

Livingstone was now writing direct to Hamilton, exhorting him on January 16 not to 'trouble the Government with prisoners'; and on the 30th of the month we have seen that the Master wrote to Livingstone with an ominous postscript, and to Hill urging him to make the King's justice as conspicuous in the case of the MacIans as his clemency had been in other cases. But Hill was of no account now, and only Hamilton mattered. He it was who fixed the day for the attack, arranged the different parties, and selected the leaders. He seems to have been a competent soldier, ambitious to succeed in his profession, and apt to complain of slow promotion. We find both Livingstone and the Master telling him that his future depends upon how he makes use of the opportunities they offer him. The men he picked were mostly Breadalbane's own people, and, though no letters on the subject are extant, it is certain that the most heinous treachery in the business was devised by Breadalbane and ordered by Hamilton. Treachery, indeed, was, as we have seen, inherent in the plan if it was to be 'secret and sudden,' but the special form adopted was in such utter defiance of every Highland tradition that it could only have proceeded from the brain of one long destitute of honour, and have been executed by a time-serving Lowlander to whom Highlanders were no better than beasts of chase and warren. The actual operations, too, could only be entrusted to men who, body and soul, were Breadalbane's creatures.

The general scheme of netting Glencoe, though not its exact details, was known to the whole staff of the Inverlochy garrison. Hill did nothing. Two officers protested, and were put under arrest and sent prisoners to Glasgow. We do not know at what stage they made their protest, but it is possible that it was not till the actual day of the tragedy, when they were in Hamilton's company and saw the horrors with their own eyes. In that case their names were Francis Farquhar and Gilbert Kennedy.

The Jacobite journalist got an apt title for his pamphlet on Glencoe from the Emperor Gallienus, whose instructions to his ministers, after the defeat of Ingenuus in Illyricum, put Breadalbane's notions about extirpation in frank Latin. 'Non mihi satisfacies, si tantum armatos occideris, quos et fors belli interimere potuisset. Perimendus est omnis sexus virilis, si et senes atque impuberes sine reprehensione nostra occidi possent. Occidendus est quicumque male voluit . . . Lacera, occide, concide.'

On Monday the first day of February word came to Glencoe that a body of soldiers was approaching by the shore road from Ballachulish. The news spread like wild-fire, and every Maclan who had a sword or a musket hastened to bury it deep in the peat-stacks, or in a cairn of stones, or in some cunning place in the thatch. They had the Government's protection, but they did not wish to give up their arms, without which in those lawless times they felt themselves at the mercy of any ill-wishers. Moreover, the young men had their hunting to think of. John, the chief's eldest son, with twenty MacIans in his tail, waited at the foot of the glen to find out the errand of the strangers.

He saw a force of one hundred and twenty men in red coats

and grey breeks, and a glance told him that they were of Argyll's regiment. At the head strode one whom he knew well. It was a tall man, with a long thin face, a hooked nose, a small petulant mouth like a girl's, and a delicate pointed chin. He wore his own hair, which was flaxen and scarcely tinged with grey, though his age was sixty. His complexion was still youthful, but his eyes had the glazed look of one much addicted to the bottle. The man carried himself well, and at the first glance seemed a model of manly beauty; it was only the second that showed the ravages of time and indulgence. . . . There was no mistaking their kinsman of Glenlyon.

Robert Campbell of Glenlyon had been born to a good but encumbered estate, and in his youth he had made ducks and drakes of it. He had been a notorious gambler, a heavy drinker, and something of a dandy. His political ventures, too, had been unlucky, for he had been a friend of the ill-fated Argyll who had suffered death seven years before. Bit by bit he had to sell his patrimony, till he became little more than a hanger-on of Breadalbane. Now poverty had made him a soldier, and for two years he had had a captain's commission in Argyll's regiment. He was a man, John knew, who could have no good-will to Glencoe, for had he not lost heavily in the *creagh* which MacIan and Keppoch had driven from his few remaining lands after Killiecrankie—that exploit about which Breadalbane had been so bitter at the Achallader meeting? Yet oddly enough he was kin by marriage to his brother Alasdair. His mother had taken Stewart of Appin as her third husband, and Alasdair's wife was her granddaughter, and therefore Glenlyon's niece.

The remembrance of this marriage tie was not much comfort to John, as he advanced to meet the newcomers. If the red soldiers were coming to the glen, there was no man in the world he would not have preferred as their captain.

But Glenlyon greeted him with demonstrative affection. He had always been famous for his hearty manners.

'Here's a burden come to your back, cousin,' he cried. 'It's no doing of mine, but a poor soldier must obey orders. We've been out to redd up things Invergarry way. . . . No, that affair is not finished, but the weather was unchancy and the Colonel has called a halt. Inverlochy is like a cried fair, and they are so throng that there was no house-room for my lads. So what with that, and what with this matter of the cess and hearth-money—weary fall the Parliament that is aye laying new taxes on us poor Highlandmen!—nothing would content the Colonel but he must pack us off to Glencoe. We seek only bed and bite and sup for a week or two. I know it's a heavy affliction, but I'll see that it's made as light for you as possible. If you're to have sodgers quartered on you, it's better that a friend and a kinsman should have the doing of it.'

He laid his hand on John's shoulder, a fine figure of a man, flushed with the sharp weather, almost as tall as old MacIan himself, a trim soldier, but a fellow-Highlander too, with his green Campbell plaid buckled about his middle. He spoke with an easy geniality, before which the other's constraint melted.

'You are welcome, Glenlyon,' John said, 'you and your lads It's not much that Glencoe has to offer, but it's all yours for the taking.'

''Deed I never doubted it,' was the answer. 'And how is the good man, your father? And my nevoy Sandy?' He called up the two other officers, whom he introduced as Lieutenant Lindsay and Ensign Lindsay. 'Helen's kin,' he explained. 'Man, this is a fair family gathering, though it's a month too late for Hogmanay.'

The troops came to Carnoch with John and Glenlyon walking side by side at their head. MacIan received them with the dignity of an erstwhile opponent, but the courtesy of a chief and a gentleman. The men would be billeted up and down among the cottages, and as for the officers they were given their choice of the principal dwellings, Carnoch, Achnacon, Inverrigan and Achtriachtan. It seemed that Glenlyon had already made his choice.

'Inverrigan for me,' he cried in his hearty way. 'I'll not be putting yourself to trouble on my account, MacIan. I'll leave Achtriachtan and Achnacon, too, to the sole enjoyment of their firesides. Inverrigan is the place for us, where I'll be in the heart of my folk—and of your kind folk.'

There was a great bustle all that day allotting billets to the men and moving baggage. Glenlyon and the Lindsays dined with the chief, and the first grew merry. There was new-killed venison on the table, and mutton-ham, and salt beef from the mart; fresh oat-cakes were baked on the girdle, and MacIan set out his foreign brandy. It seemed that the Argyll men had brought few stores with them except a supply of French claret and *aqua vitae*.

'This is better than Inverlochy,' Glenlyon cried in his husky drunkard's voice. 'Here's a feast of fat things, and up yonder there was nothing but thin kale and a thrawn auld wife of a Governor.'

When the strangers had gone to their quarters, MacIan talked with his sons.

'I like it ill,' said Alasdair. 'Glenlyon never came to Glencoe for Glencoe's good. He's a fine couthy fellow, but the word I have heard of him is that his heart is rotten as peat!'

'Maybe so,' said the old man. 'But he is our guest and must be treated well. You can sleep easy in your bed, Sandy, for now we are doubly secure. We have the Government's protection, and these men have eaten our salt.'

V

The Thirteenth of February

THE hundred and twenty soldiers of Argyll's were billeted among
the cottages, three in one house and five in another, according
to the size of the cotter's family. They were given the best
entertainment the glen could offer; not very lavish since it
was winter-time, but, what with kippered salmon and occasional
deer-meat, better than the meagre rations of Inverlochy. Such
hospitality meant that the hosts had to go very bare themselves.
Glenlyon and the two Lindsays were with the tacksman at
Inverrigan, but they had few meals at home. MacIan was
living not at Carnoch but at his farm a little way up the stream
which descends from the Bhuidhe glen, and near by the two
houses of his sons John and Alasdair; at Achnacon was
Achtriachtan's brother, and Achtriachtan himself, to share
in the hospitable duties, often slept there. There were frequent
dinner-parties and card-parties for the strangers, and almost
every day Glenlyon came to Alasdair's house to drink his morning draught, and to salute Alasdair's wife, his kinswoman.

The days passed pleasantly and the weather was kind for the
time of year. Deep snow lay on the high tops and in the passes,
for the December and January drifts had never melted, but in
the valley itself the land was bare and dry. The Argyll men
were mostly Highlanders and Campbells, but there were a few
Lowlanders who hung together and talked their own talk, since
their lack of Gaelic kept them from much intimacy with the folk
of the glen. There were regular drills, when Sergeant Barber
tried to smarten up the newer recruits, and in the afternoons
there were often sports in the haugh, running and wrestling and
that *camanachd* or shinty which was the game of all Gaeldom.

Of an evening, while the gentry were at the cards or a brew
of toddy, the commonalty in the cottages had their own recrea-
tions. Stories and songs went round the fire, and among these
well-mannered people there were adroit reticences. No word

was said, no tale was told, by a MacIan which could wound the Campbell pride; they spoke and sang of the common traditions of the Gael, and of those wars of William and James, and of William and Louis, which could be freely mentioned, since with the rank-and-file politics did not go deep. Also there was piping, mostly on the *feadan* or chanter, but sometimes a *piobaireachd* on the full set by a piper who knew his trade. Here, too, the airs were tactfully chosen. There were no tribal rants to awaken memories of the ancient feud between Clan Donald and Clan Diarmaid, and the pieces played were the classics known to all Albain, *The Macraes' March* and *A Kiss of the King's Hand*, and *Desperate Battle*, and once in a while the heart-breaking *Lament of Macruimen*. Sometimes, too, a MacIan would bow to his guests and play a sprig out of Lorn or Argyll to remind them of home.

No one of the soldiers, except the sergeant, had any notion of the purpose of their visit. They found themselves quartered in a kinder place than the Inverlochy barracks, and did not ask further questions. They were absorbed into the life of the glen as if they had been in their native clachans. The gentry, too, seemed at ease. The Lindsays were lumpish, sullen youths, but Glenlyon was a travelled man and a gentleman, a merry companion, and, when sober, very fastidious in his breeding. He would talk of politics with a shrug of his shoulders and a twinkle of his eye which precluded any danger of offence; he had wonderful tales of his own doings and much scandal about the great; his manner was hearty and endearing, and if in his cups he was prone to bragging, it was done with humour and good-fellowship. There was no guile in that wandering drunken eye.

So thought all except Alasdair. MacIan himself was strong on Glenlyon's simplicity. 'A rattling through-other fellow,' he said, 'whose worst foe is himself. He was never a match for yon fox of Breadalbane, so he finds himself at sixty Breadalbane's gillie. It's the queer old *bodach* he'll be in another ten years. But I tell you the man's mind is honester than sets with his tartan or his service.'

John had agreed, but Alasdair had still his doubts. Glenlyon seemed to him to be nervous about something, to be waiting for something which he half feared and half hungered for. He had detected strange looks passing between him and the sullen Lindsays. Also his wife, Glenlyon's own kin, had a woman's forebodings. She would wake him in the night to question him. A cheerful soul, like all the Appin folk, she seemed now to have fallen into a strange depression of spirit.

So the life went on for eleven days, till Friday, the 12th of February. That day the weather changed. The wind shifted to the north-east, and whined through the gullies of Aonach Eagach. 'There will be snow ere evening,' said the old men; 'in twenty-four hours the corries will be flat with the braes.'

There was a change, too, in Glenlyon's demeanour. The anxiety which Alasdair had detected in him seemed to be sharpened. There was no drilling that forenoon in the haughs; instead he ordered a route-march and sent a half-company swinging past Carnoch along the road to Ballachulish. Alasdair had seen him in secret confabulation with Sergeant Barber; he had also observed the sergeant talking privately to some of the soldiers, and had noted how their faces after his talk grew troubled and a little scared.

In the afternoon there were sports as usual in the meadows by Carnoch. This time they were a dismal business, for the soldiers seemed to have lost their zest for games, and the air had suddenly grown piercing cold. When Alasdair went into his house at the darkening his wife had a curious tale for him. A child had brought it, a child who had been at the sports and had watched them from beside the great boulder which some glacier long ago had brought down from the hills. The story was that a soldier, an Argyll man, had slapped the boulder with his hand and addressed it in Gaelic. '*Grey stone of the glen,*' he had said, '*great is your right to be here. Yet if you but knew what will happen this night, you would be up and away.*'

Alasdair tried to reassure her. 'An Argyll-man's nonsense,' he said. 'They are the lads 'for daft speeches. Nothing will happen this night except an on-ding of snow.' But she refused to be comforted; she repeated the tale to others, and because of it there were many sleepless that night—to their own salvation.

In the evening Glenlyon recovered his composure. More, he was in wild spirits. He summoned John and Alasdair to Inverrigan to a card-party, and with the two Lindsays they played till supper-time. He had been bidden to dine next day by MacIan, he told them, and to bring his officers. Oddly enough he did not invite the brothers to sup with him, but dismissed them about seven o'clock. 'I have gotten news,' he said, 'news which will mean some work for me before bedtime. I fear our pleasant little family gathering is near its end. There's fresh trouble up Glengarry's way, and any hour we may have to take the road.' He was sober, but yet he had the same high laugh and uncertain eye as when he was drunk. Alasdair turned away from Inverrigan with a mind as heavy as the sky above him, from which were hurrying the first couriers of the snow.

The orders had gone out. That morning at Inverlochy, Hill, with a sad heart, had given Hamilton the formal instructions passed on to him from the Master and Livingstone:—

'You are with four hundred of my regiment, and the four hundred of my lord Argil's regiment under the command of Major Duncanson, to march straight to Glenco, and there put in due execution the orders you have received from the Commander-in-chief.'

His one slender comfort was that he could saddle the responsibility on Livingstone, who had been in direct correspondence with Hamilton.

Hamilton the same day sent a special runner to Ballachulish, where Major Robert Duncanson was lying. Duncanson was Argyll's man, not Breadalbane's, but his troops were mostly the latter's, and included that Captain Drummond who had been in charge at Barcaldine when MacIan journeyed to Inveraray. He thus instructed Duncanson:—

'Pursuant to the Commander-in-Chief's and my Colonell's orders to me for putting in execution the service against the rebells of Glenco, wherein you, with the party of the Earle of Argile's regiment now under your command, are to be concerned. You are therefore to order your affairs so that you be at the severall posts assigned you by seven of the clock to-morrow morning, being Saturday, and fall in action with them, at which I will endeavour to be with the party from this place at the post appointed them. It will be necessary the avenues minded by Lieut Campbell on the south side be secured, that the old fox nor none of his cubs get away. The orders are that none be spared, nor the Government troubled with prisoners, which is all I have to say to you till then.'

He added a postscript:—

'Please to order a guard to secure the ferry, and the boats there; and the boats must be all on this side the ferry, after your men are over.'

Duncanson at Ballachulish completed the chain by his orders to Glenlyon, which had only four miles to travel:—

'You are hereby ordered to fall upon the rabelle, the Macdonalds of Glenco, and to putt all to the sword under seventy. You are to have a special care that the old fox and his sones doe not escape your hands. You are to secure all the avenues, that no man escape. This you are to putt in execution at five of the clock precisely. And by that time, or very shortly after it, I will strive to be at you with a stronger party. If I do not come to you at five, you are not to tarry for me but to fall on. This is by the King's special commands, for the good and safety of the countrie, that these miscreants be cutt off root and branch. See that this be putt in execution, without fear or favour. Else you may expect to be dealt with as one not true to King nor countrie, nor a man fitt to carry a commission in the King's service. Expecting you will not faill in the fullfilling hereof, as you love yourselfe.'

Hamilton had fixed seven as the hour with Duncanson, but Duncanson, assuming with reason that Hamilton's part came later, had chosen five for Glenlyon's attack. The tone of his instructions to the latter suggests that he had some fear lest his sojourn among the MacIans might have blunted his zeal. It was an exact and comprehensive scheme of destruction. Against a little clan of two hundred, at the moment unarmed, and numbering only half a hundred fencible men, nine hundred and twenty regular soldiers were unleashed. Duncanson had only four miles to travel in the winter dawn to reach the foot of

L

the glen; Hamilton, moving through the night from Inverlochy, would, by way of Kinlochleven and the Devil's Staircase, come down on the upper end. A detachment of Argyll's men at Island Stalker would block escape through Appin, the laird of Weem was watching the Perthshire roads, and Breadalbane waited in the Glenorchy passes.

Alasdair went to bed, but not to sleep. It was his turn to be wakeful, and at last his anxiety drove him to half-dress himself and look out of doors. The snow had for the moment stopped falling, but there was promise of more in the wind, and it was bitter cold. Close to his house was an empty cottage used as a guard-room by the soldiers, and to his surprise he saw a light in it. It was just after midnight, when all should have been long in their beds. Then he heard footsteps in the snow, and several men entered the guard-room, including one who had the shape and carriage of the elder Lindsay. Much alarmed, he slipped off to his brother John's house, and woke him. John took the thing lightly and refused to move. 'They are doubling the guards,' he said, 'and a very proper course. In this devil's weather the sentries need to be relieved often. That's the reason of the extra folk in the guard-room. Glenlyon's a careful man. Back to your bed, Sandy.' Alasdair, half-frozen, returned to his own house, and presently was asleep.

By five o'clock on the morning of Saturday 13th the wind had grown to a tempest, and the snow was drifting heavily. About that hour Lieutenant Lindsay and a few soldiers presented themselves at MacIan's house, and asked civilly to see the chief on a pressing matter. They were at once admitted, and MacIan got out of bed and struggled into his trews, shouting to bring the visitors a morning draught. Suddenly two shots were fired at him from behind, one in the body and one in the brain, and the old man fell dead. Then mania seized on the murderers. Lady Glencoe—to give her the title which lairds' wives bore—had risen and dressed; they seized her, stripped her naked, and tore the rings from her fingers with their teeth. The sound of the firing had brought some of the near-by dwellers to the house. Two were shot dead, and one, Duncan Don, who had come with letters from the Braes of Mar, was badly wounded. Lindsay and his party flung the three corpses out of doors into the snow, and the wounded man whom they took for dead, and then turned to leave. . . . Through the drift came another party to meet them, buffeting their way up from Loch Leven. It was Duncanson and his four hundred.

The gale blanketed the sound of the shots, and the chief's sons, whose houses were a little way off, heard nothing. But it was now John who was wakeful. Before the shooting began he had heard the movement of troops outside his window; there was shouting, perhaps because some of the better disposed wished to give him the alarm. He rose, dressed, and ran to Inverrigan to find out what was happening from Glenlyon himself, apparently not dreaming of any danger to his father. He found Glenlyon up and dressed, and got a cheerful greeting. 'What's the steer?' he cried. 'The steer is that we're off to take order with Glengarry. What ails you, man? You're as white as the snow on your plaid.' Then he burst into his jolly laugh. 'Feared for Glencoe? Is it likely? Is it likely I would lift my hand against my good friends, or if I was so ill-minded that I would not first pass the word to my nevoy Sandy? Back to your bed and thank God that you have not to take the road in this hell-begotten weather.'

John went home, only half reassured, and lay down, but did not undress. He may have dozed for an hour, not more. A servant rushed in and told him that, in a pause of the snow, he had seen soldiers moving towards his door. John went out and saw not fifty yards off a party of twenty redcoats, with their bayonets screwed into their musket-barrels. He had never seen them before, for they were Duncanson's men. . . . He knew the truth at last, and fled to the snow-laden scrub below the screes of Meall Mor.

There he stumbled upon another fugitive. Alasdair ten minutes earlier had been waked by his servant, who asked him if it were a time to sleep when they were killing his brother, for he had seen the soldiers with bayonets fixed approaching John's house. That which he had long dreaded had come to pass, and Alasdair acted on a plan already formed in his head. He got his little household through the snow to a place of temporary concealment, while he himself took to the hillside. Like John he did not think of his father's house, but of Inverrigan and

Achnacon as the danger-points. So he ran along the slopes of the south wall of the glen in order to reconnoitre, and as he ran he met his brother. They stood and listened, for in the hollow below was the sound of guns—many guns. They came from Achnacon.

Sergeant Barber was busy there. Something had happened to alarm the household, for Achnacon himself was up and dressed, and was sitting by the fire with Achtriachtan his brother, and eight other men who had come in from the cottages. Suddenly there was a volley, and Achtriachtan fell dead, and four more. The others dropped on the floor, all of them wounded. Barber bent over Achnacon and asked him if he were alive. 'I live,' was the answer, 'and I have but the one wish—if I must die, to die out of doors.' 'I have eaten your bread,' said the sergeant, 'so I will do you that kindness.' He was led outside, and put up before the muzzles of the guns. But Achnacon was a powerful man, and wrath and fear made him desperate. He flung his plaid over the soldiers' faces, broke through the cordon, and made for the hills, while the other four indoors managed to creep out by the back of the house. Barber made short work of those left in Achnacon hamlet. One was a child who was never seen again: only his hand was found; he may have died in the snow and been devoured by fox or eagle. The bodies of the dead were flung on to the midden and covered with dung.

At Inverrigan was Glenlyon. John had not long left him before the work of murder began. Nine men were taken, bound hand and foot, and shot. Then he seems to have sickened of the business and inclined to hold his hand. But Captain Drummond arrived from Duncanson's party, and as Breadalbane's henchman he remembered his chief's orders. He and Barber seem to have been the most bloody-minded of the crew. Glenlyon had spared a lad of twenty. Drummond, who had the same military rank, reminded him of his instructions, and shot the youth dead. A boy of thirteen years ran out and clung to Glenlyon's knees; Glenlyon would have saved him, but he was pistolled by Drummond. A child of four or five years was among the victims, and a woman—an excess which even Gallienus had not commanded. The bodies were hastily shovelled into shallow graves.

It was the same in all the cottages. Wherever there was a living male who could be laid hands on he died by shot or steel. Among the victims was an old man of eighty. Then, when there was no life left, the soldiers turned to other work. They loosed the cattle from the byres, the sheep from the pens, and the shelties from the rude stables. As John and Alasdair strained their ears from the skirts of Meall Mor they heard the lowing of hungry animals, who had missed their morning meal of bog-hay. And as the February dawn turned the dark into grey, they saw the driving snow redden with a glare from the valley, and knew the cause. Every cottage and hut and hovel was going up in flames.

By eight o'clock the business was over, but Glenlyon and Duncanson had not fulfilled their masters' commands. To be sure, the Government was not going to be troubled with prisoners, but they had made but a poor killing. Thirty bodies at the most, and of them several were children and at least one a woman. Most of the younger men had escaped, and though the old fox was dead his cubs were still at large. They consoled themselves by reflecting that there was but one way out of Glencoe, and that Hamilton with his Inverlochy men was stopping that bolt-hole. So they turned to their task of burning and plundering with an easy mind.

But all was not well with Hamilton. He had marched by night down the shore road from Inverlochy, and long before dawn had reached Kinlochleven. There he split up his command into parties, each with its special instructions, but all with orders to slay every man they met and make no prisoners. But on their way across the hills by the Devil's Staircase they encountered so fierce a blizzard that they were obliged repeatedly to stop and take shelter. John Forbes, Hill's major, who unwillingly accompanied them, must have thanked Heaven for the weather. What with one thing and another it was eleven in the forenoon before they found themselves at the upper end of Glencoe.

There they were met by Duncanson, who, weary of waiting, was making a patrol of the glen. He reported that old MacIan was dead and thirty-odd of his men, but that the rest had flown to the hills. Hamilton went down the river, killed an old man, burned one or two more houses, and realised that he could do nothing further. Through no fault of his own he had failed to carry out to the full the mission which was to bring him fame and fortune. His comfort was that the refugees in the hills were doomed, though they did not fall by his guns, for no human beings could live long in such a tempest of wind and ice. He contented himself with seeing to the booty, most of which would be the perquisite of the officers. The pitiful little belongings of the clan, clothes, trinkets, spoons and cups and platters, were already in the soldiers' pouches. Fatigue parties were appointed, and by the afternoon the whole stock of the glen, nine hundred cattle, two hundred horses, and a multitude of sheep and goats, were being driven across the narrows of Loch Leven on their way to Inverlochy.

Meantime what of the survivors of the little clan? The snow was their salvation, for in five yards a man was lost to sight in the drift, and they had the advantage of knowing the ground like their own steadings. Except for a young man there were but two winter roads out of Glencoe—one by the shore to Appin, and one by the east to Rannoch and Glenorchy. The first they knew was blocked by Duncanson, but they did not know of Hamilton's purpose to net the upper end. There was a third, which an active man might manage, the pass of the Laroch between Meall Mor and Ben Vair, but there, too, Duncanson was the barrier. The only hope was to go up the glen.

One or two hunters escaped by the mountain gullies, north into Mamore, and to the Macdonald dwellings on Loch Treig. But these routes were only for the mountaineer, and many desperate miles had to be covered before a place of safety was reached. In such weather it was necessary not only to get out of the clutches of the assassins but to find food and shelter, for even the hardiest could scarcely survive a night among the blizzards and snow-wreaths of the high corries.

There was only one ultimate sanctuary—Appin—for Keppoch was too distant. In Appin there would be refuge with a friendly people, a people strong enough, too, to defend the refugees. But how to get to Appin since the coast road was shut. There were two possible routes—one by the Bhuidhe glen: a second through the Lairig Gartain, between the Shepherds of Etive to Dalness; after that the way lay down Glen Etive, where there were only shepherds' bothies, to the head of the sea-loch, and then across the low *beallach* to Glen Ure and Glen Creran. Local tradition declares that most of the people escaped by the first road, but it is certain that in winter weather it was possible only for the young and the strong. The weaker folk must have followed the second. Before it was yet light, while Glenlyon and Duncanson were burning the clachans and driving out the cattle, men, women and children, old and young, many of them half-naked, were struggling up the glen in the teeth of the storm. Once they were past Loch Triachtan they were out of the danger of the troops. The Devil's Staircase descends the northern wall opposite the opening of the Lairig Gartain, but the fugitives were inside the pass long before Hamilton appeared from Mamore.

It was a cruel journey, for the snow still drifted. There were grandfathers and grandmothers among them, women heavy with child, mothers with infants at the breast, sick folk and the very young. To their bewilderment and terror were soon added the pangs of hunger, fatigue and an extreme cold. Such as reached Dalness found temporary shelter and entertainment, for the tenant was a MacIan whom Breadalbane's men had strangely omitted to molest. But some died on the road thither, and more on the further road down the Etive or over the *beallach* to Glen Ure. Among the latter was Lady Glencoe, her fingers torn by the teeth of Lindsay's troops. Some thirty were murdered in the glen, and as many perished from the hardships of the flight. But in the end Appin was reached, and there the MacIans found roofs to cover them, and a share of Appin's scanty winter pro-vender, and armed Stewarts to protect them should their enemies follow. In Appin the little clan was nursed back to life.

By the afternoon of the 13th Glencoe was a silent place. Scorched thatch still smoked among the snow-drifts, and ravens barked above the blood-smears on the blackened thresholds. From Aonach Eagach and Aonach Dubh the eagles and buzzards were gathering where the corpses had been left unburied. Except for these there was no sound—save that from Loch Leven shore came the far-away echo of Glenlyon's pipes. The tune they played was *The Glen is Mine*.

VI

The Reckoning

GLENCOE was left to the peace of death, and soon the snow shrouded the charred roof-trees and the bloody hearthstones. Hamilton, Duncanson and Glenlyon reported at Inverlochy. Their plan had somewhat miscarried, but the MacIans were fugitives in the winter hills, and it was predicted that the weather would complete the half-done job. That the affair had been bungled could not be denied. The alarm had been given by using muskets instead of cold steel, and Hamilton had signally failed to stop the main exit. Both Hill and Hamilton made their reports to the Master of Stair, who could only express a very moderate satisfaction. 'All I regret is that any of the sept got away, and there is necessity to prosecute them to the utmost. If they could go out of the country, I could wish they were let slip, but they can never do good there. Appin, who is the heritor, should have encouragement to plant the place with other people than Macdonalds.' By way of a reward to Hill he promised to look into his money claims against the Government, and to take up the matter of the civil jurisdiction for which he had long been pressing.

But strange rumours were beginning to spread, coming from the talk, perhaps, of the more merciful among the soldiers, or by devious ways from the fugitives. By March 5 there was a story in London that the MacIans had been murdered in their beds after taking the oath; the Master of Stair denied the latter part of the report, but not the first. In Edinburgh the rumour was more detailed. Argyll's regiment had been ordered south, and Glenlyon was in Edinburgh on his way to England. He was drinking heavily, and boasting at large in the coffee-houses. People noticed the wildness of his manner and the uncertainty of his eye, which belied his bold words. Bit by bit from his babbling the story came out. He was robustly impenitent. He declared that he and his colleagues were supplicating the

Council for some special recognition of their meritorious services. 'I would do it again,' he cried. 'I would stab any man in Scotland or England, if my master the King ordered me, and never speir the cause. He who would not do that is no loyal subject.' But he was like a 'fey' man, with a catch in the voice and sudden terrors in the face.

In April Glencoe was the chief talk of the Scottish capital. On April 12 the Paris *Gazette* published a summary of the doings there, accurate except in so far as it said that MacIan's two sons had perished with him. The Jacobites had been miraculously given new powder and shot, and they were not slow in using it. In April a pamphlet appeared in London, in the form of a letter from Scotland, which told correctly the full tale. At first its horrors were not realised, for the Jacobite journalists were fond of making people's flesh creep, and did not enjoy any very high repute for veracity. But bit by bit came confirmatory evidence, damning proofs that could not be denied, and by the summer responsible people in Edinburgh and London knew that beyond question a horrid barbarity had been committed. Argyll's regiment was now quartered at Brentford on its way to Flanders, and its private soldiers were talking. Charles Leslie, the Jacobite, went out on June 30 to see them and got the full details. Both Glenlyon and Drummond were there, and, said one of the men, 'Glencoe hangs about Glenlyon night and day, and you may see him in his face.' But William had gone to his glorious and inconclusive wars, and the fall of Namur and the preparations for Steenkirk left him no time for the trivialities of Lochaber.

Secretly during the spring the MacIans began to slip back to Glencoe. First went the young men to bury the dead and report that there was nothing stirring in the glen. Then a few of the half-burned cottages were made habitable, and when the fine weather began some cattle were brought to the haughs, the gift of kindly neighbours. John and Alasdair, who knew that Hill was not ill-disposed to them, approached him for help, and accordingly on May 3 the Scottish Privy Council authorised him to grant provisional protection—'to these persons, either in general or particularly, of all security to their persons, lands and goods, and a cessation of all acts of hostility, trouble or molestation to them, upon the account of their having been in arms and rebellion against their Majesties, and to take what security he shall think meet for their living peaceably until his Majesty signifies his pleasure therein.'

It was not much of a grace, for the MacIans had no goods to protect, but it enabled them to set to work to rebuild their shattered life. On October 3, Hill, having got the royal assent, formally received Glencoe into the King's peace, Alasdair acting on behalf of the clan. Four days later he wrote to the laird of Culloden: 'The Glencoe men are abundantly civil. I have put them under my lord Argyle, and have Arkenloss' surety for them till my lord comes; for they are now my Lord Argyle's men; for 't was very necessary they should be under some person of power, and of honesty to the Government.' Ardkinglas throughout the whole miserable business showed himself consistently honourable and humane.

But this formal pacification, and the paradox of a Campbell becoming surety for a Macdonald, did not silence the rumours. It was the interest of the Jacobites to foster them, and even the tough conscience of seventeenth-century Scotland was disquieted. In April 1693, Livingstone wrote to Hamilton that 'some in Parliament make a talking about the business of Glencoe, and give out that they design to have it examined,' and a month later he grew seriously concerned, and told the same correspondent that Hill must come to Edinburgh to tell all he knew. 'It is not that anybody thinks that thieving tribe did not deserve to be destroyed, but that it should have been done by such as were quartered amongst them, makes a great noise. I suppose I may have pressed it somewhat upon your Colonel, knowing how slow he was in the execution of such things.'

It was a great noise indeed, for every opponent of the Government was soon in full cry, not from love of Glencoe, but from hatred of Stair. Some honest souls had indeed been horrified by the tale, and for humanity's sake would fain have punished the guilty. When the Master of Stair resigned the office of Lord Advocate, Sir John Lauder of Fountainhall refused to accept it unless he were permitted to prosecute the Glencoe murderers. But the main motive was politics, not justice. The Master was too powerful not to have numberless enemies, and too passion-lessly wise to have many friends among the *politiques*; Johnston of Wariston, his colleague, was intriguing against him; while, of the extremists, the Jacobites hated him as a traitor and the enthusiasts as the enemy of true religion.

In 1693 William, induced by his tender-hearted Queen, ordered the Lord High Commissioner, the Duke of Hamilton, to institute an inquiry into the methods used in Glencoe, of which the tales grew daily wilder. But Hamilton died, and nothing was done in that Parliament. The scuffling of kites and crows in Lochaber seemed to the King of small importance compared to the thorny ecclesiastical questions which were obtruding themselves in Parliament and General Assembly. But when the House met again in the early summer of 1695 it was clear that an inquiry would be insisted upon. William anticipated the demand, and, before leaving for the Continent, he appointed a commission, under the presidency of Tweeddale, the new High Commissioner. After three weeks Parliament began to clamour for the report, and, though technically it should have first been submitted to William in Flanders, the agitation was so great that Tweeddale was compelled to produce it on June 24.

The commission did its work with expedition and thorough-ness. It took the evidence of the chief surviving MacIans, and of other Highlanders, and it had before it the letters which had passed between the Master of Stair, Livingstone, Hill, and Hamilton. Its decisions may be briefly summarised. A great wrong had been done in not presenting MacIan's certificate of submission to the Scottish Privy Council; not a very relevant point, considering that his submission was known in London, and one probably introduced to make prejudice against the elder Stair. The Master knew about MacIan's oath, and, though aware that the King had admitted Glengarry, who was in worse case, into mercy, did not countermand the general order for a massacre. The Master's letters showed that he had interpreted 'extirpation' in a different sense to the King, and had thereby exceeded his instructions and caused 'a barbarous murder.'

Parliament proceeded to debate the matter in detail. Hill was called before them and exonerated. A warrant was granted for the citation of Hamilton, who fled the country. The King was asked to send home for trial Major Duncanson, Captain Drummond, Lieutenant Lindsay and Sergeant Barber, who were serving in Flanders and so beyond the reach of the ordinary law. On July 10 the House in an address to the King extolled his mercy, for reasons which are not apparent, demanded the prosecution of the minor offenders from Hamilton downwards, and decided that Hill and Livingstone were covered by the orders of the Secretary of State. Then it turned to the Master, the true quarry that the hounds had always in view. 'We beg your Majesty will give such orders about him, for vindication of your Government, as you in your Royal wisdom shall think fit.'

The inquiry had been honest, but not so the findings of the commission or the resolution of Parliament. It is difficult to resist Macaulay's argument that the subordinates were covered by their military duty, and, whatever their moral guilt, were legally blameless. If this plea be disallowed, then why did not the blame attach throughout the whole hierarchy, up through Hill and Livingstone to the King? If it be argued that the worst horror, 'murder under trust,' which especially shocked the public mind, was due to Hamilton's specific orders, it may be answered that some kind of treachery was implicit in all the orders both of Livingstone and the Master, since they insisted on quiet and secrecy, though they did not contemplate the barbarity of the actual deeds. It was a mere quibble which exonerated William while it condemned the Master, and a worse quibble which concentrated on the minor malefactors and did not ask for the Master's trial. Policy over-rode justice, for Parliament knew that the King would never surrender Stair, and moreover that, if he were brought to trial, that trial would be a farce without the King as a witness. No doubt it was also aware that Breadalbane stood behind the whole business, but had been too wary to leave one scrap of incriminating evidence. He was indeed arrested and sent to Edinburgh Castle for the treasonable secret clauses arranged at Achallader in June 1691, but his defence was accepted that he only arranged these clauses to get to the bottom of the Jacobite plots, and he was presently released.

William did nothing. In common decency he could do nothing, for he knew that a great part of the moral responsibility

was his own.   He removed the Master from the Scottish Secretaryship—he could hardly do less in view of the finding of Parliament;
and the Scottish politicians, having got their way, turned joyfully
to the Darien adventure.   But he gave him an indemnity, 'his
Majesty being willing to pardon, forgive and remit any excess
of zeal in going beyond his instructions by the said John Viscount
Stair, and that he had no hand in the barbarous manner of
execution'; and as a token of his favour granted him the teinds
of the regality of Glenluce in his own Galloway country.

The Jacobite hope *Qui Glencoat Glencoabitur* was never realised.
Hamilton was indeed put to the horn and disappears from
history, but no punishment fell on the Lowlanders who were
guilty of the worst barbarities—Drummond, the Lindsays and
Barber.   Hill got his knighthood—and, let us hope, his pension,
for he was an honest if ineffectual being—but he did not live
long to enjoy it.   Livingstone became Viscount Teviot.   Glenlyon had risen to be a colonel before he died at Bruges in August
1696.   As for Breadalbane, he continued his infamies to an
extreme old age.   He was deep in the Jacobite attempt of 1707,
and, when he was nearly eighty, he rose with Mar in the 'Fifteen,
and managed to shuffle out after Sheriffmuir.   He advised Mar's
officers, since they were good for nothing else, to buy a printing
press and start a newspaper!   The old reprobate had not one
rag of virtue, but he had a sense of humour.

Of the two greater figures in the tragedy, the Master of Stair
was occluded for a brief time from the service of the State.   He
ventured a thousand pounds in the Darien scheme, which he
doubtless lost.   In 1695 he succeeded his father as second
viscount; in 1702 he was a privy councillor, and in 1703 Anne
made him an earl.   He was the ablest Scotsman of his day—
the man, said Defoe, 'of greatest counsel in the kingdom.'   He
was among the chief architects of the Union, but died of apoplexy
at the age of fifty-nine, on the eve of its final ratification.   Un-
loved and unloving, careless of common esteem, he found such
happiness as was permitted him in the exercise of his fine
intelligence and in a cynical condescension to the follies of
mankind.

As for the King, he marched resolutely upon his appointed

way, through success and unsuccess, bereavement and broken
health, till that February day in 1702 when the molehill of the
'little gentleman in black velvet,' long to be toasted by the
Jacobites, brought down his horse at Hampton Court, and he died
a few months after the exiled James. William was a great man
and a great European statesman, but to Scotland he meant little.
He never crossed the Border. He had to bear much of the blame
for two dismal tragedies, Glencoe and Darien. The Edinburgh
mob forced the bell-ringers of St. Giles's to play the tune of
'Wilful Willie.' Seasons of bitter famine, for which he got the
credit, coincided with his continental wars. On the 8th of
March 1702, the day of his death, a Highland widow announced
to her neighbours the good tidings. When asked how she knew,
her answer was that her cow had given twice as much milk as
she had had from her for seven years.

The Parliament of Scotland recommended that the survivors
of Glencoe might have some reparations made to them for their
losses and be supplied with the necessaries of life. Nothing was
done, except that the Privy Council instructed the authorities
of Argyll not to press for payment of the cess. Yet the little clan
managed to creep back to a certain stability. John, as chief,
drew the survivors together, and, aided by Appin and Keppoch
and Glengarry, built up their shattered life. He died, after
building a new house at Carnoch, and his successor was the child
of two who had been carried to the hills by his nurse on the
morning of the massacre. The clan would appear to have
grown in numbers. In 1745 Duncan Forbes, the Lord President,
put the fighting men at one hundred and fifty, and the report
of the minister of Inverness a year later rated them at one hundred.
Better seasons and the growing wealth of the Lowlands had no
doubt improved the trade in black cattle and skins and increased
their means of livelihood.

There was to be one final drama in the story of the glen before
the broken lights of its past faded into common day. The chief,
Alasdair, and his twin brothers, James and Donald, rose in the
'Forty-five. They joined Prince Charles Edward on August 27
with one hundred and twenty men; Alasdair was a member of
the Prince's Council and fought in all his battles. After Culloden

he was attainted, and lay some years in prison, but he was alive in the glen in 1773. The high moment of the MacIans was in the march to Edinburgh, when the Prince's army occupied Linlithgow. Near by stood the house of Newliston, a Stair dwelling which the Master had got in virtue of his wife. Alasdair demanded that his men and no others should guard Newliston, that they might prove to the world that the purity of the cause for which they fought was smirched by no 'vileinye of hate.'

The last word—and a great word—was with Glencoe.

BIBLIOGRAPHICAL NOTE

IN this essay in reconstruction I have tried to include no detail which has not a warrant from contemporary evidence, or is not a legitimate deduction from such evidence. The only liberty I have taken is now and then to state boldly as a fact what should strictly be qualified by a ' probably.'

The principal authority for the massacre of Glencoe is the report of the inquiry by the Commission of the Scottish Parliament, presented in June 1695. It was published as a pamphlet by B. Bragg, ' at the Blue Ball in Ave-Mary-Lane,' in 1703, and it is reprinted in Howell's *State Trials*, vol. xiii., in *Somers Tracts*, vol. xi., and in *Highland Papers*, 99-116.

The first account of the affair was given in a pamphlet published in 1692, ' A Letter from a Gentleman in Scotland, to his Friend at London, who desired a particular account of the Business of Glenco.' This was reissued, with a commentary, in *Gallienus Redivivus, or Murder Will Out*, in 1695, after the publication of the Parliamentary Commission's report. *Gallienus Redivivus*, whose author was Charles Leslie, the Jacobite pamphleteer (for whom see *D.N.B.*), was reprinted in *Miscellanea Scottica* (Glasgow, 1820), vol. iii. In the same year appeared a second pamphlet, also in *Somers Tracts*, which was partly a defence of the Master of Stair,—' An Impartial Account of some of the Transactions in Scotland, concerning the Earl of Breadalbane, Viscount and Master of Stair, Glenco-men, Bishop of Galloway, and Mr. Duncan Robertson. In a Letter to a Friend.'

The other contemporary authorities are the *Leven and Melville Papers* (Bannatyne Club, 1843); *Papers Illustrative of the Political Condition of the Highlands of Scotland from 1689-1696* (Maitland Club, 1845); *Culloden Papers* (1815); *Memoirs of Locheill* (Abbotsford and Maitland Clubs, 1842); *Memoirs of Hugh Mackay* (Bannatyne Club, 1833); Mackay, *Life of Hugh Mackay* (Bannatyne Club, 1836); John Macky, *Memoirs of Secret Services* (1733; and Roxburghe Club, 1895); *Lockhart Papers* (1817); and *Memoirs of Great Britain and Ireland, 1681-92*, by Sir John Dalrymple of Cranstoun (3 vols., 1790).

The story has been retold by all the modern historians of Scotland, such as Hill Burton, Hume Brown, and Andrew Lang— by the last most judicially. It is also the subject of one of Macaulay's most famous chapters, which has been controverted, and partly corrected, by John Paget in his *Paradoxes and Puzzles* (1874), 33-76.

In my boyhood I used to hear local legends in Appin; but their evidence is scarcely to be trusted, for Glencoe became almost at once a literary theme, and the local traditions must have been coloured and supplemented from outside sources. The topography is based on my own stalking and mountaineering recollections.

M

IV
GORDON AT KHARTOUM

My dear Evelyn Baring,

I have heard part of the story which I have told in these pages from the lips of those who shared in it; from Kitchener, from Slatin, and especially from your father. As a young man I owed so much to Lord Cromer that I should like to inscribe this chapter to his son.

J. B.

I

Prologue

In the first days of November in the year 1883 an observer on
the palace roof at Khartoum would have been struck by an
unwonted quiet. The great spaces around him were as they
had always been—the blue waters of the two rivers sweeping
to their junction, the green patches of dhurra and the fronded
palm-trees on their banks, the tracts of tawny grass and thorn
and sand stretching to little ribs of hill, black in the noon sunshine and rose-red at twilight. But in the sprawling city of mud
and brick at his feet there was an ominous stillness. There was
some stir indeed at the new fortifications which were being
constructed two miles to the south, but the troops there wrought
languidly, for they were mostly old and crippled. The racial
hotch-potch in the streets, Cairene officials, Coptic clerks, Greek
and Arab traders, and negroes of a hundred tribes, had been
solemnised into a painful expectancy. Rumours came hourly,
the wild tattle of the East, and all the rumours were bad. The
new prophet of God, the Mahdi, was master of Kordofan. His
lieutenant, Osman Digna, the slave-merchant of Suakim, had
fired the eastern Soudan. The provincial governors, Slatin
in Darfur, Lupton in the Bahr-el-Ghazal, Emin in Equatoria,
were in deadly peril. An army of 10,000 men under Hicks
Pasha, a British officer, had marched into the western desert
to deal with the enemy—a ragged, ill-trained army, but the
only thing that stood between Khartoum and ruin. The word,
the too true word, which was being whispered in the bazaars was
that that army had perished.

At the moment Egypt bore nominal rule over a domain
extending from the Mediterranean to the Equator, and from the
Sahara to the Red Sea. But in most of the country south of
Wadi Halfa, which we know as the Soudan, the writ of the
Khedive ran limpingly or not at all. The territory was larger
than all western Europe, nearly a million square miles, and it

was held by scattered Egyptian posts who at that time ranked as among the worst soldiers in the world.

Till the second decade of the nineteenth century the Soudan had had no history. The great empires of the ancient world had done no more than touch its fringes. It was a mystery land out of which came tales of snow mountains, and monstrous beasts and men, and fabulous treasures of gold. Broken tribes from Arabia crossed the Red Sea, intermingled with the negro inhabitants, and spread the faith of Islam, but to Europe it was only a name till that 'barbarian of genius,' the Albanian tobacco-seller, Mohammed Ali, made it part of Egypt. Like Cambyses he sought an El Dorado in the south; he desired for the sake of Egyptian irrigation to secure the upper waters of the Nile; visions of Napoleonic conquests, too, surged in his fantastic brain. Khartoum ceased to be a collection of reed huts and became the capital of a new empire, and a mighty emporium of the slave-trade. But the empire was miserably and corruptly governed, and instead of an asset it proved a mill-stone round Egypt's neck. Ismail, who came to the throne in 1873, was also in his own way a man of genius. He essayed reforms, but no patching could preserve a structure so ill-founded. He would have crushed the slave-trade, but his officials battened on it. He would have introduced order and justice, but his mudirs and beys were incompetent and his soldiers ran away. In 1883 the government of the Soudan was a jerry-built monstrosity which would have fallen from its own weight even if there had been no alien force to batter it. Ismail was the typical Oriental despot whose imagination, especially in money matters, far outran the prosaic fact. But there was an element of greatness in his folly. When he was asked concerning the gauge of his proposed Soudan railway, he replied, 'Make it the same as South Africa; it will save trouble in the end.'

Misgovernment was universal and enormous. A plague of rapacious underlings covered the land. The slave-trade, officially forbidden, was unofficially encouraged. There was little law at the centre, and only anarchy at the circumference. Small wonder that the name of Egyptian or 'Turk' stank in Soudanese nostrils. Efforts to sweep the chamber only meant that seven new devils arrived when the broom was withdrawn.

But let it be admitted that in 1883 the task was not easy. Egypt had neither the money nor the quality of man for so great an undertaking. The vast distances and the inadequate transport made a tight hand difficult. The land was an ethnological museum, and there was no economic or racial unity among its people. The population of the shabby little towns and villages was as mongrel as that of a seaport in the Levant. North of the thirteenth parallel of latitude lived the tribes of camel-owning Arabs, such as the Kababish and the Hadendowa. South of it, where the rainfall was heavier and there were pastures and forests, dwelt the cattle-owning Arabs, including the great clan of the Baggara, and south again the negroes of Equatoria. These last formed the hunting-ground of the slave-dealers, notably the Baggara, whom Sir Reginald Wingate has called the Red Indians of the Soudan. In such a racial medley there were only two elements of union. There was a universal hatred of the Cairo government; and, in the priest-ridden villages and among the nomads of the wilds, there was a smouldering fire of religious fanaticism, which might break forth with the suddenness and fury of a desert sand-storm.

The Soudan, as I have said, had no unity and no history, nothing to bind it together except the long silver thread of the Nile. In 1883 to the Western world it was still largely unknown, though Speke and Baker, Gordon and Stanley had interested Europe in its southern fringes. . . . Suddenly the fates set the play. From Darfur to the Red Sea, from Assouan to the Great Lakes, it became a single stage, lit by the fires of death, and as the months passed the drama drew to its climax in the few square miles of land where Khartoum stood at the junction of the two Niles. The ancient river of Egypt, which had witnessed in its lower course the making of so much history, now saw in its southern wilds a tragedy evolve itself with half the world as breathless spectators.

II

Dramatis Personae

It was no drama of blind, illogical happenings. The action was determined by the character of four men whom destiny brought into ironic conjunction. Let us glance at these in turn, beginning with the most distant and the most potent.

I

Mr. Gladstone in 1883 was in his seventy-fourth year. For the second time he was chief Minister of the Crown, and the year before he had celebrated his parliamentary jubilee. He had been returned to power in 1880 with a great majority, after a campaign of brilliant electioneering devices, in which, in spite of his age, he had played the major part. By millions of his countrymen he was passionately hated and distrusted, and by millions he was passionately adored. He had long ago formally discarded the Tory faith in which he had begun his career, but his mind remained tenaciously conservative, and the half-dozen Liberal principles which made up his professed creed were held with as blind a devotion as any Tory ever gave to Church and King. He had received, as he thought, a mandate from the nation for a programme of reconstruction at home and peace abroad—a widening of the franchise, a generous settlement of the Irish imbroglio, land reform, economy in expenditure, and, abroad, a recoil both from Palmerston's habit of light-hearted foreign adventure and from Disraeli's policy of imperial expansion. So far he had not been fortunate. Ireland was proving a thornier problem than he had thought; in South Africa he had had to face disaster and humiliation; and in Egypt he was confronted with a situation which promised much embarrassment and little profit.

'The difficulties of the case,' he told the House of Commons two years later, 'have passed entirely beyond the limits of such

political and military difficulties as I have known in the course
of an experience of half a century.' By that time some of the
troubles were of his own making, but when he took office he
inherited a quandary for which he was in no way to blame.
The cutting of the Suez Canal had involved Britain irrevocably
in Egypt's affairs, both as a shareholder in the Canal and as
the guardian of the road to India. Mr. Gladstone, anxious
to have as little as possible to do with the Nile valley, had been
compelled by the force of circumstances to armed intervention.
Alexandria had been bombarded by British warships, and
Arabi's rebellion had been crushed at Tel-el-Kebir by British
troops. There was a force of British regulars in Egypt, and
the Egyptian army and the Egyptian police were under British
officers.

Lord Granville, his Foreign Secretary, had been dragged
by Gambetta into the policy of the Joint Note, which made
foreign intervention inevitable, but France had drawn back
and left Britain to face the consequences. It was necessary
to get the finances straight in the interest both of the foreign
bondholders and the Egyptian people. It was necessary to
liquidate many of the valueless territorial assets which Ismail
had accumulated. No mere appointment of commissions to
report would meet the need; nor could a public declaration
of non-responsibility make Britain irresponsible. She was in
military occupation of a country which the native rulers and the
suzerain Turkey were alike incompetent to govern; and, since
she had the power, the civilised world and her own conscience
saddled her with the duty. But it was a duty which in the nature
of things could be neither simple nor clear, for Egypt was a
labyrinth of paradox. 'One alien race,' in Lord Milner's
words, 'had to control and guide a second alien race, the Turks,
by whom they were disliked, in the government of a third race,
the Egyptians.' And there was the eternal international paradox,
that France laboured to put obstacles in the path of a British
policy for which Britain was utterly disinclined, and by her
efforts succeeded against her will in forcing an unwilling Britain
to do what neither Power wanted.

Mr. Gladstone was not altogether fortunate in his colleagues.
Lord Morley has told us that 'no more capable set of ruling men

were ever got together than the Cabinet of 1880.' Such can scarcely be the verdict of history. The Cabinet in 1882 was a mosaic of old Whigs and new Radicals. There was a Palmerstonian strain in it, and a restless experimental yeast, and a considerable spice of the bland and leisurely eighteenth-century tradition. It was not a body from which in a crisis the nation could look for a shrewd reading of facts, instant decision, and swift action. Only two members had that rare thing, political genius—Mr. Chamberlain at the Board of Trade, who was immersed in departmental business, and the Prime Minister himself. The old man of seventy-four so towered above his colleagues in popular prestige, in parliamentary skill, and in moral force that when he bestirred himself his will was law.

As compared with the riches of his great rival Mr. Gladstone's mind was equipped like a Victorian dining-room—a few heavy pieces of furniture and these not of the best pattern. He cannot interest his successors as Disraeli interests them, for he had nothing of the artist in him, and little of the philosopher. He was without the gift of style, and has left no spoken or written word by which the world can remember him. We cannot recapture the impression of his uncanny House of Commons dexterity, or his Sinaitic platform thunderings, or his wonderful presence—the grim lips, the great nose, and the flashing aquiline eye. He was a supreme master of a talent by which Britain was governed for two hundred years, but now the fashion has passed away, and that intricate and sonorous declamation is as remote from reality as church bells heard among the guns of war. The causes he fought for have been won and forgotten, or rejected and forgotten, and give small title to immortality.

But the man himself remains a marvel and a mystery—a character far subtler and more baffling than Disraeli's. Like some mediaeval ecclesiastic he professed the half-dozen dogmas of his faith as a rigid and infallible canon, but, like such an ecclesiastic, he showed supreme ingenuity in their interpretation. He had as high a courage as was ever possessed by an English statesman; no man cultivated the masses more assiduously— or feared them less. He was not inaccessible to the teaching of facts, but his nature was such that he would ignore facts unless he could subsume them under one of his fixed categories of thought. The self-deception of which he has been accused was the effort of a mind fundamentally rigid to keep its orthodoxy inviolate, and yet continue to guide affairs and to master men. He convinced himself that he longed for retirement, but the powers which nature had given him of dominating his followers could not be laid down till the grave.

He was as sensitive as Disraeli on the question of national prestige, and would tolerate no incivility from Bismarck or anybody else. It made him furious to think that any foreign Government should have the notion of him that the Emperor Nicholas had of Lord Aberdeen. As a man of deep religious convictions and high and humane instincts he was sensitive, too, about the honour and morality of any course. But in a sudden crisis in foreign affairs he might be a dangerous leader. In the first place he was slow to realise a situation, having a short-range imagination and little power of visualising unfamiliar things. Again, his habit of mind made it a laborious task for him to admit concessions or changes into a policy which he had once accepted, the more if such changes infringed ever so slightly one of the cast-iron articles of his creed. Again, the leisurely administrative ritual in which he had been trained made him averse to any swift action; emergencies he held to be a word which should be omitted from a statesman's vocabulary, since it was his business to see that they did not arise. Above all, his enormous self-confidence inclined him to defy the clamour of fact as he would have defied the clamour of a mob. . . . Such an one might well be a protagonist in an Aristotelian tragedy, if circumstances arose which made certain elements in his strength a deadly weakness.

II

In September 1883 Sir Evelyn Baring arrived in Egypt. He was then a man of forty-two who had had much varied experience since he began life in the Royal Artillery. His earliest connection with the Nile valley was in 1846, when as a child he watched Ibrahim Pasha driving in St. James's Park. Under Disraeli's Government he had been one of the Commissioners of the Egyptian debt, and in 1879 had resigned the post in despair. On Ismail's fall he returned to Egypt as Controller of the Debt, and after a year went to India as Financial Member of Council. In 1883, when Sir Edward Malet was promoted to the Embassy at Brussels, he returned to Cairo as his successor.

The maker of modern Egypt began his career there as British Resident, a post anomalous and undefined; the authority of the office was only such as its occupier could make it. Baring was unknown to the British public, but he had a considerable reputation among men associated with imperial affairs, and he had some prestige with Mr. Gladstone's Government. In politics he was a Liberal; he was a friend of the Prime Minister; his cousin Lord Northbrook was in the Cabinet. His proved competence in financial questions seemed to mark him out as the man to handle a problem which was believed to be mainly financial. He had no melodramatic imperial dreams, and would gladly have seen Britain rid of Egypt altogether, believing that we needed it no more than, to quote Lord Palmerston, a man with an estate in the north of England and a residence in the south needed the possession of the inns on the North Road. But he recognised that Britain had assumed responsibilities which she could not relinquish, and from India he had observed with some bewilderment Mr. Gladstone's behaviour about Alexandria—his refusal to allow the landing of any force to protect life and property on the ground that such an act would constitute an 'assumption of authority,' while he considered that the bombardment of the Egyptian forts was not such an assumption. He embarked upon his Egyptian duties with an uneasy feeling that he might find Downing Street a little difficult.

But in one matter he was wholly in accord with his superiors. He saw before him a gigantic task: the rescue of a land from insolvency and a people from beggary, overdue schemes of public works, legal, educational and administrative reform, and a perpetual diplomatic strife with obstructive Powers. Egypt must begin by cutting her losses and getting rid of the Soudan. His view was that of Lord Granville. 'It takes away somewhat of the position of a man to sell his racers and hunters, but if he cannot afford to keep them, the sooner they go to Tattersall's the better.'

The quality of the future Lord Cromer was in 1883 not
revealed to the world, but the man was already formed, and
the hour for him had come.   In his leisure he had made himself
an excellent scholar; he was widely and deeply read and full
of the spirit of old good books, so he had a philosophy of conduct
behind him.   But he was above all a practical man, with a keen
eye to discern and a just mind to weigh the facts of a case.   In
all heart-breaking tangles there is usually one problem which
is the key of the whole.   The ordinary man fusses about among
a multitude, tinkers a little here and a little there, finds nothing
come of it, and gives up the business in disgust.   The wise man
seizes upon the one thing needful, and discovers when he has
achieved this that all things are added unto him.   Baring saw
that the key of Egypt was finance, that everything depended
upon financial solvency, and that his first duty was to nurse her
assets.   In this task he had only the official status which he could
create for himself.   To many at first he seemed brusque and
imperious.   Gordon, when he met him, thought him 'pretentious,
grand, patronizing.'   He certainly did not suffer fools gladly,
and he had a detestation of all tall talk and bravado and advertisement.   But in his own way he was an incomparable diplomatist,
for he diffused an atmosphere of goodwill and utter sincerity.
His brusqueness was not due to restless nerves, for he had the
patience of a sculptured king on a monument.   His motto was
that sentence from Bacon which he often quoted: 'It were good
that men in their Innovations should follow the example of Time
itself, which, indeed, innovateth greatly, but quietly, and by
degrees scarce to be perceived.'   In action he showed a wise
parsimony, the courage to do nothing when action was futile,
to go slowly when a thousand hysterical critics urged him to
speed.

In all this there was some surface resemblance to Mr.
Gladstone's own creed, the dislike of adventure, the insistence
upon prosaic economic truths, even to Lord Granville's urbane
impassivity.   But the difference was profound.   Baring was
incapable of dawdling.   His caution was the consequence of
a true reading of the case, not of setting it aside.   His patience
was a reasoned policy, and not due to a vacant brain or a halting
will.   When the time came no man could strike more swiftly

or more surely. Above all he had a mind wholly honest with itself. He did not believe that an ugly fact could be got rid of by pretending that it was not there, or that a plain moral duty could be ingeniously explained away.

III

In the early 'forties there was born in Dongola a certain Mohammed Ahmed, the son of a priest who belonged to a noted family of boat-builders. His father died while he was young, and he grew up with his uncle and brothers on the wooded island of Abba, in the White Nile above Khartoum. Very early he discovered a vocation for the religious life, but he could find no place for himself in the local hierarchy. He saw the practice of his faith clogged with impurities, he saw the children of Islam ground under the heel of foreign oppressors who in the name of the Prophet betrayed the Prophet's cause, so he retired into solitude to wait for a revelation. For some years in a cave on the island he lived the life of a hermit. He was a most impressive young man, of great physical beauty, with a voice which thrilled his hearers, and with a power of oratory which turned their heads. He preached a doctrine of poverty and abstinence, and something more—a restoration of Islam to its primitive purity and of his countrymen to power and freedom. The fame of the recluse at Abba spread far and wide through the Soudan, and his mystical prophecies were whispered from mouth to mouth. Legends grew of his miracle-working, and of his visions when the Prophet communed with him in the night watches. People journeyed from great distances to sit at his feet, among them an obscure man of the Baggara, one Abdullah, who was not interested in mysticism, but who was determined to rid his land of foreigners and rule in their stead. The young prophet was known as Zahed, the Renouncer, but there were already many who called him the Redeemer.

In 1881 the moment arrived for his epiphany. He cunningly knit up various legends of the Mohammedan world into one. The Twelfth Imam had been long hidden from men: he was the Twelfth Imam. A Messiah had been promised, a Mahdi or 'guide,' who would convert the whole world to the faith of

Islam: he was that Mahdi. In May he sent round a proclamation to the neighbouring tribes announcing his advent, and his

MAP OF THE SOUDAN

mission to purify and lead to victory all true believers and to regenerate the land. He had many things in his favour. He claimed to be of the blood of the Prophet. His age was forty, the traditional age for a Messiah. He had the mole on the cheek and the V-shaped gap between his front teeth which were looked on as proof of a high destiny. Above all he had his name for saintliness and austerity, his magnetic personality, his winning eloquence, his repute for miraculous powers and for converse with the unseen. In all likelihood he was wholly sincere in his claims, for years of seclusion and introverted thought may well pervert a man's vision.

The Egyptian authorities at Khartoum had hitherto respected the saint, but they were bound to take order with the rebel. They stumbled from blunder to blunder. In August an attempt was made to arrest him, and the police force sent for the purpose was ignominiously beaten off by men armed only with clubs. The story of the victory flew through the Soudan. Mohammed Ahmed, realising that he had burned his boats, followed the example of the Prophet and made a *Hejira* into the mountains of southern Kordofan and the country of the Baggara. There he proclaimed a *Jehad*, a holy war to free the Soudan, conquer Egypt, take Constantinople, and convert the world. Like the Prophet he appointed four caliphs, of whom the chief was the fierce Abdullah. Men flocked to his standard, slave-raiders who had chafed at Gordon's restraint, wandering tribes of the desert who saw a chance of war and plunder, all who had suffered injustice from the tax-gatherer and the kourbash. Soon he had an army of thousands, called 'dervishes,' which means poor men, wearing the patched cotton smock or jibbah, which was the mark of poverty. Abdullah and his brother caliphs presently organised them into some semblance of an army. The governor of Fashoda sent an expedition against them, and the expedition did not return. Some months later Khartoum sent 3000 men, and they too were utterly destroyed. With three victories behind him the Mahdi in the summer of 1882 descended from the mountains and entered upon his career of conquest.

The capital of Kordofan, El Obeid, to begin with made a stout resistance, and in the first action the Mahdi lost 10,000 men. But the flame of fanaticism was only kindled to greater fury by the check, and the straw tents of the besiegers crept like a locust drift around the city. In January 1883, El Obeid capitulated. Egypt made one last crazy effort at reconquest.

Troops were hurried to Khartoum, and Hicks Pasha was despatched in September with 10,000 men, to crush the rebels and relieve Slatin in Darfur. On November 3, in a forest near El Obeid, he met an Arab army 40,000 strong, and few of his command survived to tell the tale. The Mahdi celebrated his victory with a salute of many guns. Before the end of the year Slatin had surrendered Darfur, and Osman Digna was mopping up the garrisons in the eastern Soudan. South of Berber only the Khartoum area and a few isolated posts were outside the rule of the new Messiah.

The man who had wrought these miracles was no mere charlatan. He had put life into a dead people, and turned beasts of burden into warriors, and such a feat is beyond the common impostor. He had a quick sense of the theatrical and knew how to stage his appearances so as to impress his followers ; but, though he might put pepper in his finger-nails to expedite the flow of tears and paint his eyes to enhance their lustre, he believed in his mission as fervently as any Christian saint. He organised his following on a basis of extreme puritanism—the simplest food and dress, shaven heads, the prohibition of wine and tobacco, oaths and gaming and dancing—and any offence, however slight, was savagely punished. Had he been also a military genius, he might have built up a new and most formidable type of army. As it was he created a fighting brotherhood, sustained by religious ardour and a long tale of past wrongs. Like many prophets he did not practise what he preached, for in the seclusion of their inner tents he and his caliphs wallowed in debaucheries. But when he showed himself in public, to the wild Baggara and the credulous Soudanese he must have seemed indeed the chosen of Heaven. Not for centuries had the faith of Islam, 'There is but the one God and Mohammed is his prophet'—the eternal truth and the necessary lie—been preached by such compelling lips. He was tall and strongly built, with a carefully trimmed black beard; his colour was the light brown of the Dongolawi; he had a noble head, well-cut features, a mouth that was always smiling, dark eyes that both wooed and commanded, and an exquisite voice. His jibbah, as became a Messiah, was not dirty and patched, but speckless, and he exhaled a delicious perfume. Men said it was the odour of Paradise, and that it

N

was natural that it should attend him, for was he not always communing with God and the Prophet and the great Angels?

IV

In the autumn of 1883 a certain major-general in the British Army was coming to the end of a leisurely tour of Palestine. He had been studying the sites of famous Scriptural places, notably Golgotha and the Temple of Jerusalem, staying with missionaries and with the eccentric Laurence Oliphant at Mount Carmel, varying his reflections on religion with schemes for letting the Mediterranean into the cleft of the Jordan valley and so making a new canal to the Red Sea. This soldier, Charles George Gordon, was now fifty years of age, but his spare figure and scarcely grizzled hair suggested a younger man. He was about the middle height, with a slight stoop, as if he were looking for something just beyond his reach. Everything about him, his light step, his quick impetuous speech, spoke of intense vitality. He smiled much, but his face in repose was stern and rather melancholy. Tropic suns had not spoiled the freshness of his skin. The forehead was broad, and he had the high cheekbones of his Scottish ancestry; the jaw was strong, and the mouth under the small moustache was firm and a little grim. But the arresting feature was the eyes. They were of a brilliant blue, set far apart, restless, ardent, capable of melting into an infinite kindliness but also of blazing into a formidable wrath. His whole aspect suggested simplicity and modesty, but also an extreme tenacity of purpose. It was the face of an adventurer in the worlds of both flesh and spirit.

He was a lonely being, whose mind was always turning inward. In his own profession he had a multitude of acquaintances, but few friends. His intimates, with whom he constantly corresponded, were certain parsons at home and his elder sister Augusta. He was shabbily dressed, and seemed to desire above all things to escape notice and to be left in peace with his thoughts. Yet this man had behind him a career which for varied and desperate enterprise had no parallel in the world at that day. More than once he had been in the glare of publicity, and his name was somewhere at the back of people's memories, much like that of Colonel T. E. Lawrence in our own time after his Arabian exploits were ended.

Gordon was born of one of those peripatetic soldier families which have long lost any territorial link with home. He entered the Royal Engineers, and in his early twenties went through the Crimean War with distinction, making there two lifelong friends, Garnet Wolseley and Gerald Graham. At twenty-seven he went to China, and at thirty found himself in command of a Chinese army. The tale of his doings in the Far East is in itself an epic, which cannot be told here. Suffice it to say that by his courage and military capacity he suppressed a dangerous rebellion, won the admiration and confidence of so formidable a figure as Li Hung Chang, was made a Mandarin and a Field-Marshal, and was offered and refused vast wealth and many honours. Another man might have used his power to win a kingdom and to found a dynasty, but Gordon's thoughts were not on such things. He returned home with a prodigious reputation, for he was 'Chinese Gordon' to the English people, but this young man of thirty-two declined to be lionised and shunned the mention of his exploits as if they had been a disgrace. He was content to settle down to prosaic regimental duties at Gravesend, where he filled his leisure with good works, especially the care of poor boys, and with preaching quietly his religious faith. He lived bare, spending most of his small income in charity, and he sent the gold medal which the Emperor of China had given him to be sold for the relief of the Lancashire cotton famine. But he was always a keen professional soldier, and he was still worldly enough to pine for more active service. The chance came when he met Nubar Pasha at Constantinople in 1872 and was offered the governorship of the Khedive's Equatorial province in succession to Sir Samuel Baker. On January 28, 1874, he left home to take up the post. It was his forty-first birthday, and the day when the news of the death of David Livingstone came to England.

Equatoria was the second epic tale in Gordon's life. He had two main purposes; to suppress the slave-trade, and, as a means to this end, to open up communications with the Great Lakes and once for all to dispel their mystery. He served Ismail with the same single-hearted zeal with which he had served the

Chinese Emperor. He had able lieutenants, among them that great gentleman, the Italian Romolo Gessi, but he himself with his hard body, tireless energy, and unfaltering courage was the inspiration of every enterprise and the executant of most. It was a thankless labour to make a civilised state out of the squalid little towns and the immense trackless hinterland, and to enforce law and order with penny-steamers and fever-ridden soldiers 'as brave as hares.' But he never faltered and rarely despaired. He dreamed of a great Central African state where the well-being of the natives would be the Government's first care, a state extending through the present Kenya to the sea, and he conceived that he might be the man destined by God to redeem Egypt, that famous Bible land. He wrote in his journal:

Comfort-of-Body—a very strong gentleman—says, 'You are well; you have done enough; go home; go home and be quiet and risk no more.' Mr. Reason says, 'What is the use of opening more country to such a Government? There is more now under their power than they will ever manage.' . . . But then Something (I do not know what) says, 'Shut your eyes to what may happen in the future; leave that to God, and do what you think will open the country to both lakes. Do this, not for H. H., or for his Government, but do it blindly and in faith.'

Such are the doubts which must always attend a crusader.

Equatoria was mainly a business of administration and exploration. The third epic tale in Gordon's life moved to a brisker tune. In 1877 Ismail made him Governor-General of the whole Soudan from the Tropic of Cancer to the Equator. Now began those marvellous camel-rides when Gordon sped like a flame across the deserts and surprised his enemies while they were still conspiring. He dismissed incompetents whole-sale, and built up some semblance of a civil service and an army. He clipped the wings of Zobeir, the great slave-dealer of the Bahr-el-Ghazal. On one occasion he covered on his camel eighty-five miles in thirty-six hours and rode alone into his enemies' camp, paralysing their hostility by his naked courage. But meantime the affairs of Egypt were hastening to perdition, and he was summoned to Cairo to discuss financial problems

which he did not understand. He liked Ismail and thought that
he was hardly treated by the Powers; he regarded the bondholders as common usurers: his health was beginning to crack
and he believed that he had *angina pectoris*; in any case his work
in the Soudan was at an end if Egypt had to think twice about
every piastre. He accepted a last mission to the lunatic King
John of Abyssinia, a potentate who was drunk every night and
up at dawn every morning reading the Psalms. Early in 1880
he was back in England.

Then followed two years of odd jobs. Gordon had returned
with a great repute among all those interested in African problems,
but, as after China, his one desire seemed to be to bury himself.
He rejoiced at Mr. Gladstone's victory at the polls, and accepted
the post of private secretary to Lord Ripon, the new Viceroy of
India. Within a week he resigned. He went to Peking, where
his influence prevented a war with Russia. Then he went on
regimental duty to Mauritius, to oblige a brother officer, and
spent some peaceful months in that island in religious meditation.
'God has been very merciful to me,' he wrote, 'in the thoughts
I have had here (in Patmos) regarding the Scriptures and the
motives of one's actions: and now, through His mercy, I see
lakes and seas of knowledge before me.' After that he was
summoned to South Africa, where he gave his mind to the
native question, but found it impossible to work with the Cape
Government. In January 1883 he was in Jerusalem, taking a
holiday at last, and feeling himself a hopeless misfit. Africa had
laid its spell upon him, and meditations as to the exact measure-
ments of Solomon's Temple could not oust his interest in the
Nile valley, of which the northern part seemed to be now in
chaos and the centre in flames. The King of the Belgians was
making overtures to him, and he was seriously thinking of going
to the Congo. He still felt within him the conviction that he
was born to rule men and that war was his true province, and
he had reasons for his belief. In China he had shown the
talents of a commander-in-chief, and in the Soudan those
of an incomparable cavalry leader. He had the gifts of
foresight, judgment, swift decision, and lightning execution.
His old comrade Wolseley was now the soldier best spoken
of in Britain, but Gordon for all his modesty knew that

he had powers in him to which Wolseley could make no claim.

Let us look more closely at the character of this man, now waiting at Jaffa for a cable from King Leopold, and about to enter upon the fourth and greatest epic of his life. He had a mind which was a strange blend of crudity and power. He had little knowledge of the world outside his profession; his education had been slight and was not supplemented by later study except constant reading of the Bible: his views on ordinary questions, economic, educational and political, were often shrewd but were not based on any considered philosophy of life, and the cosmogony in which he believed was mediaeval in its simplicity. He had a quick eye for facts, and his judgment on matters with which he was acquainted was mostly sound and penetrating, but on other subjects few men could talk wilder nonsense. Like Cromwell, he relied more on instinct than on reason; his first summing up of a situation, his first impression of a man, was commonly his last.

His heart was tender, and he hated all cruelty and injustice. 'I am averse to the loss of a single life,' he was always declaring. But his temper was often out of control, and he was capable of great harshness. His humility before his Maker did not make him humble before his fellow-mortals, and he bore himself to British and Egyptian grandees with a pride which in another would have been arrogance. The result was a good deal of friction. 'What a queer life mine has been,' he wrote to his sister, 'with these fearful rows continually occurring.' He was not an easy man to work with, for he had moods of extreme irritability and petulance, which he sincerely repented. 'Talk of two natures in one,' he said. 'I have a hundred, and they none think alike and all want to rule.' With a deep love and charity towards mankind, he could be grossly uncharitable in his behaviour to individuals, and men whose affections he had won by his gentleness would be amazed when his eyes—'like blue diamonds'—blazed at some trifle with wrath or hardened into a stony hostility. To Cuzzi and Slatin he was relentless even in his own extremity, for they had committed the unforgivable sin of denying their Lord. In that he was a crusader, but he could also be the knight-errant, and he would have challenged Nubar to a duel because the Egyptian had insulted a fellow Companion of the Bath. His instincts were not harmonised and were often at war. His habits were temperate, indeed ascetic, for he had trained his body to need little nourishment and little sleep, but now and then he had unregenerate longings for home when he could have oysters to lunch and not get up till noon. He made sparing use of wine and spirits, but he smoked incessantly, though he tried often to give up tobacco, reminding himself that his body was the temple of the Holy Spirit. The smug gentility of Victorian England he had at all times detested, and he carried his dislike so far as to be scornful even of ordinary etiquette, perhaps because he knew that in his inmost heart he had a liking for ceremonial. When the Prince of Wales asked him to dinner, he declined on the ground that he always went to bed at nine o'clock.

Gordon was so unlike other men, so apparently single-hearted, and radiating such an atmosphere of moral fervour, that he readily acquired a spiritual ascendency over all who knew him well and many who did not. Wolseley, who did not lack self-confidence, felt that he was 'not worthy to pipe-clay his belt.' But the dualism which was notable in his lesser qualities was also in the very foundation of his being. The impression of single-heartedness was an illusion, for all his life his soul was the stage of a conflict.

Like Lee and Stonewall Jackson and many another great soldier, he had that scorn of death which comes from an abiding sense of the littleness of life. Man's efforts seemed to him only a child's game played out under the calm eyes of God. He had moments of self-abasement. 'If a man speaks well of me, divide it by millions and then it will be millions of times too favourable. If a man speaks evil of me, multiply it by millions and it will be millions of times too favourable.' The world of sense shrank to a pin-head when he contemplated the eternity beyond the grave. The rush of Time's winged chariot was never out of his ears. The irony of human life weighed on him, the fragility of its hopes, the comedy of its trivial ambitions. 'It matters little,' he wrote to Lord Lyons. 'A few years hence a piece of ground six feet by three will contain all that remains of Ambassadors, Ministers, and your obedient humble servant C. G.

Gordon.' And in a robuster mood he could even laugh at it all.

In ten or twelve years' time, Baring, Lord Wolseley, myself, Evelyn Wood, will have no teeth and will be deaf; some of us will be quite *passé*; no one will come and court us. New Barings, new Lord Wolseleys will have arisen, who will call us 'bloaks' or 'twaddlers.' 'Oh! for goodness' sake, come away, man! Is that dreadful bore coming? If once he gets alongside you, you are in for half an hour,' will be the remark of some young captain of the present time on seeing you enter the Club. That is very humiliating, for we, each one, think we are immortal.

Such a habit of thought should have made its possessor a mystic and a recluse. But it was constantly jostled by another; in Raleigh's famous image, if one gate of his soul was open to 'divine contemplations,' the other was thronged by 'manifold vanities.' Conscious of great powers, he burned to use them, not for the sake of gauds and titles, but for the delight of their exercise. He longed for the joy of battle even when he knew the ultimate triviality of the issue. All his life this combat lasted. He fought against it; he choked down his passionate desire to explore the Great Lakes; he withdrew himself to Gravesend, to Mauritius, to Palestine, but the craving would not be stilled. The convictions of the quietist could not bridle the instincts of the born man of action. These extended even beyond the grave. 'Look on me now,' he once told a friend, 'with small armies to command and no cities to govern. I hope that death will set me free from pain, and that great armies will be given me, and that I shall have vast cities to govern.' This dual nature was both his strength and his weakness. It delivered him from fear and from all vulgar ambition, but it made him uncommonly difficult for prosaic folk to work with or to understand.

The religion, which was the mainstay of his life, was evangelical Christianity, coloured by a singular mind and temperament. It was based wholly on his reading of the Scriptures, and for orthodoxy in the common sense he cared not at all. He got little aid from the churches though much from individual ministers; he only discovered the value of the sacrament of communion late in his life, when he resolved to take what he called the 'eating' once a month. Many of his theological speculations were fantastic and some were heterodox. He was curiously tolerant of other creeds, and, unlike Doughty, had a respect for the fierce Moslem monotheism, regretting only that it was blind to the fact of Christ. In his social work, too, he indulged in no diatribes against the rich; he pitied them as much as he pitied the poor, and, like Christ, called them not knaves but fools. He accepted in the simplest sense every word of the Bible as a direct revelation, and was satisfied with even the rudimentary interpretation of the popular tract—at Gravesend he was a great tract distributor. The Apocalypse was his special delight, and he looked forward to the literal accomplishment of its tremendous prophecies, the Last Trump, Christ throned in the skies among flaming myriads, and the New Jerusalem descending visibly out of Heaven. He had decided that the Mount of Olives would be the scene of the Second Coming.

The two corner-stones of his faith were the divine ordering of every detail of the universe, and his union with God in Christ. His belief in predestination was no blind fatalism, for, though he knew that his life was in God's hands, he omitted no precaution to ensure the success of his work and his own health and safety. It was his duty to keep his powder dry. But, his task in that respect being done, the rest was in higher hands. In Equatoria he wrote:

The intense comfort of no fear, no uneasiness about being ill, is very great, and more than half the cause of good health. No comfort is equal to that which he has who has God for his stay; who believes, not in words but in fact, that all things are ordained to happen and must happen. He who has this has already died, and is free from the annoyances of this life. I do not say I have attained to this perfect state, but I have it as my great desire.

And again:

I am a chisel which cuts the wood; the Carpenter directs it. If I lose my edge, He must sharpen me; if He puts me aside, and takes another, it is His own good will. None are indispensable to Him; He will do His work with a straw equally as well.

And during his wild rides in the Soudan:

My sense of independence is gone. I own nothing and am

nothing. I am a pauper and seem to have ceased to exist. A sack of rice jolting along on a camel would do as much as I *think* I do.

This conviction of all things divinely ordained abased him before his Maker, but gave him a contemptuous condescension towards the common perils of life and the rivalries and ambitions of his fellow mortals. It was united with a passionate desire for communion with the unseen, for a closer walk with God, ever since at Gravesend a text from the Bible had flashed upon his brain and he had found in nearness to God the key of life. He trod the familiar path of the mystic. It was an unbroken communion, for he had none of Cromwell's agonies of estrangement, those tortures which are the fate of subtler and profounder spirits. His religion was more like that of Major-General Thomas Harrison, who walked confidently through life, looking forward happily to the command of the left wing at Armageddon. The one cloud came from his moods of insurgent ambition, when he longed to force the pace instead of waiting upon the divine call. To learn to wait in patience was the chief discipline of his life. This mystic, when he betook himself to pure contemplation, found something lacking; he was happiest when he was busiest, and when prayer was his refreshment and not the sole occupation of his day. He prayed at all times, for in prayer he felt himself at one with God, and through prayer he could benefit the world. He had a copy-book filled with the names of people for whom he prayed daily. The devout Mohammedans around him saw in this infidel one whose trust in Allah was stronger than their own, and his fame as a holy man soon equalled his repute as a warrior. To plain folk all the world over, the soldier-saint, the practical mystic, the iron dreamer is the leader whom in their hearts they desire.

So in the year 1883 four men from the ends of the earth were being drawn together to a clash of wills and purposes on a single stage. Three were in different ways men of an austere religion. All four had the tenacity of character and elevation of spirit which make the true tragic hero.

III

ACT THE FIRST: THE MISSION

I

IN 1877 in a magazine article Mr. Gladstone had written prescient words: 'Territorial questions are not to be disposed of by arbitrary limits. . . . Our first site in Egypt, be it by larceny or by emption, will be the almost certain egg of a North African empire.' The arguments against British interference were unanswerable to a statesman whose mind was set upon home reform and who detested all grandiose foreign adventure. It would involve us in interminable diplomatic wrangles: it would vastly extend our military commitments, and in case of war it would dangerously enlarge our line of defence. Yet the logic of events had now made this discretion impossible. We had drifted into interference by steps which seemed inevitable in the retrospect. We had bombarded Alexandria and suppressed Arabi. British officers had been compelled to take in hand the reorganisation of the Egyptian army. There was a large force of British regulars in the country. The finances were under British control. The new Khedive's precarious throne was supported by British bayonets, and he had come to lean wholly on British advice. The suzerain Turkey would not, or could not, act as a protector. If Britain marched out another Power would march in, and the road to India would be in jeopardy. Besides, every consideration of public morals forbade us lightly to cast off responsibilities which we had ourselves created.

The position of supreme adviser demands that the advice given shall be continuous and shall cover the whole field of policy. It was obvious that the most difficult question was the future of the Soudan, but in this matter the British Government at first stubbornly refused to interest itself. In November 1882 Mr. Gladstone had declared that it was no part of Britain's duty to restore order there. 'It is politically connected with Egypt in consequence of its very recent conquest; but it has not been included within the sphere of our operations, and we are by no means disposed to admit without qualification that it is within the sphere of our responsibility.' The view had sound reason in it, but its logical consequence was the abandonment of the Soudan at the earliest possible moment, and the discouragement of Egypt from any attempt at reconquest. But, though this abandonment was urged by Dufferin and Malet, the British Government declined to give any advice in the matter or to prohibit Hicks's ill-fated expedition.

It is important to distinguish between the knowledge which they possessed at the time and that which they afterwards acquired. They did not then realise—no one realised—the strength of the Mahdi's power. They were not fully aware of the feebleness of the Egyptian soldiery. But, nevertheless, it is impossible to acquit them of being false in substance to their own policy. Their duty was, in Britain's interest, to make Egypt face the facts which their own representatives were pressing on them. In words which Lord Cromer wrote at a later date, they 'took shelter behind an illusory abrogation of responsibility, which was a mere phantom of the diplomatic and parliamentary mind.' Lord Granville's supineness in the autumn of 1883 was the seed of all the future misfortunes.

Before the Hicks tragedy was known Baring had endeavoured to get Britain to commit herself on the relinquishment of the Soudan, and Lord Granville had replied that, if consulted, he should recommend evacuation within certain limits. Then came the terrible news from Kordofan, to be followed by tidings of further disasters in the Suakim neighbourhood. Egypt must be advised, for she was helpless. On December 10 Baring telegraphed that he must have definite instructions, and on the 12th that the Khedive placed himself unreservedly in the hands of Britain. The British Government were in difficulties that month, for there were acute dissensions in the Cabinet on the proposed Franchise bill, and on the Egyptian question they felt that, in Lord Salisbury's words, they were 'at the mercy of any fortuitous concurrence of fanaticisms or fads.'

But the decision could not be delayed. On December 13 Lord Granville telegraphed recommending the Khedive's ministers to 'come to an early decision to abandon all territory south of Assouan or at least of Wadi Halfa.' On January 1, 1884, Baring told his Government that he was getting daily proof 'that the execution of their policy, although I believe it to be the best of which the circumstances permit, will be a work of the greatest difficulty,' and added: 'If a policy of abandonment is carried out, Her Majesty's Government should certainly be prepared to exercise a far more direct interference in the Government of Egypt than has hitherto been contemplated.' On January 4 came the final declaration of the British view. The whole Soudan, including Khartoum and the Red Sea littoral, must be abandoned. 'It is essential,' Baring was told, 'that in important communications affecting Egypt the advice of Her Majesty's Government should be followed, as long as the provisional occupation continues. Ministers and Governors must carry out this advice or forfeit their offices.' The Egyptian Cabinet promptly resigned, and their successors were virtually British nominees. Britain, with extreme unwillingness and in considerable confusion of mind, had taken over the administration of the Nile valley. In Mr. Gladstone's words, they were an Egyptian Government.

II

In Baring's telegram of December 22 there had been a significant sentence: 'It would also be necessary to send an English officer to Khartoum, with full powers to withdraw all the garrisons in the Soudan and to make the best arrangements possible for the future government of the country.' Britain had refused to despatch troops against the Mahdi to check his career of conquest, but, having put herself in Egypt's place, she was bound in common decency to extricate the Egyptian garrisons and civil population, and also to provide for some semblance of order when they had gone. So Baring thought, and he was no Quixote. The second duty was perhaps less imperative, for its possibility of accomplishment was dim, but there was no question about the first.

The Government not unnaturally desired to meet their obligations as cheaply as possible. The use of a military force might land them in a campaign; therefore a civilian must be found who had the requisite knowledge and prestige. As anxious Ministers revolved the matter in their minds they remembered the strange man, who for twenty years had been flashing in and out of the public gaze. Three years before a high official had told Lord Salisbury: 'I should never recommend your lordship to send Gordon on a delicate diplomatic mission to Paris or Vienna or Berlin, but if you want some out-of-the-way piece of work to be done in an unknown and barbarous country, Gordon would be your man.' The saying had been repeated and remembered in governing circles. Dufferin, in his despatch from Egypt about the Soudan, had suggested that Gordon might undertake its administration 'without drawing upon Egypt either for men or money.' The notion finally penetrated the languid mind of Lord Granville, who was being slowly coerced into some kind of active policy. Soldiers like Sir Andrew Clarke were pressing the same proposal. Here was a chance of getting inexpensively out of an awkward situation. The Foreign Secretary wrote to Mr. Gladstone asking if he had any objection to the use of Gordon, though he had 'a small bee in his bonnet.' The Prime Minister had none, so Baring was consulted.

At first Baring was unsympathetic. He had met Gordon when the latter had visited Cairo as Governor-General of the Soudan, and had not been impressed by his wisdom. He replied that the Egyptian Government thought it dangerous to appoint a Christian to a land which was in the throes of a religious movement. He seems to have still hoped that Egypt herself might manage the evacuation of the 21,000 troops and 11,000 civilians. But the report of Abd-el-Kader Pasha on the matter convinced him that the task was beyond the power of any Egyptian, and, after refusing Gordon a second time, he was compelled on January 16 to send a telegram accepting him on certain conditions.

Meantime the situation had changed at home. Gordon to the man in the street had suddenly become a magical name. Sir Samuel Baker had written to the *Times* pressing for his appointment with all the weight of his great experience. In the popular press what is called in modern jargon a 'stunt' was in progress. Mr. W. T. Stead, who in the *Pall Mall Gazette* appealed to both the serious and the excitable, had an interview with Gordon in his sister's house in Southampton, and came away with a copy of the *Imitation of Christ* and a sensational story which he made the most of in his paper.   In Gordon's view, as Mr. Stead reported it, Britain must either surrender everything to the Mahdi or at all hazards defend Khartoum.   His reputation had always been high in evangelical circles, but now it grew to legendary heights, not only among the devout and among those who were scrupulous for British honour, but also among the classes who were already spoken of as Jingoes.   'Chinese Gordon for the Soudan!' became a national slogan.   Gordon must be sent and no other.   It was a demand for a man and not for a policy, for very few had any notion what the policy should be.

Mr. Gladstone, we may believe in the light of after events, was little moved by the popular clamour.   He was at Hawarden when Lord Granville telegraphed suggesting that Gordon should be sent to Suakim, to use his influence over the tribes to help in the evacuation to that port of the Khartoum population which Abd-el-Kader Pasha was believed to be organising.   The Prime Minister offered no objection.   This was on January 14.   Next day Gordon saw Wolseley at the War Office and made a note of his proposed duties, the chief point of which was that he should go to Suakim, report on the military situation, and then return —a mere mission of inquiry.   It was this scheme which Mr. Gladstone finally accepted—one differing from Lord Granville's former plan, since it was advisory only instead of being partly executive, and it was this which was pressed on Baring.   The Prime Minister was in a mood of extreme caution.   He respected Gordon as a good Christian, but he had heard disquieting rumours of his difficulty as a subordinate.   'While his opinion on the Soudan,' he warned Lord Granville, 'may be of great value, we must be very careful in any instructions we give, that he does not shift the centre of gravity as to political and military responsibility for that country.   In brief, if he reports what should be done, he should not be a judge *who* should do it, nor ought he to commit us on that point by advice officially given. It would be extremely difficult after sending him to reject such advice, and it should, therefore, I think, be made clear that he is not an agent for the purpose of advising on that point.'   Now

Lord Granville's telegram to Baring offering Gordon crossed one from Baring asking for 'a qualified British officer to go to Khartoum *with full powers civil and military to conduct the retreat.*' Lord Granville had offered an adviser and Baring asked for an executant. When later in the day the latter accepted Gordon, he accepted him in the sense of his own telegram. The game of cross-purposes had begun.

Gordon after seeing Wolseley had gone to Brussels. He was recalled on the 17th by telegram, and reached London early on the morning of the 18th. He went to the War Office, where he saw the Secretary of State, Lord Hartington, and the only other Cabinet Ministers who were in town, Lord Granville, Lord Northbrook and Sir Charles Dilke. It is clear that this truncated Cabinet, having received Baring's last telegram, had on their own account gone well beyond the proposal which the Prime Minister had authorised. There was no talk now of a purely advisory mission. Gordon was not to report on evacuation but to carry it out. That at any rate was plain to his own mind, as is borne out by the three accounts he left of the interview. The shortest is as explicit as any. 'Ministers said they were determined to evacuate and would I go and superintend it? I said "Yes."'

That evening, January 18, in company with Colonel J. D. H. Stewart of the 11th Hussars, he caught the eight o'clock Continental express. Wolseley carried his solitary kit-bag, and emptied his pockets to provide him with money for the journey. Lord Granville took his ticket, and the Duke of Cambridge, who had surprisingly appeared, held open the carriage door for him. Next day the people of Britain breathed more freely; their champion had gone out against the infidel and must assuredly triumph. Queen Victoria with a truer instinct wrote in her diary: 'His attempt is a very dangerous one.'

III

Two questions must be briefly examined, for on their answer depends our judgment of the protagonists. What precisely was Gordon's mandate in his mission? Was the sending him at all folly or wisdom?

The written instructions which he received after the meeting with Ministers on January 18 empowered him to proceed to Suakim and to report on the military situation in the Soudan and the best means of evacuating Khartoum and the other garrisons. Such had been his original proposal to Wolseley. But at the close they contained the pregnant addendum that he should be under the orders of the British Minister at Cairo and should 'perform such other duties as may be entrusted to him by the Egyptian Government through Sir Evelyn Baring.' This was clearly inserted in deference to Baring's request for a British officer who should conduct the evacuation, and it made the mission executive as well as advisory. The impression left on the Ministers themselves as to what they had done was vague; Northbrook thought that the task included executive powers, Dilke, who was not present all the time, considered that it was only to report. But the written words admit of no doubt, and there was none in Gordon's mind. He held that his mandate had been enlarged since he first talked to Wolseley, and in the official memorandum that he wrote on his journey to Egypt he set out the purpose of his mission thus:

I understand that Her Majesty's Government have come to the decision not to incur the very onerous duty of securing to the peoples of the Soudan a just future Government. That, as a consequence, Her Majesty's Government have determined to restore to these peoples their independence, and will no longer suffer the Egyptian Government to interfere with their affairs. For this purpose, Her Majesty's Government have decided to send me to the Soudan to arrange for the evacuation of these countries and the safe removal of the Egyptian employés and troops.

In a crisis consistency is not possible for mortals. Baring had been inconsistent, for he began by asking for a British officer for the Soudan, then refused Gordon or any other British officer, and then was compelled by the force of facts to return to his first request. British Ministers had not been consistent, for they had started with a vague idea of a simple mission of inquiry; then under Baring's pressure they had added to Gordon's instructions the duty of taking further orders from their Minister on the spot, and they knew that Baring wanted a man who could act as well

o

as report. The change was right, for when the floods are out a bare report by a hydraulic expert is folly.

But it involved one consequence fraught with future tragedy. The Prime Minister was not present at the War Office meeting. He had had no direct part in the discussion with Gordon, and had still at the back of his mind the idea of an emissary sent only to advise. The Ministers, in spite of a slight confusion of mind, realised that they had done something momentous. 'We were proud of ourselves yesterday,' said one of them to another. 'Are you sure we did not commit a gigantic folly?' Unfortunately, Lord Hartington, in reporting the matter to his chief, did not explain the significant words at the end of the instructions and the importance of Baring's last request. He spoke only of 'advice' and of Gordon's notes of his talk with Wolseley. The Prime Minister concurred, and a few days later in full Cabinet the instructions were ratified. But Mr. Gladstone had not grasped the change, and when later he was compelled to accept executive action on Gordon's part he was naturally aggrieved.

He believed that Gordon had forced his hand. He had always been chary of high-coloured adventurers with popular reputations, and he could not forget Gordon's confidences to the dangerous Mr. Stead. Here was a man who, given a yard, would take a mile. He was aware, too, that in his Cabinet was an imperialist section who had very different views from his own, and he feared that they might be using Gordon to coerce him. In his mind were implanted suspicions which were to bear disastrous fruit. But to any candid inquirer it must be clear that Gordon did not go beyond his instructions, or Baring improve upon them. Everything that was done in the following months was covered by the letter of the Government's explicit mandate. And who shall say that the spirit was violated when that spirit was such an obscure and wavering breath?

As to the wisdom of the mission we have the considered verdict of Lord Cromer nearly a quarter of a century later, when he had seen a new Egypt rise under his hand, and could be frank about past blunders. 'Looking back at what occurred after a space of many years,' he wrote, 'two points are to my mind clear.

The first is that no Englishman should have been sent to Khartoum. The second is that, if anyone had to be sent, General Gordon was not the right man to send.' On the first point there can be little dispute. If an Englishman were beleaguered in Khartoum it must mean an armed expedition, which was precisely what the British Government desired to avoid. It meant the giving of colossal hostages to fortune, especially if that Englishman were a popular hero. Had an Egyptian or an Arab been sent instead there would no doubt have been an imperfect evacuation—but that was what actually happened. Much bloodshed would have been avoided, and the military and civilian population of Khartoum would have been no worse off in the end.

As for the character of the envoy, Lord Cromer's view is coloured by his strong prepossessions against Gordon's type. He admired him but never trusted him, and beyond question he found him a difficult subordinate. He was fond of quoting Gordon's own words in his journal: 'I know if *I* was chief I would never employ *myself*, for I am incorrigible.' But, as a plain matter of fact, putting aside the initial unwisdom of the enterprise, it is doubtful if any other Englishman would have done better. Gordon made mistakes, but so did everybody. Gordon changed his views, but so did Baring. As we shall see, in all major matters the crusading soldier was as staunch a realist as the shrewd diplomatist, and infinitely more so than Her Majesty's Government.

But even to condemn the mission is after-the-event wisdom. We must remember the 'climate of opinion' in which British Ministers were living and the meagre facts which they had at their command. They had Gordon's word for it that the thing was feasible, the word of the chief expert on the Soudan. He gravely under-estimated the Mahdi's power, and over-estimated his own. The Mahdi was to him a nationalist figure like Arabi, the kind of leader whom all oppressed peoples must sooner or later throw up—a view in which he agreed with Mr. Gladstone; in part that, and in part a figure-head set up by discontented slave-raiders against the Government. He heard that he was a nephew of a Dongolawi who had once been his guide, and he believed that no great thing could come out of that Nazareth.

So far as the movement had a popular appeal he could counter
it by his own prestige, offering himself instead of this obscure
Wat Tyler as the people's saviour. He had a contempt, too,
natural in a man who had been for years working a thousand
miles deeper in the heart of Africa, for a leader sprung of the
tame riverine tribes. What he did not realise was that behind
the Dongolawi was the flame of a religious faith, savage and
maleficent, but as fierce and forthright as his own. He communicated to Ministers and officials his own confidence, and his
known foibles did not alarm them. He was bold to rashness,
but this was a case for that kind of bravery: his religious
beliefs, a little disquieting to sober churchmen, would by
their very extravagance be a match for the fanaticism of the
desert.

There was another reason which weighed heavily with the
British Government. Humanity demanded that they should
make an effort to rescue those unfortunates whom the folly of
Egypt had marooned in the Soudan, since they had assumed
responsibility for the guidance of Egypt and therefore for the
redress of her blunders. This was felt by British Ministers, who
were honourable men, and it was deeply felt by the nation. The
flamboyant Mr. Stead expounded the views of a multitude of
wiser people than himself. The Mahdi and his hordes were
thought of as merciless savages, certain, if Khartoum were
not evacuated in time, to make a wholesale slaughter of
its people. Alike to patriot and humanitarian, to haters
of slavery and sticklers for national honour, the situation
seemed to call for immediate action. The press agitation
may have fanned the flame, but the flame was not basely
kindled.

Occasions occur, Lord Cromer has written, 'when the best
service a Government official can render to his country is to place
himself in opposition to the public view,' and he adds that he
never ceased to regret that he had not maintained his original
objection to Gordon's mission. But had that objection been
maintained it would have been against the evidence of facts and
in defiance of what was a proper instinct in the nation. Some
attempt had to be made to save the innocent, only an Englishman could make that attempt, and on the facts Gordon, in spite

of drawbacks, was the best Englishman. The course of events has shown that it would have been wiser for all concerned to do nothing; but that view in January 1884 would have been a cowardly dereliction of duty. It is better for a nation to play the fool than the knave.

IV

ACT THE SECOND: THE JOURNEY

I

As Gordon travelled through France his mind was busy on his task. He drew up and despatched to Lord Granville various proposals, that he should be given his old title of Governor-General of the Soudan that he might act with the greater authority, and that he should issue certain proclamations to the Soudanese people. These the Cabinet accepted, and authorised Baring to give effect to them. While he was crossing the Mediterranean he prepared a further memorandum for Baring. He had not forgotten the latter's desire to leave some rudiments of order after the evacuation, so he suggested that the government should be handed over to the petty sultans whose families had been in power at the time of Mohammed Ali's conquest. In some areas there were no such ruling houses, but the question what to do there could be reserved. On the policy of evacuation he was firm. 'The sacrifice,' he concluded, 'necessary towards securing a good government would be far too onerous to admit of any such attempt being made. Indeed, one may say it is impracticable at any cost. H.M.'s Government will now leave them as God has placed them.'

The original intention had been for Gordon to meet Baring at Ismailia and then proceed direct to Suakim, for he had no wish to see the Khedive, whom he had publicly criticised. But the Suakim area was in confusion, and a force of Egyptian gendarmerie under Valentine Baker had been despatched there. Baring accordingly secured Lord Granville's consent for Gordon to come to Cairo. The change of plan was vital, for had the latter gone to Suakim he would never have got through to Khartoum, and would probably have been back in Egypt within a few weeks. On January 24 a special train decanted at Cairo 'a small man in a black greatcoat, with neither servant nor portmanteau.' Gordon after his fashion stepped modestly on to his new stage.

Next day he saw the Khedive, to whom he apologised for past rudenesses, and the two became friends. To Baring and to Nubar he bore himself with the utmost cordiality. He was in high spirits, and impressed all who met him with his youth and his physical vigour. In long consultations the details of his mission were considered, and those further instructions were drafted which Baring had been empowered by the British Cabinet to give him. The area of evacuation was extended from Khartoum to the whole Soudan. The plan of restoring the petty sultans was approved. It was agreed that the work might take some months, and Gordon was allowed to retain the Egyptian troops for such reasonable period as he might think necessary. He was given a credit of £100,000 and a promise of whatever further funds he might require. A firman appointed him Governor-General of the Soudan, and he was provided by the Khedive with two proclamations which he was to issue at his discretion; one notifying the people of his new rank, and one announcing the evacuation and the 'restoration to the families of the kings of the Soudan of their former independence.'

These details the British Cabinet approved, but they pointed out that they altered Gordon's mission from one of advice to one of executive action. This, as we have seen, was not the case, since the closing sentence of the London instructions effected such a change: of this Lord Granville was perfectly aware, for on January 18 he had telegraphed to Baring about Gordon being 'on his way to Khartoum to arrange for the future settlement of the Soudan for the best advantage of the people.' There might have been some natural doubt in Mr. Gladstone's mind, but there could be none in the mind of the Ministers actually concerned.

There was another interview during these days which had fateful consequences. At the house of Chèrif Pasha, the former Prime Minister, Gordon accidentally met Zobeir, the slave-dealer of the Bahr-el-Ghazal, who had been living for six years in Cairo. He was Zobeir's sworn enemy, for he had ruined his career and had been indirectly the cause of his son's death, and on his journey to Egypt he had advised Lord Granville to intern

him in Cyprus to keep him out of the way of mischief.   But the
sudden sight of the man gave him a 'mystic feeling' that here was
one who might be used as a counterweight to the Mahdi, for he
knew his great ability, his stern and ruthless character, and his
power with the nomad tribes.   He insisted on a second interview,
at which Baring and Nubar were present.   Zobeir refused to
shake hands with him, and loaded him with passionate reproaches
for his son's death and the loss of his fortune.   Gordon defended
himself no less passionately, but the interview ended with some
approach to harmony.   The impression, however, left upon
those present was that if Zobeir were allowed to accompany
Gordon there would be murder done in the desert, and Baring
refused his consent.

That night Gordon left Cairo with Stewart by train for
Assiout, on his way to Khartoum by the Nile valley.   He had
been a little depressed during the last hours at not getting his
way about Zobeir, but he had been cheered by playing with the
children of Baring and Evelyn Wood.   To the latter's butler
he had insisted on presenting his dress-coat and waistcoat, since
he would no longer have any need for them.   Gerald Graham,
his old friend of Crimean and Chinese days, accompanied him ·
as far as Korosko.   On the journey Gordon's spirits rose.   Before
leaving Cairo, he had telegraphed to Khartoum, 'Don't be
panic-stricken; you are men, not women; I am coming.'   He
wrote to his sister, 'I feel quite happy, for if God is with me, who
can or will be hurtful to me?'   Even the spectacle of his travelling
companion, the Emir Abdul Chakour, did not depress him,
though the performance of the ruler-designate of Darfur,
smothered in an ill-fitting uniform, attended by a score of wives,
and drinking steadily, augured ill for the success of his plan of
installing the Soudan's ancient chiefs.

Graham has left us a picture of Gordon in these days, the last
glimpse of him permitted to his old friends.   He was sometimes
preoccupied with his future task, discussing plans for handing
over the southern provinces to the King of the Belgians, for
relieving Slatin, and for driving the Hadendowa from Suakim.
But often he would gossip about his old days in Equatoria, and
expound his theories about the Holy Land, and talk bad Arabic
to the Nile boatmen.   When the time came for the friends to part,

Graham walked for a little beside Gordon's camel, while in front rode the Arab escort, armed with rhinoceros-hide shields and

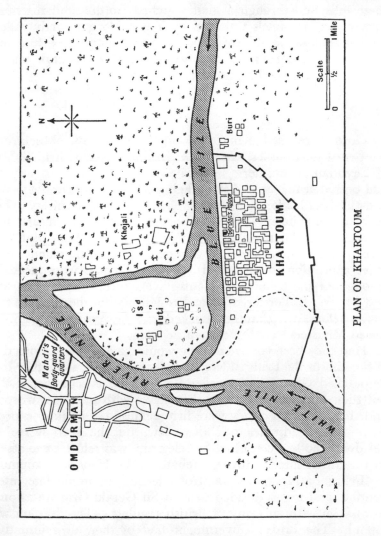

PLAN OF KHARTOUM

great cross-hilted swords. 'At last I left him, saying "Good-bye" and "God bless you." The place where I last saw Gordon is wild and desolate . . . nothing between the hills but black basins or ravines, dry, dark, and destitute of all vegetation, looking like separate entrances to the pit where those who entered might leave hope behind. . . . I climbed up the highest of these hills, and through a glass watched Gordon and the small caravan as his camels threaded their way along a sandy valley, hoping that he would turn round that I might give him one more sign; but he rode on until he turned the dark side of the hills, and I saw him no more.'

II

Gordon reached Khartoum on February 18. Much had happened since he left Cairo. Valentine Baker with his rabble of Egyptian gendarmerie had failed against Osman Digna; he had been defeated at El Teb on February 4 with the loss of nearly two-thirds of his force, including eleven European officers. The garrison of Sinkat had been overpowered and massacred; Tokar was in hourly danger of falling; and Suakim itself was threatened. Immediately a clamour arose in England for a relief expedition to the eastern Soudan. There were meetings throughout the country, the anti-slavery forces were mobilised, and Mr. W. E. Forster, who had resigned from the Cabinet two years before, trenchantly attacked the Government. Embarrassed Ministers were forced to a decision.

Had they been consistent they would have left the protection of Suakim to the British Fleet, and declared that, since they had despatched Gordon on a general mission of evacuation, it was not their business to concern themselves with isolated garrisons, and that in any case they were firm against any military expedition. Mr. Gladstone took this view, but he was overruled. Gordon, who was consulted by telegram, was reluctant to assent to the use of force. But the debate in the House of Commons on February 12 revealed a strong feeling for immediate intervention, and it was decided to send Sir Gerald Graham at once to Suakim with an army of British regulars. The decision was fateful. The British Government had of their own initiative, and under no pressure from Gordon, abandoned their policy of a wholly peaceful evacuation. If Gordon later asked for British troops he was only following the lead of his superiors. Ministers had been rudely shaken out of their frugal optimism.

Meantime on his journey south Gordon's eyes were being opened to the immense difficulties of his mission. It was his habit, which he had acquired under Ismail, to put his views at once on paper and communicate them to his chiefs, even though he might change his opinion radically once a week. This method enabled them to see the processes of his mind. But in a land where transport was difficult the custom had its drawbacks, for it meant often that an early message arrived after a later one, and the recipient was left in confusion. He was clear about his two tasks, to evacuate the garrisons and to leave behind some makeshift system of law and order. Baring had been as insistent upon the second as upon the first. It was this latter that most troubled him. The alcoholic Abdul Chakour had disillusioned him about his plan of setting up in power the old Soudanese families. He must leave a man behind him, a man fit to govern and to defy the Mahdi, and his mind returned to his old enemy Zobeir. Something also might be done with the King of the Belgians; if King Leopold took over the Equatorial provinces he himself might go south when his work in Khartoum was over and take service under him. He had an idea, too, of paying a personal visit to the Mahdi, and reasoning with that disturber of the peace. All these views he communicated seriatim to the puzzled Baring.

At Berber he summoned a council of notables, and showed them the Khedive's firman announcing Egypt's withdrawal from the Soudan. It was a dangerous step. On January 8 he had told the *Pall Mall Gazette*: 'There is one subject which I cannot imagine anyone differing about. That is the impolicy of announcing our intention to evacuate Khartoum. The moment it is known we have given up the game, every man will go over to the Mahdi. All men worship the rising sun.' No doubt he had good reason for his action, but it would appear that later he came to doubt its wisdom. The truth is that he still under-estimated the Mahdi's power, thinking him no more than a local upstart. He sent him robes of honour and offered him his friendship and the rank of Sultan of Kordofan; the Mahdi replied with point that he was already Sultan of Kordofan and much more, and returned the compliment by sending a patched jibbah and inviting his opponent to turn Moslem and save his

wretched soul. At Berber Gordon did another thing which
made a great outcry in England. The Anglo-Egyptian Con-
vention of 1877 would bring slavery in the Soudan to an end in
1889. When the notables asked him if this provision would
apply, he replied that it would not, since the Soudan was now
independent of Egypt, and he issued a proclamation to that
effect. It was obvious common sense, but it alienated some of
his noisier supporters at home.

At half-past nine on the morning of February 18 Gordon
landed at Khartoum at the stage opposite the palace. Thousands
pressed about him to kiss his hands and feet. He struck while
the iron was hot. First he made a bonfire of old instruments
of oppression, the books of the tax-gatherers, the bonds of the
usurers, and the kourbashes of the police. In the gaols fetters
were removed from the limbs of prisoners. Certain Egyptian
units he despatched at once to Cairo, and he formed a council
of Arab notables. 'I come,' he told the people, 'without soldiers,
but with God on my side, to redeem the evils of the Soudan. I
will not fight with any weapon but justice.' The city rang all
day with plaudits and blazed all night with fires of joy. Gordon
had touched the heart and kindled the spirit of the mixed multitude within the walls.

As he looked round him his mind was divided between hope
and fear. He believed that the Mahdi's levies would only fight
within tribal limits, and that if he could hold the tribes between
Khartoum and Egypt the evacuation was safe. By his concessions he thought that this might be possible, for the news of
his first deeds in the city would soon be spread over the land.
But for the rest? Of one capital danger he had as yet no knowledge. The news of his safe arrival had enabled the British
Government to rebut triumphantly the vote of censure, but the
Cabinet had relapsed in their relief into a mood of stubborn
illogicality. They would send British soldiers under Graham
to Suakim, because Suakim belonged to Egypt and they were
responsible for Egypt. But, though the Red Sea coast was
nominally part of the Soudan, it was somehow different from the
rest, and they would admit of no armed intervention in the
Soudan. 'I contend,' said Lord Hartington with a fine inconsequence on the last day of the debate, 'that we are not respon-

sible for the rescue or relief of the garrisons either in the Western
or the Southern or the Eastern Soudan.'   At first, in their anxiety
during Gordon's journey across the desert, Hartington, Dilke
and Chamberlain had been ready to press for British troops to
support him, and, if necessary, relieve him, but now all three
had been shepherded back to Mr. Gladstone's fold.   Daily the
Prime Minister was growing more malcontent with the mission
and more suspicious of the missionary.

The vacillation of London was mercifully hid from Gordon's
knowledge, but he had one gnawing anxiety ever present—the
future ordering of the Soudan, which even the cautious Baring
had considered a primal duty.   His imagination swept over the
vast country, noting the tiny 'pin-point garrisons, each smothered
in a cloud of Arab spears.'   By his proclamation he had given
this land back to its people, but what could they make of it?
Someone must exercise a nominal sovereignty.   Egypt could not;
Turkey would not; then Britain must.   Why not establish a
buffer state like Afghanistan, where Britain was not responsible
for the government but gave moral support and a subsidy?
But if a second Afghanistan was created, there must be an Amir
—someone to succeed himself as Governor-General.   For that
post there was only one man, Zobeir.   On the day of his arrival
in Khartoum Gordon telegraphed to Baring urging this plan,
and Stewart sent a telegram in its support.   He had not
changed his mind, and enlarged his mandate; he was only
proposing means for carrying out the second and, as he considered, equally vital part of his orders.

III

If the Zobeir question is to be fairly judged, the different
points of view must be remembered, for it is not a case for sweeping conclusions.   Gordon's mind had been made up on the matter
ever since his arrival in Cairo, and his 'mystical feeling' about
the ex-slave-trader had been reinforced by what he had learned
on his journey to Khartoum.   Zobeir, he was convinced, was the
only man capable of holding his own against the Mahdi, and,
when Khartoum was evacuated, of preventing the Soudan from
becoming a cockpit.   He had been the conqueror of Darfur and

was a born ruler of men. He was of the blood of the Koreish, a descendant of the Abbaside dynasty, and had therefore an ancestral religious authority which with Moslem fanatics might outweigh the Mahdi's spurious claims. He was feared by the commonalty, but, as Baring discovered thirteen years later, he was also revered. Zobeir alone could fulfil what he believed to be an integral part of his own instructions, and preserve order when he had gone. As for the personal vendetta he would take the risk. These considerations he pressed upon Baring in the long telegram which he despatched as soon as he arrived in Khartoum.

Baring to his credit was open to conviction. He, too, realised the need of finding a successor to Gordon, for he had never wavered about the duty of establishing some post-evacuation authority. He was prepared to accept Zobeir under strict conditions, not to provide 'moral support' but to announce the British Government's 'approbation'; he thought that there was something in the Afghanistan precedent. He accordingly urged the appointment upon Lord Granville, who replied discouragingly. Gordon was informed, and answered that he could suggest no other name to meet the case. He added some sentences of prescient wisdom, but of doubtful prudence in view of the mood of the Home Government:

My duty is evacuation, and the best I can for establishing a quiet Government. The first I hope to accomplish. The second is a more difficult task and concerns Egypt more than me. If Egypt is to be quiet Mahdi must be smashed up. . . . Remember that once Khartoum belongs to Mahdi, the task will be far more difficult, yet you will, for safety of Egypt, execute it. If you decide on smashing Mahdi, then send up another £100,000, and send up 200 Indian troops to Wadi Halfa and leave Suakim and Massowah alone. I repeat that evacuation is possible, but you will feel effect in Egypt, and will be forced to enter into a far more serious affair to guard Egypt. At present it would be comparatively easy to destroy Mahdi.

After events were to justify every word of this message, but the effect on the British Cabinet was disastrous. To Ministers it seemed that Gordon had gone far beyond his powers, and was changing his views with a disquieting speed. First, on the

Zobeir question. He had wanted Zobeir exiled to Cyprus; he now wished him to be a kind of Afghan Amir in the Soudan. Baring had telegraphed on February 28: 'Whatever may be said to the contrary, Her Majesty's Government must be in reality responsible for any arrangements which can be devised for the Soudan, and I do not think it is possible to shake off the responsibility.' Dare they take on themselves the burden of Zobeir's appointment? Not even Gordon's name would sweeten the pill to a suspicious public. The Anti-Slavery Society would arise in its wrath, and a watchful Opposition would seize the chance to wreck the Government.

Two Cabinet meetings considered the matter, the Prime Minister being absent. Three Ministers were in favour of Zobeir on general grounds, but all were clear that the House of Commons would never permit it. The question was raised there, and Mr. W. E. Forster fulminated against the proposal. The Liberal press was furiously hostile, the Conservative press critical. Mr. Gladstone alone supported it. Coming of a family which had owned many slaves, he had not in his blood that detestation of the very name of slavery which most Englishmen possessed; he saw, too, in Zobeir's appointment a means of bringing to an end the perilous mission of a man whom every day he distrusted more profoundly. But he was overcome by the argument about the hostility of Parliament, though he believed that had he himself been able to be in his place he might have swung the House to his side. A year later he said: 'It is well known that if, when the recommendation to send Zobeir was made, we had complied with it, an address from this House to the Crown would, before forty-eight hours were over, have paralysed our action; and although it is perfectly true that the decision arrived at was the judgment of the Cabinet, it was also no less the judgment of Parliament and of the people.' So far as it goes the defence is sound. No British Government could have sent Zobeir to the Soudan and survived for a week. Gordon continued to plead for him, and Baring to press for him with all the weight of the man on the spot, but on March 11 the Cabinet finally refused.

Had Gordon's proposal been accepted, would Khartoum have been saved? Lord Cromer believed that it might. To me it seems more than doubtful, for Zobeir with all his power would have found himself faced by something greater than himself, an incalculable, whirlwind, fanatic horde drunk with visions of Paradise. Nevertheless it is likely that if he had gone south at once he would have delayed the attack long enough to permit of at least a partial evacuation and to ensure Gordon's own safety. But for that he should have left Cairo before the end of February: by March 11, when the British Cabinet decided, it was already too late.

The difference over Zobeir was only one of the grounds of quarrel between Gordon and his superiors at home. Far graver was the effect of his other message, which to Ministers seemed to imply an amazing fickleness of mind and a determination not to evacuate but to conquer. He had proposed a friendly visit to the Mahdi, and then wanted to make him Sultan of Kordofan; now he was eager to smash him. He had wanted Suakim to be left alone, and now he proposed that the Suakim-Berber route should be opened and British troops sent to the latter place. He was announcing to the people of Khartoum that British soldiers were on their way; he was talking wildly of breaking through to Equatoria. Clearly he was trying to force Britain into a military adventure. Ministers could not make allowances (even Baring found it difficult) for a man who telegraphed whenever an idea struck him, and for the desperate expedients of one confronted with an insoluble problem. They did not know, as we know now, that all the while Gordon was labouring at the hopeless task of evacuation, that he had already got rid of the sick and feeble, and that it was principally to help him in that work that he suggested the sending of British or Indian troops to Wadi Halfa and Berber. The short-range imagination of Ministers prevented them from grasping the rudiments of his difficulties. Even Dilke and Chamberlain turned against him, and Mr. Gladstone's attitude became that of the whole Cabinet. Gordon had lost their confidence, and therefore it was their plain duty to recall him. They did not do this, for they feared the people, and presently it was too late.

For on March 12, the day after the Cabinet had finally refused him Zobeir, a force of 4000 Arabs came down upon the Nile nine miles north of Khartoum, cut the telegraph line, and blocked all movement to and from Egypt. Zobeir might have prevented it, but there was no Zobeir. What was at stake now was not the success of the mission but the life of the envoy.

V

ACT THE THIRD: THE FORLORN HOPE

I

FROM the first day of his arrival at Khartoum Gordon set himself to his primary task, the business of evacuation. He separated the Egyptian from the Soudanese troops, for the latter must be retained as a police force for Zobeir or whoever was to take charge of the Soudan. The former he removed across the river to Omdurman to await transport to Berber. He asked Baring to make provision for their reception at Korosko, and arranged with his agent at Berber for the despatch of boats southwards. The sick and the widows and orphans were sent away at once. Altogether some 600 soldiers and 2000 civilians were evacuated. His duty was to perform the task without use of force, and at first it looked as if his personal prestige would achieve this end. The people of Khartoum were docile in his hands. Women flocked round him begging him to touch and cure their children, and he was hailed as Father and Saviour. For a moment it seemed as if the Mahdi's spell was to be nullified by a greater. Even the Khartoum notables, who were nervous about the removal of the Egyptian troops, were silenced by his serene faith.

But the main problem was not the people of Khartoum but the neighbouring tribes, and here dangers at once presented themselves. The Mahdi's emissaries were busy among them, and the Egyptian posts on both the Blue and the White Nile were threatened. Gordon was compelled to send a small relief expedition which did not fire a shot, but distributed his peace proclamations, what he called his 'paper warfare.' News travels fast in the desert, and his pacific overtures were not helped by what was happening on the Red Sea littoral. Sir Gerald Graham with British troops had defeated Osman Digna at El Teb, and a little later at Tamaai he completed the dispersal of the rebels in that area.   Thousands of the Hadendowa tribe lay dead on the field, but it was a meaningless and a fruitless slaughter.   It complicated Gordon's task at Khartoum, and Graham's success only made the situation worse unless it meant that the Suakim-Berber route would be opened and British troops would appear on the Nile.   The British Government had no such intention. To defeat the Mahdi's eastern levies with British regiments was apparently in their eyes a pacific business, but to send a handful of British soldiers to keep the Nile open for the accomplishment of the duty which they had laid upon their envoy would have been a shameful and perilous act of war.

Yet Berber was the key of the whole enterprise.   If the river route to the north was blocked a peaceful evacuation would be impossible, and already the dervishes were drifting Nile-wards. Gordon, busy with the evacuation at the Khartoum end, pled with Baring to send him Zobeir, and to despatch a British contingent, however small, to Berber to hold that key-point.   From Berber the refugees must go either by river to Abu Hamed and then by the desert route to Korosko, or straight to Suakim, and in either case the neutrality of the local tribes must be assured. This seemed so self-evident that he could not believe that his request would not be granted, for surely a Government that willed the end would will the only means.   If not, he told Baring, there was nothing for it but that Khartoum should be given up, that Stewart should take the Egyptian troops and employees to Berber and try to hold the place, and that he himself should resign his commission and retire with the remaining steamers and stores to Equatoria.

Baring was in a hopeless position.   Every morning he found a sheaf of telegrams from Gordon, which were virtually a diary of the thoughts that had passed through his mind.   To the recipient they seemed a tangle of confusion, but he had the wit to see the inexorable facts.   Gordon was in a dilemma which fate, not himself, had created.   The question was rapidly becoming not whether Khartoum could be successfully evacuated, but whether Gordon and Stewart could be got away.   Since Zobeir was refused him, the only hope lay in a dash across the desert to Berber by some of Graham's cavalry so as to impress the tribes and make the place defensible.   Military opinion in

Egypt was on the whole against this, and the Home Government seized the excuse to veto the plan. On March 26 Baring put before Lord Granville his considered view, the view of a cool and impartial mind:

Let me earnestly beg Her Majesty's Government to put themselves in the position of Gordon and Stewart. They have been sent on a most difficult and dangerous mission by the English Government. Their proposal to send Zobeir, which, if it had been acted on some weeks ago, would certainly have entirely altered the situation, was rejected. The consequences which they foresaw have ensued. . . . Coetlogon, who is here, assures me that so long as the rebels hold both banks of the river above the Sixth Cataract, it will be quite impossible for boats to pass. He does not believe that Gordon can cut his way through by land. He ridicules the idea of retreating with the garrison to Equatoria, and we may be sure that Gordon and Stewart will not come away alone. As a matter of personal opinion, I do not believe in the impossibility of helping Gordon, even during the summer, if Indian troops are employed and money is not spared. But if it be decided to make no attempt to afford present help, then I would urge that Gordon be told to try and maintain his position during the summer, and that then, if he is still beleaguered, an expedition will be sent as early as possible in the autumn to relieve him. This would, at all events, give him some hope, and the mere announcement of the intention of the Government would go a long way to ensure his safety by keeping loyal tribes who may be still wavering. No one regrets more than I do the necessity of sending British or Indian troops to the Soudan, but, having sent Gordon to Khartoum, it appears to me that it is our bounden duty, both as a matter of humanity and policy, not to abandon him.

Meantime since March 12 the telegraph line had been cut, the river route blocked, and Khartoum in a state of siege. Baring's messages could only reach Gordon from Berber by slow and devious ways, and Gordon's could only get to Cairo by being carried on small strips of paper by native runners through the enemy lines. The result was that they arrived irregularly and many did not arrive at all. A thick mist had crept between Khartoum and the outer world.

II

All through March and well into April Gordon believed that Zobeir would be given him and that a small detachment of British troops would be sent to keep the Nile route open. Graham's operations in the eastern Soudan had greatly increased the difficulties with the local tribes; but he could not believe that if British soldiers could be used around Suakim, which was not a vital point, they could not be used to assist the central duty of his mission. Knowing the desert as no other man knew it, he was convinced that a light force could cover the 250 miles between Suakim and Berber, the same distance as separated the Mahdi's headquarters at El Obeid from Khartoum. For three weeks he never fired a shot. Then he was forced to defend himself, for on all sides, from south and west and east and north, the enemy began to close in on him. Dervish bullets were killing men at the palace windows. He wrote that he was as safe as if he was in Cairo, but that was only the bravado of a good soldier. He knew that he was defending a forlorn hope, that he had with him a feeble garrison and many thousands of helpless civilians, and that at home there was a Government which could not grasp the truth.

During the long summer months he received only belated and disjointed news from Baring, and he could not be certain that his pleas for help—for Turkish troops, if British were not forthcoming, or for a levy of adventurers financed by private friends—ever reached their destination. He could not conceive that Britain would forsake him, and he had a fixed hope of a relief expedition when the Nile rose. The few messages that reached him from the north infuriated him by their apparent blindness to the crisis, and he raged against diplomatists and politicians and all their works. But in the meantime he gave every power of mind and body to the task of performing the impossible. In all the history of war there are few records in which the spirit of man shines so triumphantly as in Gordon's desperate toil at the defence of a sprawling city and a scared people, with dwindling supplies and raw troops that drew their only virtue from his courage.

His first duty was to strengthen the ramparts so that the

place could not be taken by a sudden assault. On the north and west was the river; east and south he completed the half-moon of fortifications, extending from the Blue to the White Nile at a distance of about two miles from the city. Here the former officer of engineers was in his element. He had redoubts at the eastern angle, at a point about a mile to the west of Khartoum, on the south bank of the Blue Nile, and on the north bank south of Khojali. He held also the mud town of Omdurman as an outpost on the west bank of the White Nile. He supported the defence with an elaborate system of wire entanglements and land mines, which latter had a tremendous moral effect upon the attacking dervishes. Having the resources of the old Egyptian arsenal at his disposal, he was also able to armour his steamers so as to enable them to run the gauntlet of rifle fire from the shores. The rising of the Nile towards the end of April provided him with a new protection on the west, for now a broad lagoon lay between him and Kordofan. He had been doubtful from the first about his Egyptian troops. In March a handful of Arabs had put a thousand of them to flight, and he had court-martialled and shot the two officers responsible—an act which he bitterly regretted afterwards, but one which doubtless tightened discipline. Slowly he built up a more effective force of volunteers, chiefly of negro slaves, and he put a negro, Faragh Pasha, in command. By the end of April he had beaten off the first dervish attack, and won a breathing space.

He was also civil governor and had to order the life of the beleaguered city. He sent out expeditions far and wide to collect food, and, though Coetlogon in March had estimated that there were supplies for no more than one month, he managed to hold out for ten. Not only did he feed the people, but he nursed their spirit. He told the ulemas what they should preach, and, stern disciplinarian as he was, he was gentle to the *bouches inutiles* and bore in public always a smiling face. Though he toiled to the last limit of human power, he made it his habit to appear unruffled and confident. He slept mainly in the afternoon, for most of the night he was up and visiting the ramparts. 'I am always frightened,' he told a friend. 'It is not the fear of death—that is past, thank God, but I fear defeat and its consequences. I do not believe in the calm, unmoved man.' But the anxious inhabitants saw only a serene competence; he kept his exasperation and his fears for his messages to Cairo. No detail of the city's life escaped his notice. He issued paper notes, he manufactured and awarded decorations, and he supervised to the last ounce the issue of food.

The besiegers were kept at a respectful distance, but every day shots from Khojali fell into Khartoum, and soon ill news came from further afield. At the end of April a post on the Blue Nile, half-way to Sennar, was forced to surrender with large quantities of food and rifles and one of his precious steamers. On May 27 Berber fell, and five thousand of its people were massacred. The place had ceased to be the key of the evacuation, since that had long ago become an impossibility, but it remained a strategic point for any British advance, and it was never out of Gordon's mind. He dreamed of so strengthening his position that he would be able to send an expedition to recapture Berber, and then join hands with the British advance which must be now beginning. At the end of June he scornfully rejected a demand from the Mahdi for his surrender. 'The Mohammedans who are with me do not wish to surrender, and do you expect that I, who am a Christian, should set the example?' On July 13 he sent out a batch of messages by native runners, five of which reached the outer world by the end of August, to say that Khartoum could hold out for four months. In July and August things went better for the defence. Gordon's ablest native officer, Mohammed Ali, won a victory on the Blue Nile and cleared a considerable extent of country, while another victory at Halfaya opened up part of the road to the north. He had plans now for the recapture of Berber, and informed Baring that he would send an expedition under Stewart for that purpose, and would hold the town till reinforcements came—or burn it and fall back.

It was the gleam of sunshine before the storm. Before moving on Berber it seemed wise to meet a new enemy threat twenty-five miles up the Blue Nile. Mohammed Ali, in his desire to capture the dervish chief, was betrayed into an ambush in difficult country, and perished with a thousand of his men. Gordon had to revise his plan, for the Nile would soon be beginning to fall, leaving Khartoum more exposed on the Kordofan side, and he could not afford to deplete his garrison. The messages, too, that were coming through from Cairo showed him that England was grossly ignorant of his plight, and he began to fear for that British advance upon which he had based all his hopes. He resolved to make a desperate effort to let the truth be known. Stewart should go down the river to Dongola with despatches. He wrote his last letter to Baring.

How many times have we written for reinforcements, calling your serious attention to the Soudan! No answer at all has come to us . . . and the hearts of men have become weary at this delay. While you are eating and drinking and resting on good beds, we and those with us, soldiers and servants, are watching by night and day, endeavouring to quell the movements of this false Mahdi. . . . The reason why I have now sent Colonel Stewart is because you have been silent all this while and neglected us, and lost time without doing any good. If troops were sent, as soon as they reach Berber this rebellion will cease.

Tragically, Gordon thought that the chief cause of his predicament was the one man who had been loyal to him from the day he reached Cairo, and had damaged his prestige with the British Cabinet by telling it unwelcome truths.

Stewart, accompanied by the *Times* correspondent and the French consul, set out in the *Abbas*, escorted by two other steamers to see him past the danger-point of Berber, and a couple of feluccas. Berber was safely passed, and then unfortunately Stewart decided to send the escort back. When within two days of Dongola the *Abbas* struck a rock in mid-stream. Natives appeared on the bank with a white flag, and the three Europeans, believing them friendly, landed to parley with them. There they met a local sheikh, who invited them into a house, where they were instantly murdered. Gordon's diary and the key to his cyphers were captured and despatched to the Mahdi.

It was a grievous mischance, and it sealed the fate of Khartoum. Had Stewart travelled another hundred miles he would have met a man who would have learned from him of Gordon's desperate straits and would have hurried on the relief. A certain Major Kitchener had the year before been appointed second-in-command of the Egyptian cavalry, and was now doing intelligence work, his business being to keep open the Nubian desert for a possible British advance. He was a tall, very lean man, with long legs and narrow sloping shoulders, a square head, a cast in his left eye, and a face so tanned that his big fair moustache looked almost white. Sir Samuel Baker thought well of him, and Gordon, for whom he was to be soon the only link with the outer world, would have made him Governor-General of the Soudan. As fortune willed, this young sapper officer was in the plenitude of time to be his successor and his avenger.

It was two months before Gordon heard of the disaster to the *Abbas*. When Stewart left on September 9 he had no friends to talk to, so he began that journal of his innermost thoughts which has been preserved for men to read. He knew that the last struggle was approaching, for news had come that the Mahdi was on the move. The victories of the infidel on the Blue Nile had convinced Mohammed Ahmed that he could no longer afford to neglect Khartoum. He had no love of violent assaults, for he had heard of Gordon's land mines, but with his myriads he could encompass the place and starve it into surrender. Wad-el-Nejumi, one of his best captains, was entrusted with the task: he would command the fighting force, but the Mahdi himself would hallow the attack by his presence. Some 200,000 dervishes swarmed eastward from El Obeid, retracing the road which Hicks Pasha had marched to his doom. Being a cautious and sanguine visionary, the Mahdi made fresh efforts to induce his antagonist to do as Slatin and Cuzzi had done, and sent emissaries to summon him to repent and embrace the true faith.

Gordon rejoiced at the coming of his enemy, for it meant that before long the issue would be determined. 'I have always felt,' he wrote in his journal, 'we were doomed to come face to face ere the matter was ended.' Either British troops would arrive in time, or there would be that other release for which he had always longed. The sight of the hawks circling over the palace gave him strange thoughts of approaching death. . . . Soon he heard a sound other than the rattle of Arab sniping. The blowing of the ivory trumpets and the roll of the great copper war-drums told him that his master-foe was near. In numbers like a flight of locusts, the straw bonnets and the patched jibbahs, the black flags and the green, the bright spears and the long swords had come out of the west.

VI

IRONIC INTERLUDE

THE Cabinet meeting of March 11 which refused Zobeir inaugurated five months of dire misunderstanding. British Ministers had argued themselves into two convictions: that Gordon had illegitimately extended his mandate and had thereby relieved them from responsibility for his fate; and that he could leave Khartoum if he chose, and only stayed there because of his obsession by wild dreams of conquest. The answer to the first lay in the letter of the documents, to which they were strangely blind. The answer to the second was to be found in Baring's repeated solemn warnings, though these were to some extent discounted in their mind by the confident tone of the few messages which came through from Khartoum. The Cabinet, with no experience of wild lands and with little imagination, seemed incapable of realising the situation in the Soudan or the plight of their envoy. Military opinion assured them that it was impossible to send British troops from Suakim to Berber, and in any case they believed that it was unnecessary. Not even Baring's urgent telegram of March 26 could move them. 'He makes a recommendation,' the Prime Minister informed the Queen, 'that amounts to a reversal of policy; he overrides the most serious military difficulties ; he acts, so far as it appears, alone; he proposes to provide for dangers to General Gordon, of the existence of which at the present moment Your Majesty's Government do not possess evidence; and he does this in ignorance of what are at the time General Gordon's circumstances, opinions and desires.' That is to say, they declined to accept the evidence of the one man who might be supposed to understand the case, and who had never given them cause to suspect him of lightness of mind.

The decision of the Cabinet was unanimous, but some of its members were perturbed in spirit. The radical section was indeed heartily behind the Prime Minister. Sir William Harcourt, the Home Secretary, had threatened to resign if there was any talk of an expedition. Mr. Chamberlain had at first been uneasy, and had had the notion of sending Dilke to Egypt to find out the truth, but by the end of March he had come to share Mr. Gladstone's view. Lord Granville was well content to do nothing. But Lord Selborne, the Lord Chancellor, had shown signs of revolt unless an expedition was promised for the autumn, and Lord Hartington cannot have been comfortable. Six months later, on September 24, he wrote of Gordon to Lord Granville: 'We have no proof that he could have done anything different from what he has done and is doing, or that he has wilfully disregarded our instructions.' Something of that sort must have been in his mind in March, but Lord Hartington's ideas took a long time to solidify into convictions.

On April 3 the Prime Minister returned to the House of Commons after a slight illness, and the question of the Soudan was raised by Sir Stafford Northcote on the adjournment. Mr. Gladstone repeated that Gordon's mission, so far as the British Government was concerned, was advisory and not executive, and he hotly denied the report of the *Times* correspondent that he had been abandoned. Gordon, he announced, had permission to leave Khartoum if he so desired. He lashed the Opposition for taking their information from journalistic tattle, and declared that discussions on Egypt, when there were so many weightier matters on hand, were simply a waste of parliamentary time. The speech was a debating success, and it ravished the soul of Sir William Harcourt. A few days later the latter described the occasion to his constituents in his familiar vein of pious truculence. 'He (Mr. Gladstone) had been ill, and they thought that they could play tricks with the sick lion; but they were mistaken. He just put out his paw and there was an end of them. It was a wonderful scene. I have never seen the like of it in my political life. With his unparalleled eloquence he withered them with the blast of his scornful indignation, and he laid bare their inmost souls.' The speech scarcely deserved these heroics. It was based upon fallacies which Baring had exposed, and deductions for which there was no warrant. The word 'abandonment' which stung the Prime Minister was strictly justified.

Mr. Gladstone was less fortunate in his defence when the House met again after the Easter recess. The idea of a relief expedition was beginning to creep into the air, private instructions had been sent by the military authorities to make inquiries about the best routes, and the possibility of such a course being forced on him stiffened the old man's temper. He had made up his mind that he would not be coerced by an insubordinate envoy, by the British representative in Cairo whose good sense had unaccountably failed him, by imperialist colleagues, or by sentimental public opinion; and, according to his habit, he seized upon any plea to justify his obstinacy. On April 21 he told the House of Commons that Gordon was 'hemmed in' but not 'surrounded'—a distinction the meaning of which was a secret between himself and his Maker. On April 23 he declared that there was 'no military or other danger threatening Khartoum.' A relief expedition would be needless, impossible, and immoral. It maddened him to think that with so many grave preoccupations the Government should be harassed by this gadfly. The situation with Russia in Central Asia was full of menace. Germany under Bismarck was waiting maliciously to catch Britain at a disadvantage. Any forward move in Egypt would make trouble with France, and a good understanding with Paris was a primary aim of his foreign policy. Besides there were difficult times ahead at home. Ireland was a powder magazine waiting the spark, and over his cherished Franchise Bill he was having trouble with the House of Lords. The Prime Minister had many excuses for his irritation. A little firmness, he decided, and the agitation would die, for stalwarts, like Mr. John Morley, believed that people were growing tired of Gordon. There were even soldiers who looked askance at him; it was reported that Sir Redvers Buller, when a dash across the desert was proposed, had declared that 'the man was not worth the camels.'

But when on May 12 a vote of censure was moved in the Commons, he found that all his parliamentary arts were insufficient to allay the anxiety of members, not only of the Opposition, but of his own party. He repeated the familiar arguments—orders disobeyed, messages unanswered, no immediate danger. To send an army to Khartoum would be 'a war of conquest against a people rightly struggling to be free'—a description which future events were to render fantastic in the extreme, since within ten years those aspirants after liberty caused seventy-five per cent.of the Soudan population t perish. He was answered with effect by Mr. W. E. Forster, and orly Lord Hartington's foreshadowing of an autumn expedition saved the Government from defeat. The bitter comment of Lord Randolph Churchill on Mr. Gladstone's speech showed how alien it was to the temper of the House. 'I compared his efforts in the cause of Gordon with his efforts in the cause of Mr. Bradlaugh. If one hundredth part of those valuable moral qualities bestowed upon the cause of a seditious blasphemer had been given to the support of a Christian hero, the success of Gordon's mission would have been assured. But the finest speech he ever delivered in the House of Commons was in support of the seditious blasphemer; and the very worst he ever delivered, by common consent, was in the cause of the Christian hero.'

At the end of April Baring was brought to London for a financial conference, but during his two months at home he was unable to make the Government understand the facts. It would appear that they considered their Egyptian duties to be fulfilled for the moment by attending to Egypt's finances. The question of Gordon received only a perfunctory five minutes at the end of the Cabinet meetings. The Government continued to ask him for full reports on his exact situation, and when they got no answer, since their requests never reached him, decided that he was insubordinate or sulky. They wanted to know the reason why he did not leave Khartoum; the formidable reason was Mohammed Ahmed. They took no steps about the relief expedition which Lord Hartington had hinted at, except to make a few inquiries about routes, though, if such an expedition was to start in the early autumn, the preparations for it should have begun in May. They were determined to wait and see, confident that Gordon could at any time escape if he wished. So no doubt he could. It would have been possible for him with the help of friendly natives to slip through the lines of the besiegers, but he would have left to their fate the people of Khartoum who had given him their trust. 'How could I look the world in the face if I abandoned them and fled?' he had written to Baring. If a desirable quality in an envoy is concern for his own skin, it is unwise to select a soldier—still less a crusader.

The temper of the country was rising. On July 24 Wolseley, with the authority of Britain's most successful soldier, protested strongly against this insane procrastination. Before the end of June the news of the fall of Berber had reached England, and by July 20 at long last a message came through from Gordon, dated June 23, asking for word of the relief expedition. To this the Government only replied by demanding more information as to the situation in Khartoum—a piece of futility which ultimately reached Gordon, but which fortunately he could not read, his cyphers having been lost with Stewart. On July 25 the Cabinet met, and the main business was the question of an expedition. To Mr. Gladstone's chagrin only Sir William Harcourt, Lord Kimberley and Lord Granville among his colleagues stood out against it. But he himself was immovable, and he would not bow to the majority's view. More than ever he was determined that a refractory subordinate of a melo-dramatic turn of mind should not dictate to a British Prime Minister. Besides he was sallying forth to do battle with the House of Lords over his Franchise Bill, and the faithful Mr. John Morley was delighting Liberal audiences with delicious witticisms about 'mending or ending' that chamber. No distraction must be permitted in so high a task.

But Mr. Gladstone was first and foremost a politician, and on the last day of July he saw reason to change his mind. On the 29th Lord Selborne and Lord Hartington circulated memoranda to the Cabinet urging immediate action. On the 31st the latter announced that an expedition must forthwith be authorised or he would resign his office. The slow mind which had been long in travail had at last given birth to a decision. The Prime Minister, insensible to the persuasion of facts, bowed before party exigencies. He knew that when Lord Hartington spoke of 'a question of personal honour and good faith,' he meant business, for he was not wont to use these spacious words. He knew that the defection of the head of the house of Cavendish would bring down his Government and rend his party. He surrendered at discretion. On August 5 he himself moved in

the House of Commons for a grant of funds 'to undertake operations for the relief of General Gordon, should they become
necessary, and to make certain preparations in respect thereof.'
That day the War Office set to work on plans, and on
September 9 Wolseley arrived in Cairo.

Mr. Gladstone had yielded, but without conviction. Public
opinion at the time saddled him with the guilt of what was to
prove a fatal delay, and beyond doubt it was the prepotent force
of his character that kept the Cabinet inert. But, since a man
is what God made him, it seems to me that the major part of the
blame should rest on Lord Hartington for his tardy resolution.
Lord Hartington from the first more or less understood the
situation, which the Prime Minister never did. Mr. Gladstone's
mind was cast in a rigid, antique mould, and he would not yield
on a principle except in the last necessity. He detested war,
both for its own sake, and because it meant a diversion of national
interest from what he regarded as worthier matters; he would
only sanction it if the need were proved to the hilt, and the kind
of evidence which he considered essential was not forthcoming.
He had no instinct for things which cannot be formulated in
black and white, and no imagination to construct a true picture
out of scattered details.

Gordon in his journal on September 23 set down with uncanny
intuition his habit of mind. 'It is as if a man on the bank, having
seen his friend in the river already bobbed down two or three
times, hails: "I say, old fellow, let me know when we are to
throw you the life-buoy. I know you have bobbed down two
or three times, but it is a pity to throw you the life-buoy until
you are really *in extremis*, and I want to know exactly, for I am
a man brought up in a school of exactitude."' Facts, when
they ran counter to Mr. Gladstone's wishes, had to be massed
in overwhelming myriads before he could realise them. He
was not unlike the Lord Aberdeen of the Crimean War.

The truth is that he had no single gift of the man of action,
except in the sheltered arena of domestic politics. Nearly a
quarter of a century earlier Lord Salisbury in a *Quarterly* article
had acutely diagnosed one part of his psychology. 'His mind,
with all its power, has this strange peculiarity that his reason

will not work vigorously on any question in which he does not take a hearty interest; and he can only take a hearty interest in one question at one time. On any question therefore, which crosses the subject of his heart . . . his perceptions are blunted and his reason will not work true.' Again, he wholly lacked the gift of reading characters different from his own and appraising situations outside his narrow experience. Gordon from the start had been antipathetic to him. He had never been properly informed about the first negotiations, and had come to regard him as a dangerous, mercurial being who must be kept in strict subjection: when the relief expedition was authorised, he insisted on his being put formally under Wolseley and his powers limited to the Khartoum neighbourhood. How could one who thought in flashes be understood by one who thought in paragraphs! As for the dervish army, drunk with blood and dreams of Paradise, he seems to have envisaged it as a collection of dark-skinned Midlothian radicals.

Such were the limitations of the man—a great man. The tragedy lay in the fact that, being what he was, he was faced with a task in which his weaknesses became clamant and his virtues silent. But he should not be left to bear the blame alone. Lord Northbrook, when disaster came, nobly resolved never to serve under him again. It would have been more to his credit if this resolve had come earlier, and if the old man had been brought to reason by those colleagues who lacked his faults, as they assuredly lacked his genius.

VII

Act the Fourth: the Race against Time

I

ILL-LUCK dogged from the start the expedition thus tardily sanctioned. There was a delay of a fortnight before the Nile route, which Wolseley favoured and on which some preliminary work had been done, was finally approved. Sir Frederick Stephenson, commanding the British troops in Egypt, preferred the Suakim-Berber road, but he had argued against it in March, and the objection to it had been increased by the loss of Berber. Wolseley, with his Red River campaign in mind, desired to follow the same methods, with Canadian flat-bottomed boats and Canadian boatmen, and these took time to collect. He had a series of difficult cataracts to pass, and, since food could not be obtained locally, he must carry supplies for a hundred days. He was determined to leave nothing to chance, and the transport of 7000 men in such a terrain required elaborate preparations. Bases were established along the river, and at Dongola an advance guard was stationed, the nucleus of a flying column, the Camel Corps, which was to strike across the Bayuda desert from Korti to Metemmah, thereby cutting off the great bend of the river. These advance troops were intended to enter Khartoum, and hold it till the rest of the army arrived, when the relief and evacuation could be completed.

Wolseley was a competent soldier, and his deep friendship for Gordon—the two men remembered each other every night in their prayers—gave him the most urgent motive for speed. But it was his custom to make war disposedly, taking all due precautions, and he was not the man for a swift and hazardous enterprise. From Suakim to Berber the distance was 250 miles; from Cairo to Khartoum it was 1000 miles as the crow flies, and 1650 miles if the river were followed. If it was to be a race

Q

against time for Gordon's life, the Nile route seemed impossibly slow, especially when the nature of the flotilla was remembered—steamers which, in Lord Charles Beresford's words, 'had the appearance of a boat and the manners of a kangaroo,' which leaked at every rivet and whose boilers 'roared like a camel.' There was another soldier, Sir Frederick Roberts, who five years before had made a brilliant dash to Kandahar; had he been given the task with Indian troops he might have crossed the desert from Suakim and have been in Khartoum in November. Mr. Chamberlain, who knew nothing of the art of war but had often an uncanny *flair*, would have put the little-known Major Kitchener in command of a flying force. But though part of Wolseley's delay came from his too meticulous methods, the purpose of his enterprise involved elaboration. For it was not a hussar-ride for the rescue of one man or a handful of men, but for the evacuation of a multitude. Nothing less would fulfil Britain's pledge, and nothing less would Gordon accept. To succeed, any relieving force must hold the river and stave off the Mahdi for many months.

On September 27 Wolseley left Cairo. On October 5 he was at Wadi Halfa, where he established a temporary base and spent a month in supervising the transport. There he heard of the disaster to the *Abbas*, but he was not yet greatly alarmed about the situation in Khartoum. He was busy organising the Camel Corps in four regiments, two of cavalry, one of the Guards, and one of mounted infantry, with a detachment of Royal Marines, and he could not expect it to be ready to leave Korti for the desert journey much before the end of the year. He arrived at Dongola on November 3, and on November 17 received a message from Gordon, which gave some account of the Khartoum position, advised the crossing of the desert to Metemmah, and promised that four of his steamers would be waiting there. The message contained these significant words: 'We can hold out 40 days with ease; after that it will be difficult.' Since the letter was dated November 4, this meant that by December 14 the position would be grave. But Gordon's friends were always confident that he could better his best, and that if he spoke of holding on for six weeks he could hold on for six months. The concentration at Korti could not be completed before Christmas, and the crossing of the desert and the advance to Khartoum would take at the best a fortnight. That is to say, Gordon could not be rescued till six weeks or more after the last date which he had given as his limit of endurance.

Still Wolseley does not seem to have been specially anxious; at any rate he took no steps to expedite the pace of his movements. Slowly with immense labour the flotilla struggled up the river through the rapids from Wadi Halfa to New Dongola, from New Dongola to Old Dongola and open water, from Old Dongola to Korti. Wolseley was well behind his time, and his original hope of spending Christmas in Khartoum had gone. By December 15 only the advance guard was at Korti, and it was not till a fortnight later that the concentration there was completed. The Commander-in-chief proceeded to divide his forces. The Nile Column, 3000 men under General Earle, should continue up the river, deal with Berber, and at Metemmah join the Desert Column, which was to strike direct across the Bayuda wastes.

At 3 o'clock on the afternoon of December 30 the latter force rode out of Korti, a little over a thousand strong, under the command of Sir Herbert Stewart, with Major Kitchener to lead the way. The same day an Arab brought a message from Gordon, a twist of paper dated December 14, with the words 'Khartoum all right.' But he brought also a verbal message: 'We are besieged on three sides. Fighting goes on day and night. . . . Bring plenty of troops if you can. . . . Food we still have is little—some grain and biscuit. We want you to come quickly. You should come by Metemmah or Berber. Make by these two roads. Do not leave Berber in your rear.' These words made Wolseley realise the gravity of the situation, but they also convinced him that he must not go direct in force to Khartoum, but must first take Berber. That might be a slow business, including the passing of two cataracts, and it was not till the bend at Abu Hamed was reached that the boats could get the favouring north wind. The one hope of speed lay in Sir Herbert Stewart and his camelry, now cut loose from their base and launched into the desert.

II

Meantime during the last three months of the year Gordon was fighting his desperate battle against odds, and he was fighting it alone. He had no confidant except his journal, and no counsellor except the valour of his heart. On the technical side his resistance was an astonishing feat. With 7000 inferior troops he had to defend a wide periphery against twenty times their number of intrepid fanatics. Within his defence zone he had a multitude of scared civilians, who had to be fed and comforted. He was short of food, and had to scrape it together and deal it out like gold dust. He was short of ammunition and guns, while the besiegers had ample supplies. The contemptuous message which Wad-el-Nejumi sent him on September 12 was a fair picture of the Mahdi's army. 'One man of them in battle is better than a thousand of you. He has provided us with weapons of war, in which thou thinkest there is victory, with Krupp cannons, with mountain guns for battle, in which thou shalt taste of evil, if thou turn aside from the way of God.' Moreover Gordon had to keep the river open down to Shendi and Metemmah for the relief expedition which was his only hope. Up and down the falling Nile plied his penny-steamers, getting fuel from the banks when and where they could, running the gauntlet of a ceaseless bombardment, the only link with the outer world, except the occasional Arab spies who bore Major Kitchener's messages to the beleaguered city.

As the days passed Gordon found his tools breaking in his hand. There were few men whom he could trust. Officers neglected their duties, and stole the soldiers' rations; there were plots to blow up the magazine and to betray the city; there was a perpetual purloining of grain. He had to keep his eye on every detail of the defence work or it would be scamped. In such circumstances he had to rule largely by terror, and his punishments were instant and severe. Often he repented of his severity, for he detested harshness, but there was no other way. The shivering townspeople clung to his skirts, supplicated him, cursed him, blessed him. He had to drive them with a light rein, for they were on the near edge of panic.

So he encouraged them with announcements of the speedy

arrival of British troops, and assurances that he would not fail them. 'Know,' he declared on November 26, 'that if Mohammed Ahmed should call me for three years to surrender Khartoum, I will not listen to him, but will protect your wives and families and possessions with all energy and steadfastness.' He had a band to play every Thursday on the palace roof—boys, for the men were all in the trenches—and when the palace was bombarded he directed that it should be kept brilliantly lit up to show his scorn of the enemy. Such *panache* was the only chance of keeping civilian spirit from cracking. 'When God was portioning out fear to all the people in the world,' he told Bordeini the merchant, 'at last it came to my turn, and there was no fear left to give me. Go tell all the people in Khartoum that Gordon fears nothing, for God hath created him without fear.'

Yet he jumped when a shell dropped near him, and had to remind himself that 'judicious bobbing' under fire was permissible. We can learn from his journal that his nerves were strained to the last limit with overwork, anxiety, and hope deferred. He was no doubt impatient and sometimes unjust, but another man would have gone mad. He vented in writing his grievances against Baring and Granville and all that world which was daily growing dimmer, and then set himself patiently to the realities of his task. Sometimes he had strange fancies. He heard that the Mahdi had a French prisoner and decided that it must be Ernest Renan, whom he had met once in London. He wanted to meet Renan again; Renan had not, like Slatin, betrayed his Lord, for he had been always an unbeliever. He thought much of death, and decided that, if the city fell, he would not blow up the palace and perish with it—that would be too like suicide; he would let himself be taken and, if called upon, die a martyr to the faith. Sometimes he was sustained by the conviction that his defence had been rather a fine thing—at least as good as Sebastopol. Not that he thought much of fame— 'if we analyse human glory, it is composed of nine-tenths twaddle, perhaps ninety-nine hundredths twaddle.' But his professional pride was not quite forgotten. What might he not have done, he asked himself, if he had only had trusty troops whom he could use for counter-attacks 'in a real siege with no civil population or robbers of officers'?

The Moslem year begins on Trafalgar Day. The Mahdi had his new year's text from the Koran: 'Victory from God, conquest is at hand.' He sent one last summons to surrender, and Gordon's reply was, 'I am here like iron. . . . It is impossible for me to have any more words with Mohammed Ahmed—only lead.' November compelled him to revise his old view of the poor quality of the dervish troops, for on the 14th came a terrific Arab attack on the fort of Omdurman on the west bank of the White Nile. The place was sturdily defended, but the enemy succeeded in cutting the fortified lines which connected it with the river and thereby isolating it. Unless the English came soon Omdurman must fall, and that would mean the end of Khartoum. But the Arabs did not at once press their advantage. They established a battery at Khojali across the Blue Nile, from which at a range of a mile and a quarter they bombarded the palace. One unpleasant result was that his few steamers were in constant danger.

Sunday, December 14, was the last of the forty days which Gordon had given Wolseley as the limit of his power to hold on. On that day he made the last entry in his journal.

Now mark this, if the Expeditionary Force, and I ask for no more than two hundred men, does not come in ten days, the town may fall; and I have done my best for the honour of my country. Good-bye. C. G. GORDON.

On the 15th the little *Bordein* set off down the river, with the journal, and letters, official and private. Among the latter was one to his sister Augusta, which had this postscript: 'I am quite happy, thank God, and, like Lawrence, I have tried to do my duty.'

III

Between Korti and Metemmah lay 176 miles of desert. The route had been surveyed by Ismail for a railway, and the Desert Column had his map to guide them. Since the enemy was known to be near it was necessary to establish supply posts and to leave guards at the few water-holes. The scarcity of camels prevented the expedition from making the whole journey at once, and it was decided to establish an advanced base at the wells of Jakdul, 98 miles off, and return for the rest of the troops and supplies. This double journey was the first delay.

Riding through nights of brilliant moonlight the column reached the Jakdul wells, three deep pools in the clefts of the black hills, on the morning of January 2. It had been on the march for sixty-four hours with only four hours of sleep. There the Guards battalion was left as garrison, and the rest returned to Korti. It was not till January 8 that Sir Herbert Stewart set out again, with his strength now increased to 1600 British troops, 300 camp-followers, and some 2400 camels and horses. He had also part of the Naval Brigade under Lord Charles Beresford, which was intended to man the steamers believed to be waiting at Metemmah. On the 12th Stewart reached Jakdul, where he found all quiet, and on the 13th resumed his advance. Nine days had been occupied by the double journey.

Meanwhile the Mahdi's picked troops, whom the delay had amply warned of the British movements, were hastening north to bar the way. When on the evening of the 16th Stewart reached the ridge which looked down on the wells of Abu Klea, he saw 10,000 dervishes encamped beneath him. The night was made hideous by the beating of their war-drums, but there was no attack. On the morning of the 17th the British advanced in a square, which presently halted when it was seen that the Arabs were moving forward. Inside the square were the camels and the ammunition; it stood in the trough of a little valley, with the enemy in front and on the adjoining hills. Suddenly on its rear appeared a cluster of green and white flags, and 5000 dervishes swept down upon the Heavy Camel Regiment and the Naval Brigade, 'an immense surging wave of white-slashed black forms brandishing bright spears and long flashing swords.'

What followed was a second Inkerman, a soldiers' battle. For such fighting the Arabs were as well equipped as the British, and they had the fury of their wild faith to nerve them. Stewart's troops had the wretched Gardner gun, which perpetually jammed in action. They had the old Martini-Henry rifle, which also jammed, while the Arab Remington, using a different kind of cartridge, was free from this fault. Against the razor-edged Arab spears were pitted blunt bayonets and cutlasses that bent and twisted. In physical strength and weapon power, as in numbers, the British were hopelessly outmatched. They were saved only by their steady, disciplined courage. The enemy broke into the rear of the square and pressed his assault up to the camels, which stopped his rush and gave the front and flanks time to face inwards. For a little there was a desperate hand-to-hand struggle, officers and men fighting side by side. No Arab emerged from that broken square, and at length the enemy withdrew leaving over 1000 dead on the field. But the British had paid a heavy price for their victory, for out of their little force they had lost 18 officers and 158 other ranks. Worse still, Colonel Burnaby, whom Wolseley had destined to take charge at Metemmah, lay dead after all his journeyings, 'slain in the desert by a wandering spear.'

Abu Klea had involved another day's delay. That night Stewart bivouacked by the wells, his men without food or blankets. Next day, the 18th, the march was resumed in the afternoon, and continued through the night, till early on the morning of the 19th, the column came in sight of the Nile. It halted for a brief rest, and once again the enemy drew round it in clouds. A zariba was hastily formed, and breakfast was eaten under a rain of bullets. Stewart received a wound which proved to be fatal, and the command devolved upon Sir Charles Wilson, a distinguished intelligence officer who had never before commanded troops in the field. The new leader decided to press on to the Nile, and the square moved slowly forward, sweeping the dervish force before it by its deadly fire. The sun set, the twilight deepened to dusk, and under a your moon the British came to the river bank. The troops who had been marching and fighting for four days without sleep and with little food or water, and had lost one man in ten, could at last drink and rest, but so weary were they that, when they came back from quenching their thirst at the river, they fell down like logs.

Next day was occupied in fortifying their position, and on Wednesday the 21st Sir Charles Wilson advanced against Metemmah. The attack had not begun when four steamers, flying the Egyptian flag, were seen to be coming from the south. They were Gordon's steamers; the troops broke into cheers, and there was a rush to the river bank to welcome them.

The march through the Bayuda desert had been a splendid

feat of arms, but it had been slow, and there was no man in the column whose thoughts were not reaching beyond his present troubles to what might have happened, or be happening, a hundred miles up those blue waters to whose shores he had fought his way. The last word from Gordon had left Khartoum on December 14, and its appeal had been urgent. It was now thirty-eight days since then—the 21st of January.

VIII

ACT THE FIFTH: THE END

ABU KLEA was fought on January 17, and the news of it brought consternation to the Mahdi's camp. The sword of the infidel had proved more potent than the sword of the Prophet. A salute of 101 guns was ordered on January 20 to proclaim a victory, but this was only to delude the people of Khartoum, for in the camp itself there was lamentation. Gordon on that day saw through his telescope a multitude of weeping women and guessed the truth, and presently a spy confirmed it. Mohammed Ahmed called a council of his emirs, and all but one urged a retreat to El Obeid and the raising of the siege. 'If one Englishman,' they argued, 'has kept us at bay for a year, how much more will these thousands of English, who have defeated our bravest men at Abu Klea, be able to crush us and drive us away.' Only Abd-el-Kerim stood out; let them attack Khartoum at once, he said, and there would still be time to fall back if they failed.

For a day or two the dervish council hesitated. News came of another victory of the English and their advance to the Nile bank. The sight of a dozen redcoats would have sent the whole army westward into the desert. But the 21st passed and the Mahdi's scouts reported no British movement, nor on the 22nd or the 23rd. The courage of the dervishes revived and their temper hardened. When at last on the 24th news came that the British were advancing, Abd-el-Kerim's views had prevailed, and it was resolved forthwith to attack the city. Abu Klea had been misrepresented; the infidels were in doubt and fear, for if they had been victorious they would long before have reached Khartoum.

On January 15 Omdurman had capitulated to the enemy, and he was now able to plant guns on the west bank of the White Nile and double the fury of his bombardment. More serious, the river was falling fast, and the trenches and ramparts on the west side of the lines, abutting on the stream, had to be pushed further into the drying mud. But with the loss of Omdurman this became impossible. The river was ceasing to be a defence, and presently it had receded so far that a sand ridge appeared some 300 yards from the east bank. If the enemy landed on this he had only to wade through a shallow lagoon to be inside the lines. A spy carried this news to the Mahdi's camp.

When Gordon wrote the last words in his journal on December 14 he closed his account with the outer world. After that date we have only the fragmentary evidence of the survivors of the garrison, and of prisoners in the dervish camp. By the end of the year the state of the city was desperate indeed. There was no food ration left to issue at the close of the second week of January. Gum was served out and the pith of date-trees, and for the rest the food was lean donkeys and dogs and rats. Dysentery was rife, and the soldiers on the ramparts were almost too weak to stand, their legs swollen, and their bodies distended by gum and water. The spirit had gone out of the stoutest, and even Faragh Pasha advised surrender. But Gordon was adamant. He suffered those civilians who desired it to go to the Mahdi, and many went, but he would permit no weakening in his council of notables. Resistance must be maintained to the end. The news of Abu Klea had for a moment given hope, and he issued daily announcements that the British were coming, would arrive any hour. But when no smoke appeared on the northern horizon the last dregs of resolution were drained from the sick and starving people. 'They will no longer believe me,' he told Bordeini. 'I can do nothing more.' But he did not relax his efforts. Day and night he was on the ramparts, in the streets, in the hospitals, the one vital thing in a place of death and despair.

We have no journal to tell us his thoughts, but we can guess them from the nature of the man. He had become two beings—one ceaselessly busy in his hopeless duties, scanning the distances anxiously for the smoke which would mean relief; the other calm and at ease. On the palace roof at night with the vault of stars above him he found that union with the Eternal which was peace. His life had always hung as loosely about him as an outworn garment, and now the world of space and time had become only a shadow. 'I would,' he had once written to his sister, 'that all could look on death as a cheerful friend, who takes us from a world of trial to our true home.' The communion with the unseen which had been the purpose of all his days was now as much a part of him as the breath he drew. Like the ancient votaries of the Great Mother, he had passed through the bath of blood and was *renatus in aeternum*. His soul was already with the Congregation of the First-born.

The letters which Gordon's steamers brought to Gubat on the 21st were dated December 14 and their tone was sufficiently grave. Ten days' time was given as the extreme limit of resistance. There was another message on a scrap of paper: 'Khartoum all right. Could hold out for years'; but this was clearly meant as a device to deceive the enemy, should it fall into his hands. Sir Charles Wilson had no illusions about the need for haste, but his experience had not lain in the leading of men, and his was not the character for bold and decisive action.

Stewart's instructions from Wolseley had been to take Metemmah, which would serve as a base later for the River Column, and to send Wilson on to Khartoum in Gordon's steamers, accompanied by Lord Charles Beresford and part of the Naval Brigade. Wilson now found himself in command of the whole force, and he hesitated about his next duty. When he received Gordon's papers it is clear that he should at once have gone himself, or sent someone, to Khartoum. As it was, he delayed three days in spite of the protests of Gordon's Arab emissaries. The reason is obscure, but it is probable that Beresford was the cause. He was ill at the moment, suffering from desert boils, and he was eager to accompany the relief force, as he had been instructed. News came of an enemy advance from the south, and then of another from the north, and he induced Wilson to use the steamers to make reconnaissances in both directions, in the hope, doubtless, that he would presently be fit for duty. Two and a half days were wasted in a meaningless task.

This delay was the last and the most tragic of the tricks of fate. Had Burnaby lived it is certain that a steamer would have set out for Khartoum on the afternoon of the 21st. Had that been done, it is as certain as such things can be that Gordon would have been saved. It was not till the 24th that the Mahdi decided upon an assault, and it was not till the evening of the 25th that the details were agreed upon. Allowing for the difficulties of the journey, the steamers, had they left on the 21st, would have been in time to convince the hesitating dervishes, and turn them against Abd-el-Kerim's plan; they might even have been in time had they left on the 22nd. This was the view of the Europeans in the Mahdi's camp who were in the best position to know—of Slatin and of Father Ohrwalder. 'Had twenty red-coats arrived in Khartoum,' the latter has written, 'it would have been saved. . . . If the English had appeared any time before he delivered the attack, he would have raised the siege and retired. . . . Many survivors have said to me, "Had we seen one Englishman, we should have been saved."' By such a narrow margin did a great enterprise fail.

Wilson eventually set out on the morning of Saturday the 24th, in two steamers with twenty British soldiers and a few bluejackets—all the troops, at Gordon's request, being clad in scarlet tunics. Misfortune dogged his path. On the evening of the 25th the *Bordein* struck a rock in the Sixth Cataract, which caused a delay of twenty-four hours. Early on the 27th the Shablukah gorge was passed, and that day the voyage continued under heavy rifle fire from both banks. There were Arab cries from the shore that Khartoum had fallen, but they were not believed. Early on Wednesday the 28th, the expedition came in sight of Khartoum beyond the trees on Tuti island, and ran the gauntlet of the batteries at Halfaya. Then they opened the palace and saw through their glasses that no flag was flying. The channel at Tuti was one long alley of rifle fire. As they rounded the corner they beheld a wrecked city, with the Mahdi's banners flaunting under the walls, and knew that all was over. They were sixty hours too late.

Wilson could only turn and retreat. The little gimcrack steamers had a perilous journey. Both were wrecked and in danger of capture, and a young officer of the 60th, Stuart-Wortley, set out alone in a boat for Gubat to bring help. On February 1 at dawn Beresford was hailed by a voice from the river, which could only stammer, 'Gordon is killed . . . Khartoum has fallen.' From Gubat the news crossed the

desert, and was flashed to a world which for months had
drawn its breath in suspense. Queen Victoria at this, as at
most times, was the voice of her people. 'She went to my
cottage, a quarter of a mile off,' her private secretary wrote to
Baring, 'walked into the room, pale and trembling, and said
to my wife, who was terrified at her appearance, "Too late!"'

All day on Sunday the 25th there was a movement of Arab
troops to the east bank of the White Nile. Wad-el-Nejumi,
the commander of the storm-troops, had his camp at Kalakala, a
mile south of the defences. That evening, as twilight fell, a
boat put off from the western shore, and four figures joined him
and his emirs; it was Mohammed Ahmed himself with his three
khalifas. The Mahdi blessed the troops and gave them his orders.
In the name of God and the Prophet he bade them attack
Khartoum in the dark of the night; let them have no fear, for
those who fell would straightway enter Paradise. The four
returned as silently as they had come, and Wad-el-Nejumi unfolded his plans.

One part of the force should attack the western half of the
defences, breaking through the gap which the falling river had
left on the shore side. The second division should attack on
the east between the Messalamieh Gate and Buri, but if the
western assault succeeded this section was to hold its hand, side-
step to the left, and follow the first division. In front would
go the skirmishers, then the main force of spears and swords,
and then further riflemen, with the cavalry in reserve on the
rear flanks. Bedsteads and bundles of straw were carried to
fill up the trenches, if necessary. The Mahdi had left no precautions untaken, for he was nervous about a direct assault,
though his emirs had assured him that God had made their path
easy and plain.

As soon as the moon set the movement began. In silence
the left division crept towards the defences. Now they were
at the ramparts, and at that moment a fierce bombardment
broke out from every Arab gun around the city. Under this
cover it was easy for the left flank of the attack to break through
the gap at the river bank, which only three armed barges defended.
In a few minutes they were inside the lines, sweeping to the east,

and taking the rest of the defences in rear. Swiftly they crossed the space between the lines and Khartoum, a space dotted with cemeteries, magazines and slaughter-houses, and bore down on the helpless city. The post at the Messalamieh Gate, finding its position turned, was compelled to fall back, and through that gate poured the contingent destined for the Buri attack. By four o'clock Khartoum had fallen, and the siege of three hundred and seventeen days was over. Most of the attackers made for the streets and the business of plunder and massacre. But one body, with whom there were no emirs, rushed to the palace, and swarmed in at the garden entrance.

Of Gordon's last doings our accounts are few and bare. It appears that he had spent the day indoors, striving to put resolution into his notables, but in the evening he had examined part of the defences. From the palace roof he had his last search for the steamers that never came. He had seen the Arabs crossing the White Nile and may have guessed what was afoot, for he did not go to bed. The sound of musketry and guns after midnight told him of the attack, but he could do nothing. The end had come, and he was in the hands of God.

The firing drew nearer, and then he heard that dreadful sound which strikes terror into the boldest heart, savage men baying like hounds for lust and blood. Presently there came a tumult in the garden, and the death-cries of his black sentries. He walked to the head of the staircase, dressed in a white uniform, with a sword at his belt, and a revolver in his right hand. The darkness was passing, and the first crimson of dawn was in the sky.

He saw a mob of dark faces and bright spears, and with them no high officer. That he knew meant instant death. Not for him to be taken prisoner and confronted with the Mahdi, with the choice before him of recusancy or martyrdom. He must have welcomed the knowledge. He stood, his left hand resting on his sword-hilt, peering forward as was his fashion. An Arab— Mohammed Nebawi was his name; he fell at the battle of Omdurman—rushed on him, crying 'O cursed one, your time has come,' and struck at him with his spear. Gordon did not defend himself. He turned away with a gesture of contempt, and in a second a dozen spears were in his body, and men were slashing at him with their swords. The hour of his death was about 5.30, when it was almost full dawn.

His slayers cut off his head, and brought it in triumph to the Mahdi's camp. Mohammed Ahmed had wished him to be taken alive, but he bowed to the will of Allah. It was now broad day, and the captive Slatin, sick and anxious, crawled to his tent door. He found a group of shouting slaves, carrying something wrapped in a bloody cloth. They undid the cloth and revealed the head of Gordon, his blue eyes half opened and his hair as white as wool.

'Is not this,' cried one, 'the head of your uncle the unbeliever?'

'What of it?' said Slatin. 'A brave soldier who fell at his post. Happy is he to have fallen; his sufferings are over.'

IX

Epilogue

THE policy of Britain contained the germ of its own reversal. Gordon's prophecy was true; if there was to be peace on the lower Nile the upper river must be controlled. The white-clad figure fronting the dervish spears at sunrise on that January morning was more persuasive in his death than in his life. Wisely the first step was backward. The Soudan was evacuated, and steadily Egypt gathered her forces for the recoil. A succession of devoted British officers drilled the Khedive's troops into an army. At Ginniss, between Wadi Halfa and Dongola, towards the end of 1885 Sir Frederick Stephenson defeated the dervish forces, and thereby warded off the invasion of Egypt proper. In 1889, at Toski, Sir Francis Grenfell fought the opening battle under the forward policy; there Wad-el-Nejumi fell. He blooded the new Egyptian army, and gave it its first taste of self-respect. Two years later Osman Digna was defeated at Tokar, and the eastern Soudan was tranquillised.

In those years Egypt, fortunately for her, was forgotten by Britain, but under the major of sappers, who had been the chief link with Gordon, she was quietly and surely preparing her own salvation. In 1897 the final advance began. The railway was pushed on from Wadi Halfa to Abu Hamed. In April 1898 Sir Herbert Kitchener by his victory at the Atbara laid open the road to Khartoum. Five months later the battle of Omdurman, fought beside the Mahdi's yellow, pointed tomb, broke for good and all the power of the fanatics who for fifteen years had burdened the country. A more economical triumph was never won, for the cost of the conquest of the Soudan was only 60 British and 160 Egyptian lives, and a sum of £2,350,000, far less than that of the relief expedition which failed. In 1884 Kitchener had calculated that 20,000 British troops would be needed for the task; his judgment was sound, for at Omdurman he had 22,000. Baring, now Lord Cromer, had nothing to do

R

but, in his own words, 'abstain from a mischievous activity and act as a check on the interference of others.' Mr. Balfour telegraphed on the eve of the Atbara, 'The Sirdar may count upon the support of Her Majesty's Government whichever course he decides on adopting. Unless he wishes for a military opinion, we refrain from offering any remarks which would interfere with his absolute discretion.' A far cry from the waverings of Lord Granville!

Kitchener was hailed by Cambridge, when he received his doctor's degree, as '*Gordonis ultor*.' But Omdurman was no mere punitive act, and Gordon needed no avenger. The drama of Khartoum was more than a strife of common interests and passions; it was a clash of opposing worlds, of fervent creeds, of things not intrinsically base which could not dwell side by side in the compromise which we call civilisation. Tragedy sprang more out of rival greatnesses than out of rival follies, and it was dignified by the quality of the actors. If it revealed human weakness and perversity, it revealed—and not on one side alone—the faith and courage which ennoble our mortality. The end, as in all great tragedies, was peace—the Gordon College in Khartoum, a just law for all, protection for the weak, bread for the hungry, square miles of tillage where once the Baggara raided. . . . In 1919 the son of the Mahdi offered his father's sword to the British king as a token of his fealty. The old unhappy things had become far off and forgotten.

BIBLIOGRAPHICAL NOTE

THE principal authorities for Gordon's life are *The Journals of Major-General C. G. Gordon at Khartoum* (1885) and *Letters of General Gordon to his Sister* (1888); the British Official White Paper on China (1864) and the Blue Books on Egyptian Affairs (1884-5). The telegrams in the last-mentioned are not always given in full, but the originals are in the Record Office, and have been printed by Mr. Bernard M. Allen in his *Gordon and the Sudan* (1931). Additional material in the shape of letters and reports will be found in *Sudan Notes and Records*, vols. x. and xiii.

The early Lives (by D. C. Boulger, 1896; A. E. Hake, 1884, 1896) were apt to be uncritical eulogies. The best account of Gordon's work in Africa is that by B. M. Allen cited above, which is supplemented by his *Gordon in China* (1933). Lytton Strachey's ingenious travesty will be found in his *Eminent Victorians* (1918). An illuminating imaginary conversation between Gordon and Gladstone is in H. D. Traill's *The New Lucian* (1900). Mr. H. E. Wortham's *Gordon: an Intimate Study* (1933) is a vivid and judicial sketch of the whole career, and makes use of many hitherto unpublished letters.

The best narrative of the Mahdi's rising is Sir Reginald Wingate's *Mahdism and the Egyptian Sudan* (1891). Useful too are Sir Rudolf Slatin's *Fire and Sword in the Sudan* (1906) and Father Ohrwalder's *Ten Years' Captivity in the Mahdi's Camp* (1903). The story of the Relief Expedition is told in Lord Edward Gleichen's *With the Camel Corps up the Nile* (1886), Sir W. F. Butler's *The Campaign of the Cataracts* (1887), Sir Charles Wilson's *From Korti to Khartoum* (1886), the opening chapters of Mr. Winston Churchill's *The River War* (1899), and Lord Charles Beresford's *Memoirs* (1914).

Gordon appears in every biography and autobiography of the time. The most valuable are Lord Cromer, *Modern Egypt* (1908); Sir George Arthur, *Lord Kitchener* (1920); Sir F. D. Maurice and G. C. A. Arthur, *Lord Wolseley* (1920); Vetch, *Life . . . of Lt.-Gen. Sir Gerald Graham* (1901); John Morley, *Life of Gladstone* (1903); Bernard Holland, *Life of the 8th Duke of Devonshire* (1911); Wemyss Reid, *Life of W. E. Forster* (1888); Fitzmaurice, *Life of Earl Granville* (1905); Garvin, *Life of Joseph Chamberlain*, vol. ii. (1933); and Buckle, *Life and Letters of Queen Victoria*, vol. iii. (1928).

V

MONTROSE AND LEADERSHIP

MONTROSE AND LEADERSHIP

IT is the aim of these lectures, which have been made possible by the generosity of the Walker Trust, to expound from concrete examples in history the meaning of the word 'leadership.' I can imagine no purpose more valuable to a University, where young men are being prepared for their entrance into the world. Human nature cannot do without its human inspirations. Mankind will always brigade itself in the fashion of an army, since life is for all of us a kind of campaign; and an army must have its commander-in-chief and its subaltern officers. We must have a flag to follow, a creed for which to fight, leaders to fight under. Loyalty is one of the greatest of our mortal virtues, and loyalty is not devotion only to a cause, but to men, or to a man, in whom that cause is embodied. If we understand what constitutes true leadership, we shall know a good deal about the meaning of true loyalty.

Moreover, there is another side to it. All of us, however modest our station, are called now and then to be leaders. We must make decisions which affect not only ourselves, but a greater or lesser number of our fellow mortals. We must face situations in public or in private life where we have to choose between two roads, one hard and one easy, one, it may be, right and the other wrong. We have to take risks, to gamble in life, and we have to persuade other people to follow us in our decision and to trust us. The matter may be of small moment, or it may be of the first importance, but the nature of the decision is the same. We have to act as leaders, and therefore we have to act alone. It is useful at such crises to know something of the obligations which leadership involves, and to have in our memory, for our encouragement, the examples of men who faced similar problems in a far more difficult form, on a grander scale, and for more momentous issues.

I am going to speak to you this afternoon about a great leader who was once one of yourselves, James Graham, the first

Marquis of Montrose. Three hundred years ago he was entered at St. Salvator's College as a boy of fourteen. He did all the things you are doing to-day. He played golf; he was a reasonably assiduous student of the Latin and Greek classics; he made many friends and entertained them; occasionally he ate and drank too much and had to suffer for it. He did some things, also, which I do not suppose you do. He practised hard at the butts and won a silver medal for archery. He went out hawking. He hunted in the valley of the Eden, and used to give his horse a quart of ale after a long day with hounds. He went regularly to Cupar races, which I suspect are a thing of the past. He was rather foppish, and his clothes cost him a figure which would make the modern undergraduate stare. Many eminent men have trod in their youth the cobbles of this ancient city, and some of them, I fear, may have been rather inclined to be prigs in their young days. But Montrose, the greatest of them, was the most human kind of undergraduate, and over the gulf of three centuries a St. Andrews man of to-day may still feel a certain kinship with one who had such zest for friendship, and sport, and all the things which are the glory of youth.

Once during the War I talked to a famous French general about the soldiers of our own nation, and he said that it always seemed to him remarkable that each part of the British Isles had produced one of the four great British generals. For England he naturally gave Marlborough, and for Ireland Wellington. With some curiosity I asked for the Welshman. He at once said Cromwell; rightly, I suppose, for the great Oliver was paternally a Williams and of Welsh extraction. With still greater curiosity I mentioned Scotland. He looked surprised. 'Scotland!' he said. 'Can there be any doubt? Have you not the Great Montrose!'

My friend called him 'le grand Montrose,' as if 'great' was the natural epithet to associate with his name. That has always been Montrose's reputation on the continent of Europe. In the seventeenth century in France and Germany he was generally classed with people like Condé and Turenne, in the very front rank of contemporary soldiers. It is only recently that, owing to the work of Mr. S. R. Gardiner and Sir John Fortescue, we in Britain have been coming round to the same view. To-day I think that most students of war would rank him as Cromwell's superior, and as the chief military figure produced by the Civil War.

We might well go further. For myself, I would rank him as the greatest man of action to whom Scotland has given birth. I would rank him as the greatest Scottish soldier. At first sight it looks as if it were not easy to set up a fair calculus of military genius, since conditions have varied so much throughout the ages. It may be said that he never commanded more than a few thousands, and that the problems of war which he had to face were elementary. But I should be inclined to argue, on the other hand, that military genius and military problems have remained very much the same from Alexander the Great and Hannibal to Foch and Haig, and that the increase in numbers and in the intricacy of warfare is balanced by the facilities for dealing with them given by modern inventions. The scale is different; the kind is the same.

But however that may be, one thing assuredly has not changed, and that is the nature of leadership. The qualities by which one man exercises his will over, and diffuses his personality throughout, a great mass of men, are precisely the same to-day as in the age of Montrose, or in the age of Julius Caesar. It is not for his statesmanship, or his philosophy, or for his technical accomplishment in the art of war that I offer Montrose for your consideration to-day, but for his gift of leadership. He may not be in the front rank of the world's soldiers, but assuredly he is one of the most marvellous leaders of men of whom history has record.

Now, what constitutes this gift of leadership? Primarily it is a gift of character. There is an intellectual side to it, of course. The stupid man can never be a true leader. The leader must be the intellectual superior of at least the majority of his following. Again, intellectual gifts so high as to approach the sphere of the marvellous will give a man authority over others, due to his possession of powers which seem superhuman and beyond mortal compass. A great genius like Napoleon inspires devotion because his men have come to believe in his star; they see him perform miracles, they cannot follow the lightning processes of his mind, so they follow blindly. But there have been great leaders whose genius fell far short of Napoleon's, and I think we may say generally that the chief foundation of leadership is character. To lead, a man, whether he be general or statesman or captain of industry, must have a personality which dominates and inspires masses of people who rarely or never see him. Take the case of Mr. Lloyd George in the last year of the Great War. He was admittedly a very great War Minister, but that does not mean that he always understood very clearly what was happening in the field, or that he had any profound military insight. What he possessed in a colossal degree was the will to conquer and the belief that victory was possible, and he was a great leader because he managed to make this resolution and optimism of his permeate not only the masses of his countrymen and of the overseas Empire, but of the other Allied nations. Take, on the other hand, my old chief, Lord Milner. Lord Milner's mind was the keenest weapon I have ever known. He had superb powers of insight and comprehension; he understood, for example, the military situation as few soldiers understood it. But he had none of the gifts of a popular leader. He had a personality the quality of which could not be readily communicated to the ordinary man. One had to penetrate into the secluded chambers of his intellect before one realised his greatness.

Obviously the personality capable of this wide diffusion must be a rich and potent thing. I would go further and say that it must be fundamentally a worthy thing. To this rule I do not believe there are any real exceptions. You remember that Joseph Bonaparte was once asked what he thought about his famous brother, and replied that in his opinion future ages would look upon Napoleon not so much as a great man as a good man. That sounds a preposterous example of fraternal blindness, but all the same I think it contains an element of profound truth. Napoleon was one of the greatest of leaders, and in so far as he was great he was also, in the largest sense of the word, good. When he was base he ceased to be great and failed. When he was swinging from victory to victory, pruning the rottenness from Europe and patiently devising the rebuilding of France, he forgot his personal ambitions in something worthier.

We can make a catalogue of the moral qualities of the greatest leaders, but we cannot exhaust them. First, of course, there will be fortitude, the power of enduring when hope has gone, the power of taking upon oneself a desperate responsibility and daring all. There must be self-forgetfulness, a willingness to let worldly interests, and even reputation and honour, perish, if only the task be accomplished. The man who is concerned with his own repute will never move mountains. There must be patience, supreme patience under misunderstandings and set-backs, and the muddles and interferences of others. There must be resilience in defeat, a manly optimism, which looks at the facts in all their bleakness and yet dares to hope. There must be a sense of the eternal continuity of a great cause, so that failure will not seem the end, and a man sees himself as only a part in a predestined purpose. And another quality will not, I think, be lacking in the greatest leaders—I mean human sympathy. We see it in Julius Caesar's magnanimity, in Robert Lee's tenderness and chivalry, in that something in Napoleon at his best which bound the souls of his veterans to him, and which was far more than his record of unbroken triumph. A great leader lays his spell not only on the mind and spirit, but on the heart of his people.

Leadership, then, depends primarily upon moral endowments. And now we return to the intellectual side which we discarded, for, in the distinction between the great leaders of the world, the principal difference seems to me to be an intellectual one. Granted, in more or less degree, the moral qualities I have enumerated, there are two main schools of leadership distinguished by the type of mind possessed—the mind, and that compost of the conscious and the unconscious which we call temperament. I will call them roughly the narrow and the broad—the man with the single idea to which every force of his nature is devoted : and the man who looks calmly and steadily on the world and owes his power to the breadth and lucidity rather than to the fiery concentration of his soul. To the first school belong the great destructive forces in history, the 'Scourges of God,' the Attilas and the Timours; most preachers of new religions like Mohammed; iconoclasts like Luther and Calvin and John Knox; leaders of crusades, like Peter the Hermit and Ignatius Loyola. Such men may build, but their primary task is to break down. To the second school belong the moderates whose impulse is primarily a reasoned conviction, and whose daimonic energy is not due to any fever of the heart. These are the constructive leaders, and history has many to show. Such was Julius Caesar; such were Charlemagne and our own Alfred; such were Henri IV of France and William the Silent and (though some may not agree with me) Oliver Cromwell; such, on the whole, was Napoleon; such, emphatically, beyond the Atlantic were George Washington, Abraham Lincoln, and Robert Lee. . . . And such was Montrose.

A little more than a year ago we celebrated the tercentenary of John Bunyan, a man who had his roots very deep in English soil and understood most fully the nature of his countrymen. Now, in his writings you get a great many characters who have their counterparts in ordinary life, and in particular he has drawn many portraits of fighting men. There is one thing to be noted about Bunyan's chief figures—they use their brains. They do not fight merely for fighting's sake. His famous leaders, Mr. Greatheart, Mr. Standfast, Mr. Valiant-for-Truth, are all reasonable people who use their heads as well as their hands. He has given us portraits of the other kind, and they are rarely effective folk. There is Captain Anything, for example, a brisk lad in a broil, but of no use to any side. There is Mr. Haughty in *The Holy War*, who declared that he cared not on which side he fought so long as he acquitted himself well, and, as you remember, Mr. Haughty was duly hanged. And even when Bunyan draws a good man who has not much intelligence he makes him not a leader, but a follower, and the kind of follower who has to be constantly helped along. Take the delightful figure of Old Honest. Mr. Honest, Bunyan says, came from the town of Stupidity which 'lieth four degrees *beyond* the City of Destruction'—that is, four degrees farther off from the Celestial City. Bunyan had no admiration for an empty head, even when it was combined with an honest heart.

Now, I do not wish for one moment to deny the value of the first school I have described—the narrow, absorbed, single-ideaed leaders, whom we may call the fanatics. As compared with the false moderates who play only for safety and believe that the right course in any dispute is to halve the difference—

as compared with the intellectuals who are governed by a thin mechanical logic—they must always win. At certain stages in the world's history destruction, wholesale and single-hearted destruction, has been the one thing needful. In certain crises, when something evil has to be rooted out, moderation and toleration may be synonyms for moral apathy and spiritual sloth. Men cannot be led to a worthy purpose by one who has his flag firmly nailed to the fence. Yet—and this rule has no exception—the extremist will only be a constructive as well as a destroying force if his extremism is based upon reason, and not upon the surrender of reason—upon a clear facing of facts, and not upon their emotional simplification. We dare not underrate the power of fanaticism, even of the craziest kind. Its strength comes from its narrowness, since its spiritual force has been canalised and brought to a mighty head of water. It has done great things in history, but these things have been principally negative—necessary negations often, but still negations. Moreover, there is no finality about its work, for there is always the certainty that it will produce a counter-fanaticism, since it is based upon a half-truth, and the world will find this out. An arbitrary conception of the Divine will induce a blind denial of its existence at all. A fanatic glorification of the State will produce as its corrective a fanatic individualism. Therefore I suggest to you that the moderate is the more valuable type of leader, for, while the other type may do wonderful work in pulling down a crazy structure, it is he who has the constructive task and builds a new home for mankind. The Beatitude of the Meek, in the Sermon on the Mount, is true in the most literal and practical sense. It is the meek, the moderates, who inherit the earth.

I propose to examine with you shortly some of the characteristics of the true moderate, with special reference to the career of Montrose.

1. In the first place he makes certain of the faith that is in him. He is not content to take facts or formulas at second-hand; he tries all things; he refuses to believe on hearsay. Such an attitude involves a certain amount of honest scepticism. It was Charles James Fox who said that some measure of scepticism was the only basis of toleration. If you have thought out

your faith, and not swallowed it blindly, you will be tolerant of
those who have passed through the same intellectual process and
reached different conclusions. But none the less you will be
more firmly established in your faith than the fanatic, for you
will be secure against sceptical doubts. Having been through
that stage yourself, you will have raised the doubts and answered
them. The moderate can never be a barren dogmatist. He does
not spend his time, like Sir Walter Scott's Old Mortality, in
deepening the inscriptions on tombstones. He realises that
there are eternal truths, but that they require a frequent restate-
ment; and he knows that most of our rules of life are not eternal
truths, but working conventions, which must often be drastically
overhauled to make certain that they have not survived their
usefulness. But at the same time he will not underrate the
value of the inscriptions on tombstones, and he will treat
reverently whatever has been an inspiration to mankind, till the
last dregs of inspiration have departed.

Montrose had this intellectual courage. When he returned
to Scotland in 1636 at the age of twenty-four, he found these
islands distracted with conflicting dogmas—a theory of monarchy
which belonged to the Middle Ages set against a rootless parlia-
mentarianism for which the times were not ripe—a high-flying
doctrine of Episcopacy set against a not less high-flying doctrine
of Presbytery. What did he do ? He set himself during eight
difficult years to think out the problems for himself. He did not
drug his soul with easy loyalties, and he had the courage and
the candour to look facts in the face. For the first problem, the
problem of civil government, you will find his conclusions in his
Discourse on Sovereignty, to my mind the most penetrating study
of the foundations of government which the seventeenth century
produced. His first principle was the Rule of Law. There must
be some 'power over the people above which power there is
none on earth'; this power is limited by the laws of God and
nature, the law of nations, and what he called the 'law fundamental' of the country; but these limitations are inherent in
itself and it cannot be divided among competing authorities.
He held no brief for monarchy, except that it was a form of
sovereignty which the British people had accepted, but he held
a very clear brief for law. If law were once weakened by con-

flicting sovereignties within the same nation, then the security had gone for the liberties of the ordinary man. You cannot, he said, have a government unless it fulfils this first requirement, which is indispensable in all governments. He was a man of his age, and he did not foresee modern parliamentary developments, and the nature of modern democracy. But one thing he foresaw, the cardinal principle which alone gives value to any government. He laid down certain fundamentals which no nation, ancient or modern, has ever departed from, except to its own undoing.

As for the ecclesiastical question, he was from first to last a devout Presbyterian and loyal to the Reformed Kirk of Scotland. He began, you remember, as an enthusiast for its rights, and was one of the champions of the National Covenant, first read in the church of Grey Friars in Edinburgh on the last day of February 1638. That Covenant enshrines a logical and historically sound ecclesiastical nationalism. He drew the sword on its behalf, and, indeed, went to extreme lengths for a man of his temper in enforcing it. But when the church leaders in Scotland moved away from it to the policy that culminated in the Solemn League and Covenant, under which the Kirk encroached upon the sphere of civil government, and demanded, as the price of an alliance with the English Parliament, an enforcement of their special polity upon an unwilling England, Montrose drew back. That way lay anarchy and confusion in Scotland, for it meant in practice a theocracy on a feudal basis, an intolerant Kirk, and a free licence to a factious aristocracy, provided that aristocracy remained orthodox.

Observe the intellectual courage shown in Montrose's conduct. Here was a man who was deeply committed to the cause of the Kirk, who had been flattered and given high command by its leaders, among whom were nearly all his boyhood's friends. It took no small strength of mind to break with it and follow the path of his convictions. Montrose would far rather have been with Alexander Henderson than against him. A man of his antecedents had more in common with the minister of Leuchars, and, indeed, with many of the Covenanting nobles, than with light-headed feudal satraps like Huntly and the *condottieri* of the North. Notice another point. A weaker man, having broken with the Kirk on one point, would have broken with it on all. But Montrose never wavered in his devotion to the Church of Scotland, the Church which after a century or two of confusion was to accept his doctrine of Church polity. In his dying speech he regretted his severance from his old communion. 'I am sorry,' he said, 'they did excommunicate me; and in that which is according to God's laws, without wronging my conscience or allegiance, I desire to be relaxed. If they will not do it, I appeal to God, who is the righteous Judge of the world, and will, I hope, be my Judge and Saviour.' The day before, in his appearance before Parliament, he said, 'The Covenant which I took I own it and adhere to it. Bishops, I care not for them. I never intended to advance their interests.' It is a pleasing irony of history that one of his chief Covenanting opponents, Mr. Robert Baillie, Principal of Glasgow University, on almost the first page of his famous journal, wrote 'Bishops I love.'

2. In the second place, and as a corollary to the fruitful scepticism which I have mentioned, the moderate must keep his mind bright and clear. He must preserve a perpetual intellectual vigilance. He must never become fixed and muscle-bound in his creed. He must always be ready to change and adapt, for only thus can he remain faithful to the reason which is within him.

Montrose had no cause to change his main creed, for he had attained to it only after deep thought and heart-searching, and it remains the one rational and fruitful doctrine in that age of half-truths. But we can judge of the hard training in which he kept his mind by the way in which he adapted his military tactics to novel contingencies. I am not going to enlarge upon this subject, for it requires maps to make it clear, but it will be patent to any one who studies carefully Montrose's campaigns. Let me mention only a few obvious points. He picked up his military training in a very inferior school, but, being a great natural soldier, he penetrated very soon to the inner principles of strategy, which are eternal things, and his mental powers enabled him to revise the cumbrous tactics of his day. Long before Cromwell's New Model, he adopted the plan of Gustavus Adolphus of the three front ranks in an infantry line firing simultaneously. He was bold enough, in order to get a broad front of fire, to reduce his files to three instead of six. He was a pioneer of shock tactics for cavalry before the New Model. He insisted on his troops reserving their fire till close quarters, which, you remember, became one of the great devices of the British Army under Marlborough and after. And, to take a last instance, at the battle of Auldearn he weakened his right wing and used it as the hinge on which the rest of his force swung to break the enemy's centre—an anticipation of Napoleon's famous manœuvre at Austerlitz.

3. In the third place, the moderate has all the other kinds of courage. I have specified intellectual courage. Physical courage may be taken for granted in one who aspires to lead brave men and take the risks which leadership involves. The true moderate will also have that moral courage which is a great deal talked about and too rarely practised. The false moderate has, of course, no courage at all. He is the common trimmer whose motto is 'safety first,' and who is determined never to give himself away. The fanatic has his own kind of courage, but not, I think, the highest kind. You will hear people, in the midst of the most delicate uncertainties, talking grandly about taking a bold line, about sticking to their principles, about backing their side. But that noisy clamour is more often a sign of weakness than of strength. Extreme courses are easy to follow. They only require blind eyes and a hot temper, and the kind of Dutch courage which temper gives. It is a far rarer kind of courage to insist upon facing the facts, even when it may involve an appearance of inconsistency and the surrender of part of a man's creed. There was a famous Scotsman, the late Lord Minto, who, when he was Viceroy of India, once laid down in a public speech a principle which seems to me to deserve to rank as one of the great maxims of public conduct. 'The strongest man,' he said, 'is the man who is not afraid to be called weak.'

The final test of moral courage is the ability to stand alone. Montrose is a conspicuous example. Before his great decision in 1644 he was very nearly alone in Scotland, for he was in full agreement neither with Covenanter nor with Cavalier. When he visited the Court at Oxford in the early months of 1644 he

s

was altogether alone. He was the only man whose spirit still burned bright in the midst of perplexities. He offered, you remember, to raise Scotland for the King, but at the moment it seemed as if Scotland had effectually risen for the King's opponents. The strong hand of Parliament and the General Assembly lay over the land; the Cavalier nobles were quarrelling among themselves, and by most of them Montrose was either suspected or disliked. But so strong was his faith, so compelling was his ardour, that he forced his will upon the King and his timid counsellors. He was given his commission, and rode alone by the North road out of Oxford to conquer Scotland. Six months later, as you remember, with two companions and four horses he crossed the Border and reached the Highland line. It took a steely courage to begin the conquest of a country with such meagre strength. But, as you know, in six months more he had succeeded, and Scotland lay at his feet. You find the same swift daring, the same power of accepting any responsibility, even the most crushing, in every phase of his campaigns. You find it at Inverlochy when, pinned between two superior forces, he decided that the boldest course was the safest, and, swinging back on a flank march among wintry mountains, which is one of the great exploits in our history, drove Argyll into the sea. You find it when, after Philiphaugh, he refused to give up hope and conducted a losing battle among the snow-clad hills of the North. He had that finest of all kinds of courage which you find expressed in his own song. He was always willing 'to put it to the touch, to win or lose it all.'

If I might take a modern parallel I would take it from the career of one who was recently Chancellor of this University. On a certain day in September 1918 Douglas Haig was forced to take a great decision. He saw that it was altogether necessary in the interests of civilisation that the War should be brought to an end before Christmas. He believed that it was possible, that it could be done by flinging his main armies there and then against the fortified entrenchments which the Germans called the Siegfried Line. His French colleagues were more than doubtful. The British Government was more than doubtful. Haig had to make the decision alone. If he failed, the responsibility would lie wholly on his shoulders, and it might mean the destruction of a large part of the British forces and a colossal expense of human life. He decided to take the great hazard, because he believed it to be his duty in his country's interests. We know the result. He went through the Siegfried Line as through blotting paper, and in six weeks the War was over. There is no finer instance of moral courage in all our history, and across the gulf of the centuries the St. Andrews under-graduate of three hundred years ago and the St. Andrews Chancellor of our own day join hands in the brotherhood of those who put fear behind them.

4. In the fourth place, true moderation involves intellectual modesty and a sensitive humanity. I do not think you can have humanity without humility. You cannot understand your neighbour's point of view if you are too dogmatic about your own, just as you cannot sympathise with your neighbour's troubles if you are too much occupied with your own. One feature of fanaticism is its arrogance. It does not attempt to understand its opponents, but is content to despise them. The moderate's maxim is that of the old Irish bishop Malachi in the eleventh century, who thus summarised the stages of human progress, *Spernere mundum, spernere sese, spernere nullum*—you begin by despising the world, you go on to despise yourself, and you end by despising nothing and nobody.

For Montrose this modesty and humility were, I think, a late growth. In his youth we know that he was very stately and ceremonious, gracious to his friends, but a little haughty towards the world. That is a common trait of imaginative youth. Its sensitive pride is both a defensive armour and a defiance, and its boyish stateliness is its announcement to the world of the great part it has set itself to play. We know, too, that later, when he had begun his career of action, he was apt to despise those whom he did not like. He consistently underrated, for example, the abilities of Argyll. But he was purified by suffering, and at the last he seems to have lost every trace of that arrogance. In Bacon's great words, he has the face of one who pities humanity. If we want an instance of Christian meekness I do not know where we will find a better than in Montrose's behaviour during the long march as a prisoner from the North, and in his trial before Parliament, and in his conversations with the exultant ministers, and, most of all, in his speech on the scaffold. You remember one passage in that speech :

I desire not to be mistaken (he said), as if my carriage at this time, in relation to your ways, were stubborn. I do but follow the light of my conscience, my rule; which is seconded by the working of the Spirit of God that is within me. . . . If He enable me against the fear of death, and furnish me with courage and confidence to embrace it even in its most ugly shape, let God be glorified in my end, though it were in my damnation. . . . I have no more to say, but that I desire your charity and prayers. . . . I leave my soul to God, my service to my prince, my love and charity to you all.

5. Lastly, the moderate having brought all the powers of his mind to the shaping of his creed, will lose himself in that creed. He will become the most formidable type in the world, far more formidable, far more intransigent than any fanatic, for he has behind him not only the powers of emotion but the powers of thought. He will not be like Lord Falkland, troubled with doubts, doing his duty sadly and despairingly. He has no doubts, for he has gone through them all and reached the other side. He has become, if I may use a phrase I have used before, Reason armed and mailed, Philosophy with its sword unsheathed. He fights for his cause for its own sake, and not because of any ulterior rewards. You remember Robert Louis Stevenson's fable, in which a priest, a fakir, and an old rover with an axe go on a pilgrimage. The first two are fanatics in their creed, but in each case the belief is shallow, and depends on the future rewards of belief. But word comes that Odin has fallen, and that the Powers of Darkness have triumphed. Both priest and fakir are in a hurry to make terms with the conqueror, but the old rover with the axe goes off to die with Odin. That un-self-regarding virtue was the creed of the ancestors of some of us—the Norsemen who lived on the coast of Norway and harried these coasts a thousand years ago. In their creed Odin was destined some day to fall. Some day the Powers of Evil would be triumphant, and Odin and all his bright company would be overwhelmed in darkness. But that strange fatalism did not make the votaries of Odin falter in their worship, though they knew that their god was doomed, and that evil would triumph. They were

prepared to fall with Odin rather than triumph with the Powers of Darkness.

That is the only true and manly morality. I will give you another example, this time from the Old Testament, from the story of the three Hebrews, Shadrach, Meshach, and Abednego, whom King Nebuchadnezzar commanded to worship the golden image he had set up. You remember their answer? 'O Nebuchadnezzar, we are not careful to answer thee in this matter. *If it be so*, our God, whom we serve, is able to deliver us from the burning fiery furnace.' Well, you will say there is nothing remarkable in that. It is a cautious defiance; they were fanatics in their creed, and thought themselves safe. But how does it go on? '*But if not*' (no caution there), '*but if not*, be it known unto thee, O King, that we will not serve thy gods nor worship the golden image which thou hast set up.' Even though their God failed them they were determined to be true to themselves.

I think we may fairly say that Montrose before the end of his short life attained to this high virtue. He triumphed over fear in the completest sense; he triumphed over the world; he triumphed over himself. So purged were spirit and heart that to some of us he seems, before his actual death, almost to have shed the garments of mortality. I cannot find better words to describe that mood and that triumph than those with which Shelley concludes his noblest poem:

> To suffer woes which Hope thinks infinite;
> To forgive wrongs darker than death or night;
> To defy Power, which seems omnipotent;
> To love and bear; to hope till hope creates
> From its own wreck the thing it contemplates;
> Neither to change, nor falter, nor repent;
> This like thy glory, Titan, is to be
> Good, great and joyous, beautiful and free;
> This is alone Life, Joy, Empire, and Victory!

One last word. We may analyse leadership meticulously, like a chemical compound, but we shall never extract its inner essence. There will always be something which escapes us, for in leadership there is a tincture of the miraculous. Take Montrose and his rough following. I do not suppose there were more heterogeneous materials on the face of the globe than

the various elements which he combined into an army. For a
year he united the whole of the central Highlands, and he won
his authority, not by pandering to the vices of savage warfare,
but by a scrupulous and chivalrous observation of the decencies
almost unknown among his contemporaries. What gave this
slim, grave, scholarly young man that iron authority over fire-
eating giants like Alasdair Macdonald, and his fighting men of
the Homeric age? Take that occasion at Dundee when in the
middle of a sack he drew off half-tipsy troops in the face of a
superior enemy force, and led them, weary to the bone as they
were, over thirty miles in the darkness of night to the safety of
the hills. Take that last great pageant of his entry into Edinburgh as a doomed man.˙ He was tied with cords and set up
in the hangman's cart, and the Edinburgh populace, the men
and women who had lost their kin in his wars, lined the cause-
way with stones and mud. But not a stone was thrown. Instead,
the curses of the people were turned into tears and prayers.
What was the reason of these miracles?

I should define the miraculous element as a response of
spirit to spirit. There is in all men, even the basest, some
kinship with the divine, something which is capable of rising
superior to common passions and the lure of easy rewards,
superior to pain and loss, superior even to death. The true
leader evokes this. The greatness in him wins a response, an
answering greatness in his followers. Montrose appealed to that
god-like something in his rough levies so that even in their cups
they followed him blindly. He appealed to that divine something in the Edinburgh mob when, for one moment, bound
and despised as he was, he became their leader, and they his
followers. You will find it all through history, whether it be
the response to the appeal of saints and crusaders and great
captains, or Mazzini winning ignorant men to an unselfish
ideal, or John Wesley evoking the spiritual power of the rudest
and most degraded classes in England. The task of leadership
is not to put greatness into humanity, but to elicit it, for the
greatness is already there.

VI
LORD ROSEBERY

LORD ROSEBERY

In the roll of the more eminent British statesmen during the last two centuries there is evident, it seems to me, a certain broad uniformity of talent. Their gifts, it is true, varied surprisingly, but they were all gifts for politics and the conduct of public affairs. The instances are few where we can detect abilities wholly divorced from those desirable in public life. One thinks of Canning and Disraeli, and in both cases their non-political aptitudes were drawbacks in popular esteem; and the versatility of the latter was only forgiven when it became apparent to all men that affairs were his true passion. Britain demands that her statesmen shall be whole-hearted servants. She loves the professional, and will accept the amateur only when his conduct makes it clear that his chief desire is to rise to professional status.

But what makes for success in a public career does not as a rule give assurance of immortality. The great figures, who during their lifetime were the idols of the people and the autocrats of the State, are apt to become to posterity dim shadows, which only to the historian attain a simulacrum of life. Walpole is remembered better perhaps by his after-dinner talk than by his years of adroit government. What are now the omnipotent Whig Lords, who staffed the Georgian cabinets? No more than names, while Edmund Burke, who never held high office, is an influence more potent than in his life. For immortality a statesman must either play so sounding a part in the world, that, like Chatham and Pitt, his speeches become deeds, and his life has the drama of that of a great soldier, or he must have qualities which are communicable to later generations. Speeches will not often do it, for the oratory of Gladstone and Bright is already as dead as Queen Anne; it was successful because it was topical, satisfying a temporary mood, which cannot be recaptured. Books may do it, or some whim of personality or oddness of mind which made its possessor a centre of good stories. We remember Halifax and Bolingbroke and Fox and Canning, when political careers of greater achievement are thick with dust. Disraeli is a never-ending interest to his successors, while Peel and Gladstone are only notables in the history books.

I

Lord Rosebery has left so much for the world to judge him by that I am inclined to the belief that, after Disraeli, he is the figure in recent statecraft which will most interest posterity —he, and for very different reasons, Mr. Lloyd George. There is, first, the interest of his personality and career. He came of a curiously varied stock; on his mother's side a nephew of Lord Stanhope the historian, and a great-nephew of Lady Hester Stanhope, and so kin to the Pitt family; on his father's side sprung from the Scots *noblesse de robe*, one of whom took the side of Montrose. At Eton his tutor, William Cory, described him as 'a portentously wise youth, not, however, deficient in fun,' and the young man, who chose to be sent down from Oxford rather than give up his racehorses, was clearly modelling himself on some grand seigneur out of history or Disraeli's novels, to whom versatility and a certain easy condescension upon accomplishments were the first of the virtues.

In those early years he must have worked hard behind the scenes, for when he appears in public he is precociously mature, not only abundantly well read, but the master of a style which has an eighteenth-century rotundity and finish. It is a marvel that a young man, who had so many preoccupations other than scholastic, should have entered upon the world so well equipped. In 1871, at the age of twenty-four, he addressed the Philosophical Society of Edinburgh on 'The Union of England and Scotland,' an address abounding in happy phrase and pregnant epigram. James had 'turned the Privy Council Chamber of Scotland into a dissecting-room'; the career of Hamilton 'is one which may well be spared from history to be framed in fiction, for it derives but little lustre from facts'; 'that they (Belhaven's speeches) were absurdly pedantic, that they were painfully prepared to the very least monosyllable, that the delivery no less than the style was intolerably affected, are hindrances perhaps to our pleasure in reading them, but formed no obstacle to their popularity in Scotland.' And he concluded in that high manner which he was afterwards to make familiar to the world :—'Our ancestors put their hands to a mighty work, and it prospered. They welded two great nations into one great Empire, and moulded local jealousies into a common patriotism. On such an achievement we must gaze with awe and astonishment, the means were so adverse and the result so surprising. But we should look on it also with emulous eyes. Great as the Union was, a greater still remains.' In 1871 there was no one speaking with quite the precision and perfection of this young gentleman of twenty-four.

Nine years later he is addressing the students of Aberdeen as their Lord Rector, and his subject is again taken from Scottish history. He is the patriot, but he is also the moralist, who sees as a background to all temporal triumphs the Dance of Death, and knows how to solemnise as well as to kindle. Yet he is a young man addressing men little younger.

And how solemn a moment is that passing forth from the cloisters of learning into the great Vanity Fair of the world, there to make, for good or for evil, the choice of Hercules and to abide by the result. Even I may, without presumption, indicate to you the crucial importance of that crisis of your lives, when it lies with you to decide whether your career shall be a heritage of woe or a fruitful blessing and an honoured memory. Day by day the horizon of human possibility, which now lies so unbounded before you, must contract; the time must come when, under the stroke of illness, and the decay of nature, hope, and health, the pride and power of life and intellect, which now seem so inseparable from your triumphant youth, will have passed away.

The man who could strike such notes, who could on the right occasion force his hearers to view a topic *sub specie aeternitatis*, was clearly cast for a great part in public life. It was in a sense an advantage that he was excluded by his birth from the House of Commons, for, not being content with the narrow arena of the House of Lords, he was able to speak *urbi et orbi* and reach directly the masses of his countrymen. He was especially fitted to capture the heart of Scotland; his quick sentiment for her past, his gift of hero-worship, his emotional power, his grave and exalted rhetoric, his subtle humour, soon gave him a position only second to Mr. Gladstone's. In the early 'eighties, after the famous Midlothian campaign, in which he played Eugene to Mr. Gladstone's Marlborough, he was by far the most promising and interesting figure in politics. He had not yet developed a political creed of his own, but was still the faithful Gladstonian, with perhaps a more democratic flavour in his faith than was possible to a product of early nineteenth-century Oxford. The young nobleman with popular sympathies is apt to be a somewhat ridiculous figure, like some virtuous character out of *Sandford and Merton*; the world, judging by the Rockinghams and Lafayettes of history, suspects a lack of humour and of common humanity. But Lord Rosebery had both humour and fun; moreover, he was already known as an enthusiastic sportsman. He seemed to be able to combine every appeal; a lofty puritanism, like Cromwell's, which, like Cromwell, he united to a passion for horses; a glowing liberalism, an imaginative patriotism, and that gift of shining words which is independent of creed and even of character.

II

In 1885 he entered the Cabinet, and in 1886 he was Secretary for Foreign Affairs. In those days, when politics for him were still touched with glamour, he was one of the most industrious and indefatigable of Ministers. For foreign affairs he had a natural talent, since his imagination gave him insight into the hearts of other peoples, and travel and reading had amply informed his mind. His influence determined British policy on several critical questions, and in the St. Lucia Bay negotiations he was credited by no less an authority than Bismarck with proving 'too sharp' for Germany. Few more laborious and business-like statesmen have presided at the Foreign Office, and he took his full share also in the work of Parliamentary debate, though the fact that his speeches were made in the House of Lords a little detracted from their public appeal. Here is an example of his Parliamentary manner:

'You should forget party,' said the Duke of Argyll. . . . The

Duke of Argyll cannot forget his party, because his party is himself. Whatever may be your wisdom, however noble may be your aspirations, when you have a party in that compact and singular, I might almost say that portable form, it is one of which you cannot divest yourself, and it is one of which I think the Duke, on reflection, would be unwilling to divest himself.

And later in the same speech:

Now, if all hope of union has not fled before this, it is due, in my opinion, mainly to the patience of our leaders, who, when they have been buffeted on one cheek, have meekly offered the other. But I am bound to say this, that the time may come when we shall reach an end both of our patience and of our cheeks.

At this period in his career he had an extraordinary appetite for work, even for its dry-as-dust details, for he had always an imaginative vision to console him. In 1889 he took up the business of London municipal politics as the first chairman of the County Council, and won a high reputation for skill in the handling of both men and affairs. Moreover, he was no longer the docile Gladstonian, deep as was his attachment to his leader. He felt the great legacy of the past in every fibre, and he began to dream of an Imperial unity which should make our Empire indeed a 'blessed and splendid dominion.'

But presently came to him that 'contraction of the horizon of human possibility,' of which nine years before he had warned the Aberdeen students. The death of his wife in 1890 was the beginning of a serious breakdown in health, and he began to suffer from insomnia, that most terrible of scourges to a man who works with voice and brain.

The rest of his political career was to be somewhat shadowed. As Foreign Secretary in the last Gladstone Government he did splendid and far-sighted work with regard to Egypt and the Nile valley, Uganda and Siam; but when in 1894 the mantle of his leader descended to him and he succeeded to the Premiership, he was already a tired man. This is not the place in which to write the tale of his short administration. He was out of sympathy with most of his colleagues; he was something less than lukewarm about the principal Gladstonian policy, Irish

Home Rule; in foreign affairs he seemed to the ordinary Liberal to be too much of a Tory, and he could not speak with the proper unction of such matters as Disestablishment and Local Veto. Moreover, he had lost his hold upon the Nonconformists by the apparent levity of mind which could win the Derby two years running. Of this curious episode he has written himself.

After a quarter of a century of fruitless expectation, I won the Derby. But what was the result? . . . With very little knowledge of the facts, and with much less of that charity 'that thinketh no evil,' I was attacked with the greatest violence for owning a racehorse at all. I then made the discovery, which came to me too late in life, that what was venial and innocent in the other officers of the Government—in a Secretary of State or a President of the Council, for example—was criminal in the First Lord of the Treasury. I do not even know if I ought not to have learned another lesson—that although, without guilt and offence, I might perpetually run seconds and thirds, or even run last, it became a matter of torture to many consciences if I won.

His party was defeated at the polls, and opposition did not unite it. Mr. Gladstone in the following year raised the slogan of Armenian atrocities, and Lord Rosebery was unable to regard them as a sufficiently important cause for which to run the risk of a European war. With his old leader and the majority of Liberals against him, there could be no other course than retirement, and on October 9, 1896, at a meeting in Edinburgh, he took farewell of politics in one of the most dignified and moving of valedictory speeches ever spoken by a British statesman. The man who could thus speak of Mr. Gladstone had great qualities of magnanimity and justice:

Perhaps Mr. Gladstone has been the indirect cause, or the latest indirect cause, of the action which I have thought right to take. . . . But let none think that for that reason I have regretted his intervention in the Armenian question. It is now seventeen years since Mr. Gladstone came to Midlothian. I remember then making a speech in which I said that we welcomed the sight of a great statesman, full of years and full of honours, coming down at his advanced period of life to fight one supreme battle on behalf of liberty in Europe. Little did I think then that seventeen years later I should see a still nobler sight—a statesman—the same statesman—fuller still of years, and, if possible, still fuller of honours, coming out and leaving a well-earned retirement, which the whole world watches with tenderness and solicitude, to fight another battle, but I hope not the last, on behalf of the principles in which his life has been spent.

So ended Lord Rosebery's short enjoyment of the highest office and the leadership of a famous party. Thereafter, until the end of his life, he was virtually in retirement, although he made many public appearances and performed various pieces of work of high national importance. It has been the custom to assume that his political career was a failure, that he failed, while earnestly desiring success, because of some hidden flaw of character or mind. It has been said that he was intolerant of the drudgery and the sacrifices which are entailed in the service of the State. William Cory's phrase is quoted that 'he desired the palm without the dust.' I believe that the truth is exactly the opposite. I believe that he became disillusioned about the palm, and saw the laurels—of politics at any rate—as a dingy and fast-fading garland. Walter Bagehot once said truly that a successful English statesman should be a man of common ideas and uncommon abilities. Lord Rosebery was uncommon both in abilities and ideas. There were too many personalities bound up in him for that concentration and single-heartedness which is possible to narrower souls. In part this was due to accident; he had been born, so to speak, in the purple, and had reached the highest honours too soon and too easily to value them in the same way as a man who wins them at the end of a long and difficult contest. In part it was due to certain frailties of body and temperament. His delicately balanced nervous system was unfitted for the rough-and-tumble of politics, he was acutely sensitive, and, however impassive his demeanour might be in the face of attacks, he had not the happy gift of laughing and forgetting.

But the main reason, I believe, lay deeper, in an abiding sense of the vanity of human wishes and the transitoriness of life. His eye kept watch too constantly over man's mortality. He told the people of Bristol on one occasion that Burke's exclamation, 'What shadows we are and what shadows we pursue!' summed up 'the life of every politician and perhaps of every man.' Behind all his exterior urbanity and humour lay this haunting sense of transience, and, while to the world he seemed like some polished eighteenth-century grandee, at heart he was the Calvinist of seventeenth-century Scotland. Had he been faced in his public life with some desperate crisis like the Great War, I believe that he would have shed his temperamental weakness and become single-hearted indeed, with a spiritual force far more intense than that of any of the tribe of normal competent statesmen, who never doubted in their lives. But his work was with second-rate problems, the ordinary party scramble among half-truths, and both the task and the rewards came to seem to him too trivial to be worth his care.

It was, I repeat, not the dust that disquieted him but the frailty of the laurels. There is a passage on Sir Walter Raleigh, written by Sir Walter Raleigh's namesake, which—*mutatis mutandis*—appears to me to be applicable to Lord Rosebery:

He has the insolent imagination of Marlowe and the profound melancholy of Donne. 'The mind of man,' he says in his *History of the World*, 'hath two ports, the one always frequented by the entrance of manifold vanities; the other desolate and overgrown with grass, by which enter our charitable thoughts and divine contemplations.' Both gates of his mind stood open; worldly hopes and braggart ambitions crowd and jostle through one entrance, but the monitors of death and eternity meet them and whisper them in the ear. He schemes elaborately, even while he believes that 'the long day of mankind draweth fast towards an evening, and the world's tragedy and time are near at an end.' The irony of human affairs possesses his contemplation; his thoughts are high and fanciful; he condescends to action and fails, as all those fail whose work is done stooping. He is proud, sardonic, and aloof. His own boast is true—'There is none on the face of the earth that I would be fastened unto!' He takes part with others in no movement, and stakes little or nothing on the strength of human ties. The business of men on this earth seems trivial and insignificant against the vast desert of eternity.

III

As the years of his retirement passed, and his incursions into national affairs grew infrequent, he became more and more the Scots laird. He was at his happiest, I think, at Rosebery, his little moorland dwelling under the Moorfoots, where he shot, and walked, and entertained a few selected friends. He loved every acre of the Lothians, and took part in all the duties and interests of a country gentleman, a very full, varied, and, till his illness in 1918, active life. He kept in close touch with his political and racing friends, and one of the most valued was Lord Morley—a curious instance of the attraction of opposites. But his chief pleasure was his books. He had a noble library scattered throughout his many dwellings—the great Scots collection at Dalmeny and Barnbougle; the French memoirs and illustrated books at Mentmore; and his marvellous little library at the Durdans, so full of rarities that the casual visitor could scarcely believe them genuine. He was always a bibliophile and collector, but he was far more a reader, and there can have been few men of our time who ranged over such wide domains of literature. Everything was grist to his mill, except metaphysics, military history, and certain kinds of poetry—for his taste in poetry was strictly circumscribed.

It often happens that one who takes in a vast amount from books gives out little in the shape of books of his own, and Lord Rosebery's published list is small. He could have written the best memoirs of his day; he could have enriched the world with studies of statesmen done with an inner knowledge impossible to the ordinary historian; he could have produced an historical masterpiece on a dozen periods and subjects. But though he was more of an artist than a politician, and though literature was always his constant love, the lack of ordinary ambition prevented him from the concentration needed to produce a large work. What he has given us are mere casual studies, chips from a workshop where the *chef d'œuvre* may have been contemplated, but was never begun. But, small as the quantity is, I believe that it will endure, and will give him a permanent place in English literature. Many of his speeches must be included, for he is the only man since Burke—with

T

the exception of Disraeli—whose political orations have the salt of style to preserve them from decay. It is to be hoped that the best of them may soon be collected, for, with proper editorial explanations of the circumstances in which they were delivered, they will make a volume scarcely less fascinating than the *Miscellanies*.

Lord Rosebery's main interest was historical. It was a very practical interest. In his Rectorial Address at Aberdeen University he urged the provision of a Professorship of Scottish History, and in a Presidential Address to the Scottish History Society in November 1897 he outlined certain tasks which lay before Scottish historians—tasks which, since he spoke, have been largely fulfilled. As an historian he had all the graces desirable in that craft, and most of the more solid qualities. He was accurate; he was prepared to be laborious; he had an admirable faculty of judgment ; he had a quick imagination; he had an almost perfect style. But in a life of so many activities, lived so much in the public eye, it was impossible for him to produce any massive piece of historical work. He could not have found time to do the necessary research, and he had not that specific training which prevents an historian from being lost among his authorities. His sense of form was so acute that, if he had found himself compelled to delve among the overgrown debris of the past, he would speedily have lost patience. There is no task for which a special training is more necessary than the handling of the data of history. The circumstances of his life forced his historic interest into a special sphere— the domain of historical biography. For this particular form his talents were perfectly suited. He had no creed to preach; he left his facts, as a rule, to point the moral; he was not cumbered with any academic philosophy of history. And he possessed two rare and invaluable gifts in a high degree. One was a psychological insight which could see very deep into the heart of a character, and the other was an imagination which enabled him to reconstruct a scene of the past with so much truth and colour that it might seem as if he had himself been an eye-witness.

The chief books are the *Pitt*, the *Napoleon*, and the *Chatham*. Of these the first is the best planned, the most shapely, and the most perfect example of Lord Rosebery's urbane and classical prose—one of his two manners. Take such a specimen as this:

The uneasy whisper circulated, and the joints of the Lords became as water. The Peers who yearned for lieutenancies or regiments, for stars or strawberry leaves; the prelates who sought a larger sphere of usefulness; the minions of the bed-chamber and the janissaries of the closet; all, temporal or spiritual, whose convictions were unequal to their appetites, rallied to the royal nod.

The *Napoleon* is a brilliant *tour de force*, an acute study of character, but it is less satisfactory, for it is a defence of a paradox, and not all the author's ingenuity can command our assent. The *Chatham* is the natural sequel to the *Pitt*, and contains some of Lord Rosebery's most polished and incisive writing, but he is a little oppressed by the consciousness of the value of the new letters which he gives us, and is content too often to sink the critic in the pious editor.

It is in the two volumes of *Miscellanies*, however, that we find the most perfect and most characteristic specimens of his prose. He has two chief manners, which might be called the urbane and the apocalyptic, one derived from eighteenth-century and the other from seventeenth-century models; but both are also original in a true sense, a subtle reflex of mind and temperament. In both manners, too, we find what seems to me his greatest literary gift, his power of imaginative visualisation, as when he pictures Dr. Johnson returning to earth during the Lichfield celebrations, or the first Rector of St. Andrews living, like Swift's Struldbrug, through the centuries. He has the power of seeing the past as a pageant with no gaps in its processes, and, though he disliked philosophy, he has the philosopher's best endowment, the sense of relativity. And he has one special gift. He is extraordinarily clever at discovering small, unperceived, but significant details which illuminate the whole picture. For example, in his address on Burns at Dumfries, he points out that among the soldiers who lined the streets at Burns's funeral was one, Colonel Jenkinson of the Cinque Ports Fencible Cavalry, who afterwards became Prime Minister

as Lord Liverpool. Could anything add more to the tragic
irony of that scene than the presence of the disapproving Colonel
Jenkinson, the worthy, conventional English statesman, at the
obsequies of the dead poet?

The first manner, the Augustan, is the staple of his prose.
It is usually gently ironical, often whimsical, always full of
strong good sense, but it changes easily into a sober eloquence
which is close to poetry. It has also an agreeable and kindly
cynicism. In his address on Lord Salisbury he defines cynicism
as 'the parching up of a subject by the application to it of a
wit so dry as to be almost bitter'; and he adds, 'Is it not a
priceless advantage, when some untimely or importunate question is put, or some subject is advanced which it is not desirable
to discuss, to have the acid, the corrosive cynicism to apply
to it, to dissolve it, at any rate for the moment?'

Perhaps the best example is the paper on Lord Randolph
Churchill. It is a wonderful picture of a friend, affectionate,
discriminating, vivid in every line; but it is also a 'character'
in the seventeenth-century sense, like some excerpt from Clarendon, with a universal application, and full of insight into the
arcana of politics. There is the undercurrent of humour.
'Racing remained a passion with him to the end. Almost
every letter that I had from him in his last years of life was
about that sport. Let not ambition mock these homely joys.'
Or this: 'Poor Old Whig Party! Already moribund, if not
dead; never, at its best or worst, malignant or monstrous,
though no doubt a little hungry, a little selfish, and a trifle
narrow. It might possibly have been compared by a flatterer
to a slow-worm.' There are shrewd pieces of criticism: 'Randolph's humour may be fairly defined as burlesque conception,
set off by an artificial pomp of style; a sort of bombastic irony
. . . what one could imagine that Gibbon might have uttered
had he gone on the stump.' Or in a graver style:

No one reads old speeches any more than old sermons.
The industrious historian is compelled to explore them for the
purposes of political history, but it is a dreary and reluctant
pilgrimage. The more brilliant and telling they were at the
time, the more dolorous the quest. The lights are extinguished,
the flowers are faded, the voice seems cracked across the empty

space of years; it sounds like a message from a remote tele-
phone. One wonders if that can really be the scene that fascin-
ated and inspired. Was this the passage we thought so thrilling,
this the epigram that seemed to tingle, this the peroration that
evoked such a storm of cheers? It all seems as flat as decanted
champagne. . . . All the accompaniments have disappeared—
the heat, the audience, the interruptions, and the applause—and
what remains seems cold and flabby.

And graver still:

The fairy godmother had perhaps denied him one necessary
gift, but she had given him all, or almost all, the others. Many
have risen to the highest places with far less of endowment. And
even with his unfulfilled promise he must be remembered as one
of the most meteoric of Parliamentary figures, as the shooting-
star of politics, and as one who, when in office, strove for a
broad and enlightened policy, to which he pledged his faith and
his career. He will be pathetically memorable, too, for the dark
cloud which gradually enveloped him, and in which he passed
away. He was the chief mourner at his own protracted funeral
—a public pageant of gloomy years. Will he not be remembered
as much for the anguish as for the fleeting triumphs of his life?
It is a black moment when the heralds proclaim the passing of
the dead and the great officers break their staves. But it is a
sadder still when it is the victim's own voice that announces his
decadence, when it is the victim's own hands that break the
staff in public.

It is on the note of mortality that Lord Rosebery's prose
reaches its highest levels, when he halts to contemplate the
vanity of fame, when he watches a great career pass from light
to shadow, and most of all when, in a happier faith, he sees
in death a sowing unto life. Now and then in this mood he
becomes almost theatrical, which is perhaps the nemesis of
the great orator; but his lapses are rare. In such prose urbanity
is not the quality, but rather a lofty and solemn eloquence, a
cadence like the tolling of a bell, and an apocalyptic vision
which haunts the mind like great poetry. There are many
such passages. One of the most famous is on Cromwell:

How does he appear to us? He comes tramping down to
us through the ages in his great wide boots, a countenance

swollen and reddish, a voice harsh, sharp, and untunable, with a country-made suit, a hat with no band, doubtful linen with a speck of blood upon it. He tramps over England, he tramps over Scotland, he tramps over Ireland, his sword in one hand, his Bible in the other. Then he tramps back to London, from whence he puts forth that heavy foot of his into Europe, and all Europe bows before him. When he is not scattering enemies and battering castles he is scattering Parliaments and battering general assemblies. He seems to be the very spirit of destruction, an angel of vengeance permitted to reign for a season to efface what he had to efface, and then to disappear. Then there comes the end. The prophetic Quaker sees the 'waft of death' go out against that man, there is a terrible storm, and he lies dying in Whitehall, groaning out that his work is done, that he will not drink or sleep, that he wishes to 'make what haste he can to be gone'; and the sun as it rises on his great day, the 3rd of September, the day of Dunbar and of Worcester, finds Cromwell speechless, and, as it sets, leaves him dead.

There are other such passages in his speeches; there is the famous conclusion of his Glasgow Rectorial address on the British Empire 'growing as trees grow while others slept,' which good judges have considered the high-water mark of his eloquence. But I should select rather the meditation on the same theme in his Glasgow address on Burns:

Man, after all, is not ripened by virtue alone. Were it so, this world were a paradise of angels. No! Like the growth of the earth, he is the fruit of all the seasons; the accident of a thousand accidents, a living mystery, moving through the seen to the unseen.

He presents the combination, rare in our literature, of sagacity and vision, solid earth and 'high translunary things,' as if the gifts of Addison and Sir Thomas Browne were conjoined, and the ruffles and stiff skirts of the Georgian senator could change suddenly to the mantle of the prophet.

IV

I have left to the last that side of Lord Rosebery which will be no more than a phrase to posterity, his singular personal charm. I cannot judge how he appeared to his coevals; I can only write of how he appeared to one thirty years his junior. Our friendship began when I was a very young man at Oxford; till the War we used to walk together every August on the Moorfoot Hills; and in later years scarcely a month passed without our meeting or exchanging letters. I have been privileged to know, and in some cases to know well, most of the people of our time whose personalities have influenced their contemporaries, but I can fairly say that I never knew any one, man or woman, who diffused a charm so rare and abiding as he did. Partly it came from his physical endowments, his clear meditative blue eyes, his rich and musical voice. I have been told by those qualified to judge that no other voice of our time, except Mr. Spurgeon's, was comparable to Lord Rosebery's for compass and flexibility and beauty. Partly, of course, it was due to his great powers of mind, his deep reading, his extraordinary memory, his wide experience of men and affairs. A man who has lived in the best society of every foreign capital and has known intimately people, like Bismarck and Gladstone, who to most of us are only resounding names, starts with a considerable advantage in the art of conversation. But the quality of his talk did not depend upon reminiscence. Everything was passed through the crucible of a most critical mind.

His moods were apt to vary. He could be caustic and destructive, a master in the art of denigration; he could be punctiliously judicial; in certain matters he refused to be other than freakish, making brilliant fun out of bogus solemnities; he had also his deep and sober loves. To hear him talk of certain friends, certain books and figures of the past like Dr. Johnson and Sir Walter Scott, was to listen to a boyish enthusiasm. In all he said there was the antiseptic of humour and sound judgment. He took nothing at second hand, and his admirations were as individual as his antipathies. I have heard his talk called cynical, but the word is a misnomer. In all he said there was gusto, which is the opposite of cynicism, and when he condemned it was with a kind of frosty geniality. But the marvel of his conversation was its form. He spoke finished prose as compared with the slovenly patois of most of us, and his thoughts clothed themselves naturally with witty and memorable words. It seemed like listening to some *revenant* from the eighteenth century, except that his manner was lighter and more exquisite than the recorded specimens of Augustan talk. I have noticed the same finish in the conversation of elderly judges, but theirs was apt to be ponderous, while his was always light and delicate like the play of a rapier.

Yet, when all this is said, I think that the source of his charm lay deeper, in his large wise kindliness and simplicity: He was far too proud to show anything but a firm front to the world, and too shy to be forthcoming, and these qualities gave him a reserve of manner which to many argued a lack of heart. He seemed to a casual acquaintance to be the brilliant man who stood aside and commented, a detached and somewhat inhuman figure, remote alike from mortal frailties and mortal virtues. The impression was false; his show of detachment was the protective armour to defend a too quick sympathy and a too sensitive heart. He had won much from life in fame and honour and opportunities, but he had also suffered sorely from it, and both gains and losses were relegated to silence. As he saw his world growing empty, and the son who was the pride of his life cut off in his promise, he wrapped round him the mantle of a noble stoicism. In these last years he became detached indeed, but it was the detachment which philosophers praise—from the ambitions and pettinesses of the world. He seemed to have settled matters with his soul, and out of loneliness and sickness to have won peace. He was more gentle, and as tolerant as a mind can ever be whose critical power is unimpaired. He found his pleasure in simple things like the friendship of children and the sunshine of a spring morning and the reading of old books. He lived much in the far past, and it was rather on memories of the Scotland, Eton, and Oxford of his youth that he dwelt than on the brilliant arena of his middle years. He used often to tell me that, after the New Testament, he held Sir Walter Scott's *Journal* to be the most comforting book in the world, and I fancy that if he had written a diary it would have had some of the qualities of Scott's. He used to say, too, that he would rather have had Sir Walter's life with all its shadows than that of any other man, and the choice reveals the fundamentals of character that survived when the accretions of a glittering career had gone. Like the laird of Abbotsford, he was first and last a great Scotsman, with all the best endowments of the race— a quick sentiment for the past, zest and imagination in the business of life, seriousness in great things and humour in all, kindliness and unostentatious charity, modesty in success, and a manly fortitude in sorrow.

VII

THE KIRK IN SCOTLAND

THE KIRK IN SCOTLAND

THIS chapter is not an essay in Church history. History is an ampler thing which demands exact documentation and a multitude of details. It is no more than an attempt to sketch on the broadest lines the career of the Kirk in Scotland; the vicissitudes which it suffered from controversies within and without its bounds; the different strands interwoven in its creed; the slow stages by which it attained to a clearer consciousness of its nature and its destiny.

There is no lack of literature on the subject, but the reader may find himself in trouble if he plunges without guidance into its mazes. Much of it is uncritical and unhistorical. The chronicle of the Scottish Church has too often been compiled in the spirit of hagiography. Some writers have approached it in a mood of rapt exaltation, and produced a device in snow and ink—spotless saints and infallible wisdom set against scowling diabolists and malignant folly. There has been no lack of casuists to defend the indefensible. It may be fairly said that history conceived in such a spirit does scant justice to the Church itself. On the other hand, it is easy for the cynic so to set forth its disputes as to make them seem the merest logomachies. The old divines write often uncouth English, and they are apt to make their arguments a mosaic of Scripture texts which lends itself readily to caricature. Causes for which men freely offered their lives can be made to seem trivial or ridiculous.

Of the two faults I think this the worse, for it is the less intelligent. The blindest hagiology seems to me preferable to that detachment which never comes within measurable distance of the point. Knox, Melville and Henderson—Boyd, Durham and Rutherford—Boston and the Erskines—Chalmers, Cunningham and Candlish—all were men of remarkable gifts of character and mind; we may fairly assume that they did not give their time to wrangling about trifles; it is our business to find out what kernel of living truth is concealed in a language which may have passed out of use. We must approach the historical Church with some equipment in the way of historical imagination, for even in its blunders we may find enlightenment. We cannot afford to look scornfully on any belief which once 'taught weak wills how much they can.' And there is this reward for the honest inquirer. Without some understanding of the Church there can be no true understanding of Scottish history or of the nature of the Scottish people.

I

THE MEDIAEVAL CHURCH

The Church in Scotland has a long ancestry, but its descent is not in direct line. The Christian faith was first brought to our shores towards the end of the fourth century, when Ninian settled at Whithorn and built a church to the glory of God and the memory of St. Martin of Tours; but soon the tides of war and paganism flowed over his work. In the middle of the sixth century Kentigern became the apostle of Strathclyde, and, as St. Mungo, the patron saint of Glasgow. On Whit Sunday in the year 563 Columba landed in Iona, and he made that isle for the remaining thirty-four years of his life a light, the beams of which shone over all Scotland. We must give up, I fear, the pleasant tale derived from John of Fordun, of the early Scottish Church as being in substance Presbyterian and non-Roman. That Church was, like the Irish Church, monastic in its structure; but as soon as it becomes an organised and national institution it is part of the catholic European system, though monastic elements, like the Culdees, long remain to testify to its beginnings.

It is as unhistorical to picture an early anti-papal Scottish Church as to imagine that the niceties of Roman rule were from the first universal, or that the Middle Ages knew only one uniform ecclesiastical pattern. There was nationalism in every Church; most sovereigns had their quarrels with the Pope, and many peoples lay occasionally under his ban. In Britain there was, perhaps, a special degree of spiritual independence. James I of Scotland, a devout son of the Church, was as ready to assert himself against undue papal interference as William the Conqueror. The Scot, indeed, when he travelled abroad, carried with him a certain flavour of heterodoxy, and the validity of his orders was sometimes questioned. But in general we may say that the mediaeval Scottish Church was a normal branch of the Church Catholic whose centre was Rome.

It has been the fashion ever since the Reformation to picture that Church in dark colours, as something alien and despotic, with small hold on the affections of the people. The view has little warrant. The questioning spirit of the nation sometimes set the popular mind against its own hierarchy, and more often against the Roman Pontiff, for the Scot has always been more individualist than catholic, and his aspiration that of the old song:

> That all the world shall see
> There's nane right but we,
> The men of the auld Scottish nation.

But the mediaeval Church gave to the people all of religion and humane learning that they knew, and there is ample evidence that it played, even in its decadence, a vital part in men's lives. It produced the only sacred poetry of the highest class that Scotland can claim. From the earliest days it had its reformers and its evangelists as well as its moderates. Even at the Reformation the Christian virtues were not all on one side. The great churchmen were often, like Lamberton and Wishart, leaders in the fight for national independence. Henry Wardlaw who founded the University of St. Andrews, Kennedy who succeeded him in that see, William Turnbull to whom we owe the University of Glasgow, William Elphinstone who was the creator of King's College at Aberdeen, must rank high amongst the benefactors of their country.

The Church which had endured for nearly a thousand years disappeared almost in a night, and with it went, unhappily, most of the outward evidence of its existence. Few ancient buildings remain still in use to remind us of that vanished world. But if we lack such memorials, we may claim an ultimate shrine. If the stream of Church history seems to be long lost among sands and morasses, we can recognise its fount. The little isle with its green hills and white beaches, which looks across the ribbon of tide to the granite of Mull, is a sacred place to which the devotion of every Scottish creed and communion is vowed. For there Columba, warrior, saint, scholar, explorer and law-giver, taught a simple evangel, first to the Gael and then to the other peoples of the mainland, and thereby lit the lamp of a missionary faith which has flickered often, but has never died. Iona is the Holy Land and the Holy City of Scotland, the spring of 'the wisdom before which knowledge is as a frosty breath.'

II

THE FIRST REFORMATION

The Reformation came to Scotland in its most drastic form. There remained indeed the same major articles of the Christian faith, but, on grounds partly political and partly religious, there was a final breach with Rome, to some extent in creed and to the full in ritual and Church government. It began with the 'Band' of December 1557, which denounced Roman abuses and demanded the English Prayer-book: in August 1560 a Confession of Faith, drawn up by John Knox and his friends, was ratified by Parliament as 'wholesome and sound doctrine grounded upon the infallible truth of God's word'; a few months later the first General Assembly was held, and the First Book of Discipline was approved; and in the December Parliament of 1567, during the regency of Moray, the reformed Church was established by a statute 'declaring and granting jurisdiction' to it, and disallowing 'any other face of Kirk in Scotland.'

The keynote of the Reformation was a return to simplicity. The great structure of the mediaeval Church, with its accretions of fifteen centuries, was exchanged for a simple revelation— God speaking through His Word to the individual heart and judgment. It claimed to replace an external standard by an internal, to be a re-birth of the spirit of man and a vindication of the liberties of the human soul. Its fundamental doctrine was the priesthood of all believers. Its conception of the Church was of a free autonomous community owning no leadership but that of Jesus Christ. But, since a human institution cannot be founded upon the bare principle of liberty, the new Church was at once compelled to seek definition and discipline.

The Reformation in its extremest, or, if we prefer, its purest form, was mainly the work of John Calvin, who performed two tasks of the first importance. In his *Institutes* he codified the theology of St. Augustine, and provided a body of doctrine, differing, indeed, only in emphasis from Catholic dogma, but skilfully adapted to the new conditions. In the Church which he founded at Geneva he created a model which Knox thought 'the most perfect School of Christ that ever was on earth since the days of the Apostles,' and which had a profound influence upon the nascent Church in Scotland.

But the hardening of the molten ore of spiritual fervour in the moulds of an institution was attended with certain difficulties, and, since in them is to be found the germ of all the later troubles of the Scottish Church, it is necessary to examine them with some care.

1. The first concerned the basis of faith. The foundation of the Reformed Churches was the Bible; they accepted no truth which had not a Scriptural warrant, and they claimed that whatever they did was done by Scripture authority. But the Bible must be interpreted, and the only means of interpretation, once the authority of an infallible Church had been rejected, was the human judgment and the human conscience. That remained the view of the more liberal among the Reformed theologians. 'The authority of man,' Hooker wrote, 'is the key which openeth the door of entrance into the knowledge of the Scriptures.'

But such a view inevitably involved diversity of opinion, and it seemed an insecure basis on which to build a lasting fabric. Luther and Zwingli, for example, both founding upon the Bible, had reached different conclusions about the meaning of the Eucharist. Calvin and those who followed him saw the danger, and endeavoured to avoid it by something very like a return to the ecclesiasticism which he had rejected. We know, he held, that the Bible is the Word of God, not because

U

of the authority of an historic Church, but because of the testimony of the Holy Spirit. This testimony must be systematised by God's servants, and a Church erected which shall be the medium of the Holy Spirit and the treasury of inspired interpretation. His *Institutes* in their second edition made definite claim to be the canon of Scripture teaching; it was in his new Church and its accepted creed that saving knowledge could alone be found. This was not far from that doctrine of an external, infallible canon which the earlier Reformers had rejected.

Such an attitude towards the Bible and its interpretation was a fruitful parent of strife. In the first place, it led to the most forced and arbitrary reading of Scripture texts. The Bible was made the sole manual of practice. The Church of Calvin and Knox forgot the warning of St. Paul—that the Old Testament was a dangerous book if the letter of it was regarded to the exclusion of the spirit, and it tended to make it a storehouse of minute precedents. The Roman Church had used for its basis not the Bible only, but the writings of the Fathers, and the dictates of practical experience, and it possessed the power of regulating the whole, and providing for natural development, by authoritative decree. The Scottish Church retained this doctrine of authority, but had somehow to harmonise it with a quantum of individual liberty, and it narrowed the canon to the two Testaments, thereby perilously limiting its tools.

At the beginning there was indeed a certain laxity. In 1558 the Scottish Protestants petitioned Mary of Guise that all matters might be tried by the New Testament, the ancient Fathers, and the 'godly laws of Justinian.' Knox, when it suited him, was prepared to differ even from the New Testament, and in an argument with Maitland of Lethington, who quoted St. James's direction to St. Paul to purify himself in the Temple, was bold enough to doubt 'whether either James's command or Paul's obedience proceeded from the Holy Ghost.' When Alexander Henderson disputed with Charles I, and the King argued that, when the Bible was not explicit, it was right to have recourse to the records of the Church, Henderson met him fairly on his own ground. But in general the early history of the Scottish Church shows a steady hardening and narrowing in its apologetics.

From this constriction of basis many misfortunes were to flow. The first was a perpetual risk of heresy and a constant invitation to schism. If ancient writings were to be construed without scientific method or historical perspective, it was certain that human ingenuity would find many causes of division. A second was the ossification of the minds engaged in so barren a task. The human reason in its worthier sense was atrophied by being limited to a futile casuistry. Superstitions, such as witchcraft and demoniac possession, were given by the idolatry of the Old Testament a new lease of life. The free use of the intellect was paralysed, and honest men became sophists. Ninian Winzet in his controversy with Knox had no difficulty in showing that the Reformers went to the Bible to find proofs for their creed, not to find that creed, since they rejected certain rules of the Roman Church which had scriptural warrant, and accepted others which had none. Andrew Melville based his objection to bishops on the ground that in the New Testament there was no mention of bishops ruling over presbyteries, ignoring the fact that his own system had just as little warrant, since there was no proof of a presbytery governing more than a single church.

In the following century the attitude became still more rigid. One Johann Koch of Leyden became, as Cocceius, anathema to the orthodox, because he held the reasonable view that Hebrew sentences should be interpreted by their context. Spiritually and intellectually this searching for proof-texts became a disease, for the truth in Donne's saying was ignored, that 'sentences in Scripture, like hairs in horses' tails, concur in one root of beauty and strength, but, being plucked out one by one, serve only for springes and snares.' Considerations of expediency and common sense were banned: the Bible was made a hand-book to every aspect of life; no word of the sacred writings but was regarded as dogma; every syllable, letter, comma and full-stop was treated as divinely inspired: whatever was not contained therein was unlawful, for it was laid down as the first principle of interpretation that for God not to command was to forbid. And so we have Samuel Ruther-

ford in his *Divine Right of Church Government and Excommunication*
declaring that 'there is nothing so small in either doctrinals
or policy, so as man may alter, omit, or leave off these smallest
positive things that God hath commanded.'

This passionate formalism must obviously lead to credal
divergencies, and it must inevitably land a Church in difficulties
about rites and ceremonies. It was not easy to accommodate
Christian worship in Western Europe in the sixteenth century
to the practice of Judaean peasants in the first, or of Israel a
thousand years earlier. The immediate result was confusion.
The early Reformers in Scotland had no objection to settled
forms and prescribed prayers. Knox began by accepting the
kneeling posture at communion, though he afterwards rejected
it. Wafer bread was employed by Calvin in his own church
at Geneva. Winzet pointed out to Knox that there was no
explicit warrant in the New Testament for either the baptism
of infants or the strict observance of the Lord's Day. The first
Reformers derived from the Church they had left a preference
for a certain catholic order in worship until they were over-
borne by the Scripture literalists. This influence came chiefly
from the English Puritans; under their guidance Sunday, the
day on which Calvin had played at bowls and Knox had given
supper-parties, became the Jewish Sabbath, and selections from
the Mosaic law were dovetailed into the Christian creed. Even
the ring in marriage would have been abolished had not the
women proved stronger than the preachers.

2. If the seeds of dissension lay hidden in a basis of faith
too narrow for the human spirit, they were also present in the
new conception of the Church. Presbytery, being based on the
Word of God, was a system *divini juris*; its founders were
possessed by the mediaeval idea of a universal Church; therefore we find it speedily claiming the right to insist upon
religious uniformity. It was not only divinely founded, but,
with its Continental analogues, was the only system of divine
origin. It is easy to see how such an attitude came about,
for against the universal claim of Rome it seemed necessary
to establish a counter-universalism. But it involved two
dangerous consequences—the prohibition of variety in religious
belief and usage, and the duty of coercion. To the Scottish

Reformers it appeared that no religion was safe unless it were predominant.

The new Church held firm by the Catholic doctrine of comprehension, but it insisted also upon uniformity—an apparently irreconcilable ideal. The Church of Rome had permitted within its pale all who formally assented to its creed; the Reformers tended to make the 'church visible' also the 'church invisible.' The classic authority is the sixteenth chapter of Knox's *Confession*:

> As we believe in one God, Father, Son and Holy Ghost, so do we most constantly believe that from the beginning there hath been, now is, and to the end of the world shall be, one Kirk; that is to say, one company and multitude of men chosen of God, who rightly worship and embrace him by true faith in Christ Jesus . . . which kirk is Catholic, that is, universal, because it containeth the elect of all realms, nations and tongues. And we utterly abhor the blasphemy of those that affirm that men which live according to equity and justice shall be saved, what religion soever they have professed.

The practical doctrine, adumbrated by Knox and made explicit by his successors, was that it was God's will that the Kirk, which was scripturally the only true Kirk, should admit no rival in any sphere where it had won dominance, and should suffer no internal divergencies from its divinely-inspired interpretation of Scriptural mandates. It believed, as Rome believed, in the ideal of a single Church, a complete and exclusive system to which a single separatist was anathema.

From such a conception the duty of coercion inevitably followed. Christ never taught the exercise of coercive power, and the early Church was not in a position to attempt it. But in the fourth century, with the acknowledgment of Christianity as the State religion, the practice began; heresy became treason; and St. Augustine, building on the isolated text, 'Compel them to come in,' preached the use of force in conversion. The view was based upon his doctrine of the utter depravity of the natural man, since, if human nature was hopelessly corrupt, there was no reason to consult its wishes. 'What can be more deadly to the soul,' he asked, 'than the liberty of error?' 'Toleration,' said Richard Baxter in the seventeenth century, 'is soul murder.' The view was inevitable, granted the premises, for on them tolerance seemed no better than spiritual sloth and moral apathy. This was the belief alike of Protestant and Catholic, of Knox and of Innocent III, of Andrew Melville and of the Cardinal of Lorraine. A man like Samuel Rutherford, who was what was commonly known as an 'affectionate' preacher, taught, as has been said, 'the loveliness of Christ for thirty years without ever perceiving the unloveliness of intolerance.'

Another consequence was the institution of a drastic internal discipline, in order that the visible might be made to approximate as far as possible to the invisible Church. Evidence, indeed, could not be demanded of the possession of saving grace, but over every outward manifestation there was exercised a minute inquisition. No serious attempt was made to distinguish between moral fundamentals and non-fundamentals, and the most secular aspects of life were not exempted from oversight. Once again the conclusion followed logically from certain dubious premises. Historically we can perceive its justification, but in its results it was disastrous. 'By your hard and subtle words,' Cromwell was to tell the ministers before Dunbar, 'you have begotten prejudice in those who do too much in matters of conscience—wherein every soul has to answer for itself to God—depend upon you'; and the indictment was unhappily true.

3. The third potential source of strife was the relation to the civil power. Ever since Constantine this problem had confronted the Church, and the great *Corpus Juris* of Justinian defined the respective rights of Church and State—a definition at first accepted by the Reformers. Presently their attitude changed. Hag-ridden by Old Testament precedents, they came to believe that the visible sign of God's acknowledgment of His people was the gift of political power. The Church was not only supreme in spiritual matters, but it was the duty of a Christian State to support it and to lend the secular arm, when required, to carry out its decrees, to punish heresy and enforce discipline, and to suppress any Church which threatened rivalry. In the fathers of Presbytery there was nothing of the *politique* whose creed has been defined by Tavannes: 'Ceux

qui préfèrent le repos du royaume, ou de leur particulier, au salut de leur âme, et à la religion, qui ayment mieux que le royaume demeure en paix sans Dieu qu'en guerre pour luy.' [1]

This view involved the Church's establishment, and Knox and Melville and Henderson were Erastians in one sense of that doubtful word. Moreover, the rejection of toleration and the belief in uniformity were bound to lead to a usurpation of civil power. With such a creed there could be no real delimitation between the spiritual and the secular, between Church and State. The right of the Church to dominate personal and family life was soon extended to the duty of interference with secular government. Its maxim became *Cujus religio, ejus regio*, the converse of the mediaeval formula. Doubtless it is true, as has been argued, that the original aim, as shown by the use of the phrase the 'crown honours of Christ,' was less to aggrandise the Church than to exalt the majesty of our Lord. But in fact it was soon to develop into a claim which was inconsistent with any stable civil society.

Of this fatal heritage of the Middle Ages Knox was the chief exponent. The Reformation in Scotland was largely political, the work of laymen; its most effective champions, the nobles, owed their bitterness against Rome mainly to the desire to retain Church lands; so the relationship with the civil power was from the start a vital issue. Knox—*clarum et venerabile nomen*—one of the greatest destructive forces in our history and no mean constructive one, had immense shrewdness and practical wisdom, but he had little power of coherent thought. He is one of the most inconsistent of writers and speakers, and his mind is constantly in a passionate confusion. From such a man it was idle to expect any wise and cogent definition of the respective powers of State and Church. It was owing to him that the Reformation in Scotland went so deep; but if he left his country the bequest of a noble democracy, he left it also a tradition of rigidity and intolerance and political strife.

For the essence of his conception of the Church was really that of unlimited authority. It could not choose but interfere in civil affairs. There was no agreement on what constituted an ecclesiastical offence; an Edinburgh elder, for example,

---

[1] *Mémoires*, ed. Buchon, 269.

was ordered to do penance in the kirk for exporting wheat. Andrew Melville's famous declaration about the two kings and two kingdoms in Scotland might seem a reasonable statement of spiritual independence, but its occasion was a claim of the ministers to interfere in secular policy.[1] In theory, the Church professed to separate civil and ecclesiastical jurisdiction with scrupulous care, and it always objected to ecclesiastics holding civil offices; but in fact no barrier could long stand, the Church's claims being what they were. The doctrine of the Headship of Christ was interpreted in the long run so as to overrule all lesser sanctions. That was the true root of the trouble over Episcopacy, and not a mere difference in the reading of certain New Testament passages. The Kings, James and Charles, desired a hierarchy so as to give them more control over the Church; the Church desired the liberty of extending, when it so desired, its spiritual prerogatives into secular domains. Both based their arguments on divine right. It was a conflict of rival extremes.

III

PRESBYTERY AND EPISCOPACY

With high purpose and a sincere devotion, but with those perilous elements, which we have sketched, in its constitution, the Reformed Church of Scotland started upon its journey. It had come into being by its own act, independent of the civil power, for its birth was the General Assembly of 1560-61. At that date the national Church sprang into life; seven years later an Act of Parliament made it an established Church; that is to say, the State did not create the Church's authority, but recognised formally that which was already existing. Its organisation, its ritual, and even its doctrines were not yet wholly settled, but its spiritual autonomy was indisputable, since it owned no headship but Christ's.

It began in 1560 with a purely administrative episcopacy, not possessed of orders higher than those of the ordinary ministry. The superintendents, or bishops, were subject to the control

[1] Rait, *The Parliaments of Scotland*, 53.

of the General Assembly, and the main purpose of their office was to perform the duties of local administration, which, under the influence of Andrew Melville, were, about 1580, assigned to the newly-instituted Church courts, known as presbyteries. The position, however, see-sawed according to the prestige of the King at the moment, for James did not admit the Church's claim of spiritual autonomy, and regarded an hierarchy as a necessary protection for the throne. In 1584 the Black Acts recognised the King as the head of the Church, and made the meetings of the General Assembly depend upon the permission of King and Parliament; in 1592 the position was reversed, and a complete Presbyterian polity was established; by 1600 James had triumphed again and bishops sat in Parliament. When he succeeded to the English throne he won a new authority, the Act of 1592 was repealed, and Episcopacy became the law. In the same way the Articles of Perth, ratified by Parliament in 1621, made customs approximate to the English rather than to the Genevan code, by enjoining kneeling at communion, confirmation, and the keeping of certain Church festivals.

But neither the parliamentary Episcopacy nor the Perth Articles greatly affected the life of the Church, for the law was not strictly enforced, and James had the wisdom to call a halt in his policy of religious uniformity. The discipline and practice were in substance Presbyterian, especially as regards local government. The General Assembly lost first its authority and then its existence, and the bishops exercised such political influence as remained to the Church. Their political power encouraged among their opponents that tendency by which the Church, under the inspiration of the Melvilles, came to regard itself more and more as a self-governing commonwealth, wholly independent in all things which by any stretch of language could be called spiritual. Knox had written: 'The ordering and reformation of religion doth especially appertain to the Civil Magistrate. . . . The King taketh upon him to command the Priests.' By 1620 no leader of Presbytery in Scotland but would have repudiated this dictum of its founder.

Yet in the first decades of the seventeenth century there was no final bar to uniformity between England and Scotland. The new impulse in religion had first come north of Tweed through the study of Wycliffe's Bible, and both nations had the Word of God in the same tongue. There was some justification for James's policy. Both Churches were Protestant; both had liturgies which might have been made one had the advice of John Hales been followed, and a public form of service devised embracing only those things upon which all Christians were agreed.[1] There was an opportunity for a true eirenicon, as Archbishop Ussher believed, if bishops were required to follow the primitive practice and act on the advice of the ministers, laymen were brought into church management, and churchmen were disqualified for civil office. There was a real chance of union under James; under Charles I it vanished, and has not returned.

Episcopacy, in the attenuated form in which it had been now established, might well have been tolerated in spite of Andrew Melville's theoretic objections, since it bore so lightly on the ordinary man. It had not much prestige—the *tulchan* bishops had seen to that—but it roused no great antipathy, and it interfered little with Presbyterian usage. The trouble which began under Charles I was due not to Episcopacy but to Prelacy. 'Episcopacy,' Sir Thomas Raleigh has written, 'is a form of government, possessing a strong claim upon our respect and gratitude. Prelacy is a vice, and a vice which is not peculiar to the episcopal churches. It makes its appearance wherever a minister of the Word imagines that his office entitles him to exercise lordship over his brethren. It was in the Church from the first; for we remember how the companions of Christ disputed which of them should be greatest, and how Salome asked that her son should have the chief place in the Kingdom.'[2] The prelate, as 'one set above,' was an offence to a Church which believed in the parity of ministers, and for the King to claim to alter ritual and interfere with Church government of his own will was to undermine the spiritual freedom which was the Church's chief foundation.

So we reach what is sometimes known as the Second Reformation, which was a revolt from Prelacy, as the First Reformation had been a revolt from Rome. Charles I by his revocation of

---

[1] See his *Tract concerning Schisme*, 1642.
[2] *Annals of the Church in Scotland*, 10.

Church property in the hands of laymen had alarmed the nobles and barons, and thereby provided for the Church in her disputes a new set of Lords of the Congregation. He had established a Court of High Commission, increased the number of bishops in the Privy Council to seven, and made Archbishop Spottiswoode Chancellor—the first time since the Reformation that the office had been given to a churchman. He passed from one blunder to another, driving even royalists like Drummond of Hawthornden into opposition, till in 1637 he imposed, by an act of pure autocracy, a new Prayer-book upon the Scottish Church. The result was to fire the heather and to unite all Scotland against him, except a few Catholic nobles and Aberdeen doctors. The National Covenant was signed in the first months of 1638, a temperate and strictly legal assertion of the autonomy of the national Church. In November of the same year a General Assembly held at Glasgow, formally illegal, but with a solid nation behind it, decreed a root-and-branch abolition of Episcopacy and its ministrants.

It would have been well had the Church been content to stop there. With all the irregularities of its procedure, it had required that Scottish liberties should be safeguarded, and demanded in proof the grant of the kind of Church which the nation preferred. In its insistence upon spiritual freedom it had ample historical warrant. But the dangerous constituents in its heritage were now to come uppermost, and too many of its leaders had the vision of Hildebrand in their souls and the spirit of Hildebrand in their blood. It is a hazardous thing to claim that any system of church government is *divini juris*, unless it be granted that the claim can be shared among many systems. 'Establish,' said Coleman, preaching before the House of Commons in July 1645, 'as few things by divine right as can well be.' The claim to possess a monopoly of divine inspiration came from a casuistical and unscholarly interpretation of the Scriptures, and on the same basis Independent, Quaker, and Laudian Anglican could reach the same conclusion about his own belief. Of such a premise uniformity was the logical consequence, and to insist upon it became a duty. This was the creed as much of Henderson and Guthrie as of Laud and Charles. 'In the paradise of Nature,' wrote Henderson in 1640, 'the diversity of flowers and herbs is pleasant and useful, but in the paradise of the Church different and contrary religions are unpleasant and hurtful.' Note that 'different' and 'contrary' were conjoined. Scotland claimed to dictate to England her ecclesiastical polity.

There was nobility in the dream, but it was a noble folly. The Scottish divines had never lost the vision of a single catholic and universal Church upon earth. You will find it in Melville and Brown of Wamphray; you will find it in Samuel Rutherford and James Durham, as well as in Archbishop Leighton. They never unchurched their old enemy Rome, or treated her baptism as invalid. They were always unwilling separatists, and longed for reunion—on their own terms. Durham is vehement against the divisions 'occasioned by a carnal and factious-like pleading for and vindicating even of truth.' They had a horror of light-hearted schism and a pathetic desire to see Christ's people in concord. Durham's congested style becomes on this subject almost eloquent:

Never did men run to quench fire in a city, lest all should be destroyed, with more diligence than men ought to bestir themselves to quench this in the Church. Never did mariners use more speed to stop a leak in a ship, lest all should be drowned, than ministers especially and all Christian men should haste to stop this beginning of the breaking in of these waters of strife, lest thereby the whole Church be overwhelmed. And if the many evils which follow therefrom, the many commands whereby union is pressed, yea, the many entreaties and obtestations whereby the Holy Ghost doth so frequently urge this upon us all, as a thing most acceptable to Him and profitable to us—if, I say, these and many other considerations have not weight to convince of the necessity of this duty to prevent or heal a breach, we cannot tell what can prevail with men that profess reverence to the great and dreadful name of God, conscience of duty, and respect to the edification of the Church, and to their own peace at the appearance of the Lord in the great day, wherein the peacemakers shall be blessed, for they shall be called the children of God.[1]

But so long as there was no clear distinction between the essen-

---

[1] *Treatise concerning Scandal* (1659), 313.

tial and the inessential, so long as unity was identified with uniformity, this passionate desire for union became an explosive to shatter instead of a cement to bind.

The result was the Solemn League and Covenant, signed in St. Margaret's Church, Westminster, in September 1643, and thereafter sworn to by the Estates and the General Assembly and the Scottish people, in which the Church violently encroached upon the sphere of secular government. It was regarded as a mystical covenant with the Almighty, its acceptance a test of faith, its rejection or breach a certain proof of damnation. This method of covenant-making was a lamentable descent into a legal formalism which degraded the whole conception of the relationship of God and His people. It had immediate and disastrous results. It set Scotland in sharp antagonism to a large part of the people of England; it drove from the Scottish Church the greatest of its sons, Montrose; it intensified the spirit of sectarian bigotry into which it was drifting; it earned the hearty enmity of the foremost of Englishmen, and of all those who, like Cromwell, were striving for toleration. But the labours of the divines at Westminster, the sponsors of the Solemn League, brought forth one worthy fruit. They produced an ordinal of public worship, and they codified their theology in the Confession of Faith, which has remained ever since in substance the doctrinal base of Scottish Presbytery.

The rule of Cromwell in Scotland meant the practical curbing of the theocracy into which the Church had drifted. The Restoration of 1660 meant the upturning of its foundations. The Church, having sought too much, was now to get less than its due, and that spiritual liberty which in its pride it had denied to others was now to be denied to itself. Just as the Glasgow Assembly of 1638 had abolished James's laws, so the Act Rescissory of 1661 blotted out twenty-three years of Presbyterian legislation. The restored Episcopacy resembled that of the reign of James rather than the Laudian ideal of uniformity with England. But it was the King who dictated the Church's constitution; Episcopacy had become identified with the loss of liberty, and the issue was now not as to the merits or demerits of a form of government but as to whether the Church's autonomy was to be maintained. The Headship of Christ became the testing

question. Most of Scotland, being very weary, settled down
under the new regime, but in the south and west the flower
of the ministers and laymen opposed the King. There was
dross as well as fine gold in such men. The strife was largely
one of rival intolerances, and the Covenanters held as firmly
as Laud ever did to the principle of uniformity. They would
have had all men compelled to adopt a single creed and
practice, but that creed and practice must be their own.
Yet they fought blindly and confusedly for one lasting
truth, the Church's spiritual freedom, and, if only for th
testimony on that behalf, they deserve to be held in honourable memory.

The Revolution of 1688 saw the close of the second great
stage in the Church's history. That stage began with the
Second Reformation when Prelacy was overthrown and the
freedom of the Church was vindicated; it ended with the
Church in servitude to the civil authority, a lack-lustre nominal
Episcopacy, and some of the best of the Scottish people outlaws
for conscience sake. More serious still, the habit of separatism
had grown, and the seamless robe of the Church was rent
asunder. The quarrels of Resolutioner and Protester had
been followed after the Restoration by the Covenanting breach,
and the Covenanters themselves threatened to split up into
lesser conventicles—'a poor, wasted, misrepresented Remnant,'
in the words of James Renwick's *Informatory Vindication*, 'of the
Suffering, Anti-Popish, Anti-Prelatic, Anti-Erastian, Anti-
Sectarian, true Presbyterian Church of Christ in Scotland.'

Yet throughout that troubled age an ideal of a Church
at peace with itself was never forgotten, and there is often
more wisdom to be got from the writings of the divines than
from their public utterances and actions. The ferment of the
time produced many men of real, if one-sided, greatness. There
were fervid evangelists who made a fire in cold places; scholars
and thinkers like Robert Boyd and James Durham and Brown
of Wamphray; mystics like Samuel Rutherford, whose saccharine
sweetness often cloys, but who can rise now and then to an
apocalyptic splendour; quaint souls like William Guthrie of
Fenwick—a Scottish Traherne or Henry Vaughan—who bade
his hearers praise God, 'if ye have no more, for this good day

and sunshine to the lambs'[1]; Leighton, a bishop of the Restoration Episcopacy, whose sermons were Coleridge's delight, and who laboured for peace where peace could not be; James Renwick, the last martyr, a man of wistful apostolic power. Most of them died young, worn out with an eternal dissidence, for they had to build God's house, like Nehemiah, with trowel in one hand and sword in the other. One and all they were men of a noble fortitude, confused sometimes and a little blind, but of a great stoutness of heart. In that age of suffering and darkness their eyes were always on the world beyond time, and often, in their too ardent contemplation of immortality, they were careless of mortal wisdom and the humbler mortal duties. Each 'fired his ringing shot and passed' to the rest for which he was always longing. Their words were those of Cromwell—'We are indeed but a feeble and sickly company, yet we shall work the time that is appointed us, and after that rest in peace.'

IV

THE REVOLUTION SETTLEMENT

The Revolution Settlement—mainly the work of William Carstares, who must rank high among ecclesiastical statesmen—was a peace of exhaustion. The fact that the Scottish bishops took the side of James made it certain that Episcopacy would disappear from the national Church. For the rest, Presbytery was established, patronage was abolished, and the Confession of Faith was made statute law. It seemed that the Church had been confirmed in its exclusive spiritual jurisdiction and its intrinsic spiritual powers. There was no mention of Covenants, or of the theocratic claims which had begun with the Glasgow Assembly of 1638; it was as if it had been tacitly agreed that that stormy chapter should be forgotten.

From this fatigued unanimity there were two main dissentients. Many of the Episcopalian clergy to their honour followed the King, whose divine right to the throne had been part of their creed. They paid the price of their loyalty, and

[1] Wodrow, *Analecta*, I. 137.

the sufferings of those Scottish non-jurors are too often forgotten. There was justification for Pleydell's epithet for the communion to which he belonged—'the persecuted Episcopal Church of Scotland.' [1] But in certain districts in the north, where that Church had a large popular following, the old regime continued undisturbed. It differed from that of Presbytery only in its acceptance of bishops, and in its attitude towards the reigning house. Its ritual was of the simplest, it celebrated communion according to the barest Presbyterian fashions, and its creed was indistinguishable from that laid down in the Confession of Faith.

The other dissentients were to be found in the south-west, the men of the Societies, who followed the blood-reddened banner of Richard Cameron and Donald Cargill. They claimed to be the historic Church of Scotland, compelled through the errors of the majority to withdraw themselves into private societies for Christian fellowship. For a decade or two they led a stormy life, lit by political intrigues; the Jacobites regarded them as likely allies, and their dealings with the Society men may be read in the unedifying pages of Ker of Kersland. The Cameronians held strictly to the Covenants, and could not acknowledge an uncovenanted Kirk or an uncovenanted King. By and by, through the work of men like John M'Millan of Balmaghie, the Societies were organised into a Presbytery, which ultimately became a Church—the Reformed Presbyterian Church of Scotland, the first and not the least estimable of Scottish secessions.

In 1712, by a mischievous trick of the English Tories and the Scottish Jacobites, patronage was restored, and the dragon's teeth were sown which were to produce a melancholy harvest. The Church protested against it, but for a little it was no great grievance, since ministers continued to be placed by the will of a congregation rather than by the nomination of a patron. But presently the patrons became more active, presbyteries refused to give assent to their wishes, and the General Assemblies were congested with appeals. The device of peripatetic 'riding committees,' sent abroad to settle disputes, was a solution which had no hope of permanence. Here was one rock

[1] In *Guy Mannering*.

of offence, the more dangerous because certain younger ecclesiastics, who were afterwards to be leaders of the Moderates, were anxious in this matter to make the Assembly dictate harshly to the presbyteries.

Another was the inclination to heresy hunts, a danger in all churches which have no strong spiritual inspiration. In 1695 Thomas Aikenhead, a lad of nineteen, who favoured a fantastic materialism and considered the Pentateuch to be post-Exilian, was tried and condemned. He recanted—which would have saved his life at the hands of the Inquisition—but was duly hanged in Edinburgh. Soon controversies arose in the inner circles of the orthodox. A century before, a certain fellow of Brasenose College, Oxford, had published a book called *The Marrow of Modern Divinity*, in which the doctrine of saving grace was stated in its extreme Calvinistic form. This ancient work was seized upon by those ministers who scented latitudinarian tendencies, and the 'Marrow-men' became a dangerous left wing in the Church, trembling upon the brink of secession.

The result was an exemplification of that characteristic which Thomas Hobbes had long ago marked in Presbyterianism, a liability to hive off into sects. The first schism was that of the Erskines, who had been Marrow-men along with Boston of Ettrick; the ostensible ground was patronage and the growing Erastian character of the Church, though doctrinal dissatisfaction also played a part; they had never accepted the Revolution Settlement, and were still harking back upon the Covenants like the old Protesters.[1] 'There is a difference to be made,' wrote Ebenezer Erskine, 'between the Established Church of Scotland and the Church of Christ in Scotland'; and he proceeded to constitute the latter as a secession Church. That was in 1733, and twelve years later there was a secession within this secession. It turned on the validity of the burgess oath—whether one could conscientiously swear to uphold 'the true religion presently professed within this realm.' Those who maintained that the establishment was corrupt could scarcely approve such a form of words. So the first secession split into Burgher and Anti-Burgher, and half a century later the former split again into New Lights and Old Lights, according to the

[1] Cf. Lord Sands' paper in *Records of the Scottish Church History Society*, 1928.

x

degree of modernism among its members. The same division showed itself among the Anti-Burghers, the eternal dichotomy of conservatives and progressives. The basis was partly doctrinal, but far more that old rock of Scottish controversy, the relation of Church and State.

There was still a third hiving-off in 1761, in the Relief Church, whose founder was Thomas Gillespie, and which had a more liberal character than its predecessors. The brethren of the Relief had no enthusiasm for the letter of the Covenants. 'I do not think,' wrote Patrick Hutchison, 'that ever any part of the Church of Christ, since the commencement of the Christian era, was more deeply involved in the guilt of ignorant and false swearing than the British subjects in the last century.' [1] They held, too, by comprehensive communion, for their synod in 1773 declared: 'It is agreeable to the Word of God and their principles occasionally to hold communion with those of the Episcopal and Independent persuasions who are visible saints.'

The various secessions profoundly weakened the Church of Scotland by withdrawing from it many men of true religious genius. The ranks of the establishment closed up in a dry and formal unity against a menace which was real enough, for by 1766 there were 120 secession meeting-houses attended by more than 100,000 worshippers. The consequence was the Moderatism which for more than a century was the dominant policy of the Church. The Moderates had many merits, and it is as unfair to judge them by a pagan like 'Jupiter' Carlyle, as it would be to judge their opponents, the High-flyers, by Dr. Webster of the Tolbooth Church, the 'Dr. Magnum Bonum' of many tales, who had the bad taste to complain that while he drank with gentlemen he must vote with fools. A man like William Robertson, the historian and Principal of Edinburgh University, was as orthodox in theology as any seceder, and far more liberal and tolerant. The party did a useful work in lowering the temperature in ecclesiastical controversy, and loosening the bonds of antiquarian dogma.

But none the less they were a chilling influence in Scotland. The piety of their devout men—and they had many—was apt to be without fervour, and so without popular appeal. Their

[1] *Compendious View of the Religious System of the Synod of Relief*, 1779.

clergy were aloof from their parishioners, and inclined, under the blight of patronage, to be subservient to the local gentry. They had their own intolerances. If they were free on the whole from what Melancthon called the *rabies theologorum*, they had a stiff legalism not less distasteful. They were hostile to all missionary and evangelical effort, and Chalmers' summary was not untrue of the majority:

A morality without godliness, a certain prettiness of sentiment served up in tasteful and well-turned periods of composition— the ethics of philosophy or of the academic chair rather than the ethics of the Gospel, the speculations of natural theology, or, perhaps, an ingenious and scholarlike exposition of the credentials, rather than a faithful exposition of the contents of the New Testament; these, for a time, dispossessed the topics of other days, and occupied that room in our pulpits which had formerly been given to the demonstration of sin and the Saviour.

A religion without enthusiasm is a religion without life and without hope of growth. Also, this enlightenment had its childish side. The ministers who thronged to the performance of Home's *Douglas*, and flocked after Mrs. Siddons, and made a parade of their little liberties, have to me an indescribable air of naughty urchins.

But Moderatism, great as were its defects, made its own contribution to the development of Church and nation. It meant the abandonment for good and all of the fantastic theocratic dreams of the previous century. It was a disintegrating force when brought to bear on certain debasing superstitions. The Church, for all the dialectical power of its theology, had been slow to apply the same vigour of mind to the examination of witchcraft and cognate beliefs, and as late as 1697 we have the amazing case of Christian Shaw of Bargarran, who was tormented by devils, a story which carries us back to the heart of the Middle Ages. Good men like Wodrow and bad men like Lord Grange were alike opposed to a relaxation of the savage witchcraft laws. But, as the eighteenth century advanced, the light of common-sense began to penetrate the darkness, and we find Mr. Fraser of Tiree and Mr. Campbell of Aberfeldy treating 'Satan's invisible world' as a subject for cool scientific inquiry. Hutcheson's lectures on moral philosophy at Glasgow prepared the way for that *Aufklärung* which, however shallow its inspiration, was at any rate the foe of the blinder superstitions.

Let it not be forgotten that it is to the Moderates that we owe an infusion of the rationalistic spirit, 'sapping a solemn creed with solemn sneer,' which is an ingredient in all progress. It was the only path to toleration, since, as Charles James Fox once said, for toleration there is needed a certain degree of honest scepticism. Behind all their cant and foppery there was this solid achievement—the provision of the necessary sceptical dissolvent for belated or perverse dogmas. They preached the forgotten lesson of the importance of the human reason in all human endeavour, and they strove to link religion to those other spheres of intellectual effort from which it had too long been divorced. Without the help of this uninspired and matter-of-fact sagacity Scotland would have been slow to clear her feet of mediaeval lumber. Theirs was the same spirit which in the secular world made her turn her back upon vain dreams of separation and revolt and work out for herself her economic salvation.

It is a mistake, I think, to regard the ecclesiastical life of the capital city in the eighteenth century as truly reflecting the religious life of Scotland. The ministers satirised by Burns had no doubt their counterparts in most shires, 'cauld harangues' were varied by the 'Gospel club,' and the hungry sheep were fed now with a drab morality, now with superheated imaginings, and now with barren scholastic subtleties. But the records of kirk sessions and presbyteries show us that the plain evangel was widely taught by wise and simple preachers. Survivals of the old, stern tradition of the saints kept the spiritual fires alight, even within the Church, and most Lowland parishes could boast a David Deans or a Gifted Gilfillan. The central Borders had shared less than many districts in the Covenanting fervours, but we may read in James Hogg how real a thing religion was in the life of the Border peasant. He made the Bible the lamp of his path, and at family prayers communed fearlessly with his Maker. 'The flocks on a thousand hills are Thine and their lives and death wad be naething to Thee.

Thou wad naither be the richer nor the poorer, but, oh Lord, it's a great matter to huz.' Nor was the spirit of critical independence absent, and he was under no blind bondage to the letter of the Word. The householder would stop his reading of the Bible with the remark: 'If it hadna been the Lord's will, that verse had been better left out.' We have already travelled far from Samuel Rutherford.

With the end of the eighteenth century came the dawning of a new world. The *Aufklärung* gave place, in literature, to the Romantic Revival. Robert Burns interpreted Scotsmen to one another and wove into one poetic tradition the conflicting strains in our history. Sir Walter Scott revealed his country to itself and to the world. Scotland had set her house in order, her industries were entering upon an era of wide expansion, and her agriculture was rapidly becoming a model to all Britain. Political thought, stimulated by the French Revolution, was no longer content with a museum piece like the Scottish system of representation, and doctrines were professed by reputable citizens which would have sent their fathers to the gallows. Of this stirring in men's minds there were two main consequences. Scotland's nationalism was intensified, and her pride enlarged; she was resolved to hold by her past as well as to march boldly towards the future. Again, the critical spirit was abroad, and it was certain that no doctrine or institution would be long exempt from it.

The century closed with an established Church in uneasy alliance with the State, and a number of secession churches, free indeed from such entanglements, but shackled with heavy dogmatic bonds. Some of the old matters of dispute had been shed. Prelacy would never again interfere with Presbytery, and the removal of its disabilities in 1792 enabled the Scottish Episcopal Church to follow its own natural development. The Covenants were no longer a dead hand, even in the sects which had left the parent Church because of them. There was a movement towards a more liberal construction of the Creed, and wise men were beginning to hold the true Reformation view—that a living Church must be free to change its confessions within the wide limits of the Scripture faith. In the Church of Scotland itself the State establishment was a cardinal principle, but it had lost the dangerous rider which the seventeenth century had given it; if it still based itself on the text in Isaiah, 'Kings shall be thy nursing fathers and queens thy nursing mothers,' it did not press the second clause of the verse, 'They shall bow down to thee with their faces towards the earth and lick up the dust of thy feet.' Indeed, the Church's pretensions as regards the State had become humility itself, and patronage tended to make it a disconsidered dependent.

Yet in the minds of many there was a vision of a national religion, 'the restoration,' in Montrose's words, 'of that which our first Reformers had.' Among the seceders there was little valuing of secession for its own sake, and some of their leaders were beginning to dream of an eventual unity. And in all the various kirks there was growing up a conception of what Presbytery might yet become, a faith of which Principal Rainy, in his reply to Dean Stanley, has given a classic definition:

Presbyterianism meant organised life, regulated distribution of forces, graduated recognition of gifts, freedom to discuss, authority to control, agency to administer. Presbyterianism meant a system by which the convictions and conscience of the Church could constantly be applied, by appropriate organs, to her current affairs. Presbyterianism meant a system by which quickening influence, experienced anywhere in the Church, could be turned into effective form and transmitted to fortify the whole society. Presbyterianism meant a system by which any one, first of all the common man, had his recognised place, his defined position, his ascertained and guarded privileges, his responsibilities inculcated and enforced, felt himself a part of the great unity, with a right to care for its welfare and to guard its integrity. From the broad base of the believing people, the sap rose through Sessions, Presbyteries, Synods, to the Assembly, and, thence descending, diffused knowledge, influence, unanimity through the whole system. Presbyterianism is a system for a free people that love a regulated, a self-regulating freedom.

It was a great ideal, which still awaits its full accomplishment.

V

THE MOVEMENT TOWARDS REFORM

The nineteenth century was to see at once a movement towards union and a further disruption, for much had to be pulled down before a new and ampler building could arise. Scotland, for the better part of a hundred years, was filled with controversy, which, if less bitter and more fruitful than that of the seventeenth century, was scarcely less vehement and continuous. To the detached observer it seemed that the land was spending its strength in barren debate. In an 'Appeal to the Clergy of the Church of Scotland,' published in 1875, Robert Louis Stevenson wrote: 'It would be difficult to exaggerate the pity that fills my heart at such a reflection; at the thought of how this neck of barren hills between two inclement seaways has echoed for three centuries with the uproar of sectarian battles; of how the east wind has carried out the sound of our shrill disputation into the desolate Atlantic, and the west wind has borne it over the German Ocean, as though it would make all Europe privy to how well we Scottish brethren abide together in unity. It is not a bright page in the annals of a small country.' Yet it is hard to see how this epoch of controversy could have been avoided, though it might well have been curtailed. There were in dispute matters of moment which were capable of no easy solution, but for which a solution must be found if the Church in Scotland was to fulfil its mission.

During the first decades of the century there were stirrings of life in many quarters. Men like Erskine of Linlathen and M'Leod Campbell were feeling their way towards a more liberal theology. An evangelical movement, which may be said to represent in Scotland the ultimate ripples of the great tidal wave of Wesley's work in England, was putting life into the dry bones of orthodoxy. In the Highlands especially, the 'Men,' prophets of an antique stamp, brought to the preaching of the Gospel the passion and mysticism of the Celt. In the secession Churches scholars were arising, like Robertson of Irvine and John Cairns, who illuminated Scottish divinity with a scholarship drawn from France and Germany. Mis-

sionary enterprise was beginning—in India under Alexander
Duff, in South Africa under David Livingstone and Robert
Moffat.

But, for the rest, the rule of the past was strictly obeyed.
Church architecture retained its pristine hideousness. A Scottish
service followed the meagre Puritan fashion—not that of the
first Reformers—and was in the main a lengthy monologue
by the preacher. Patronage lay heavy on the Church, and
the dominant Moderate party were stiff legalists both in doctrine and practice. In dogma they held by the letter of the
Westminster Confession; in ecclesiastical policy they inclined
to emphasise the dependence of the Church upon the civil
law. Their conservatism was less a political creed than a
temperamental bias, for they held, like Lady Rachel Drummond,
that 'a new light could enter only through a crack either in the
head or in the heart.' They were, in Lord Cockburn's phrase,
that inexorable type of revolutionary 'which will change nothing
voluntarily, and thus compels everything to change itself
forcibly.'

As the century advanced the new forces gathered strength,
and it was very clear that ere long there must be conflict. The
new wine was too strong for the old bottles. The example of
the secession Churches made it certain that the issue would
be joined upon patronage. The majority of the reform party
were on the progressive side in politics, but their leader, Thomas
Chalmers, was a staunch Conservative, who professed a 'moral
loathing' for the Whigs. In the Assembly of 1832, under his
Moderatorship, the question was raised of a popular veto upon
the nomination of a patron. One suggestion was that the
Legislature should be petitioned to abolish patronage, a course
which might well have succeeded; but the predominant view
was that the Church itself should legislate on the matter. The
consequence was the passing in 1834 of a Veto Act, which laid
down that a majority of the male heads of households, being
communicants, were empowered to veto a presentation. At
the same time the question was raised of the new chapels of
ease, supported by voluntary effort, which were springing up
in populous parts of the country, and the ministers of which,
not being parish ministers, could not sit in Church courts.

The Chapel Act, passed in the same year, put such ministers on an equality with the rest, and thereby greatly increased the anti-Moderate element in future Assemblies.

Thus began what is known as the 'Ten Years' Conflict,' in which the whole relations of Church and State were brought into controversy. The matter at issue was not the legality of patronage, which was admitted, but the right of the Church to control its procedure. The exponents both of the new evangelicalism and of the new democracy protested against the notion of a unitary state with complete jurisdiction over all departments of life. The old war-cry of the 'Headship of Christ' was heard again, and there were wild words spoken; the extremists, like the Covenanters, were often deficient in reverence and humour; the right to veto a presentee was described as a right 'purchased by the Redeemer with His blood'; and there were evangelical leaders who seemed to advocate a new papalism. But behind the extravagance a great and historic principle was at stake, the self-governing powers of the Church. The pity was that the policy adopted in the Veto and Chapel Acts kept the quarrel inside the narrow domain of law. The difficulty lay in the confounding of two different words, 'jurisdiction' and 'authority.' The Church could claim authority derived from its divine founder, but when it claimed for its courts 'exclusive jurisdiction,' the right to declare and enforce law, it entered the perilous pale of legal subtleties. A problem, which should have been solved by statesmen, was unhappily left to the lawyers.

A crop of lawsuits, the Auchterarder case, the Lethendy case, the Marnoch or Strathbogie case, showed that the Scottish tribunals were adverse to the Church's claim, and the House of Lords affirmed their judgment. Then, too late, recourse was had to the Government. But neither Melbourne nor his successor Peel was sympathetic. It was impossible to make an English statesman understand the true inwardness of a problem with such an idiomatically Scottish background. Moreover, there were two special difficulties. The evangelical party in the Scottish Church was a High Church party, making a bold claim for religious independence; the same claim was being urged by the Oxford Tractarians, who were associated with a revolt against Protestantism, as most men understood it. The

Cabinet was staunchly Protestant, and undoubtedly in their eyes the Scottish case was fatally prejudiced by its points of resemblance with the Oxford Movement. Again, the claim of the Church, with its insistence upon 'exclusive jurisdiction,' seemed to many inconsistent with the whole genius of the common law. As Lord Cockburn put it:

A claim of jurisdiction by the Church, though only to spiritual effects, altogether exclusive of civil control, is so repugnant to modern British notions, that, after the Court decided it to be ill-founded, it is not wonderful that any Government should recoil from attempting to legalise it, even if it could be supposed that any Parliament could have been got to sanction such a measure. . . . It is plain to me that the Church of Scotland had the jurisdiction, and that its practical exercise, as proved by immemorial experience, was quite safe. But, the decision being otherwise, I do not see how any Government, relishing the decision, could do anything but adopt the law delivered by the Court. Its error lay in relishing it.[1]

For the reform party there could be no going back. In 1842, at the 'last Assembly of the united Church of Scotland,' a resolution condemning patronage was moved by William Cunningham, supported by Chalmers, and carried by a large majority. That Assembly also adopted what became famous as the 'Claim of Right,' which laid down as the basis of the national Church the sole Headship of Christ, and the government of the Church in the hands of office-bearers distinct from the civil magistrates. The Cabinet received these declarations with apathy and refused to act. Disruption was now probable; the defeat in March 1843 of Mr. Fox Maule's motion to appoint a committee to inquire into the whole question made it certain.[2] On the 18th of May the Assembly met in St. Andrew's Church in Edinburgh, a dramatic scene which has been often described. The Moderator, Dr. David Welsh, read a solemn protest, and then moved to the door, followed by Chalmers and Candlish and Cunningham and a host of ministers and elders. Through an alley in a vast

---

[1] *Journal*, ii. 35.

[2] The Scottish members voted for the motion in a proportion of two to one, and the defeat was due to English votes. History repeated itself in 1927 when the Revised Prayer-book was rejected by Scottish and Irish votes.

multitude they marched down the slopes which look upon the Firth to Tanfield Hall in Canonmills, where Chalmers was chosen Moderator by acclamation, and, after the singing of 'Durie's Psalm,' [1] the first Assembly was constituted of the Free Church of Scotland.

To Gladstone, the High Churchman, the Disruption seemed a 'noble and heart-stirring spectacle.' 'Away,' he cried, 'with the senile doctrine that religion cannot live but by the aid of parliaments!' The cool sagacity of Lord Cockburn pronounced it 'the most honourable fact for Scotland that its whole history supplies.' Such praise was amply deserved. That four hundred and seventy-four ministers should surrender a certain livelihood for a matter of conscience was a vindication of the essential nobility of human nature. Moreover, this matter of conscience was no mere pedantry, but a profound principle of Scottish religious life. But of the majority who remained behind not all were over-careful of the 'loaves and fishes,' not all were formalists and reactionaries and obscurantists. There were young men like Norman Macleod, who were afraid—and not without reason—of a new high-flying Presbyterian priestcraft, for a kind of sacerdotalism has always been a peril in the Scottish Church. And many, whose sympathies were with those who broke away, were restrained by the honest belief that the true way of reform does not lie through separation, that a schism once it has taken place is hard to bridge, and that by preserving the historic continuity of an institution there is a hope of its reconstruction which departs if it be split asunder. To such, as to the loyalists in the American Revolution, history has been somewhat less than just.

The new Free Church must remain to all time a model of bold and provident organisation. This greatest of Scottish secessions was a masterpiece of constructive genius. From the start it undertook all the duties of a national communion. In its first year it built five hundred churches; it founded and carried on schools and religious ordinances in every part of the land; it established its own colleges, and it supported its own ministry. It collected money at the rate of a thousand pounds a day, and thereby taught Scotsmen a new conception

---

[1] The 124th in the second Scottish metrical version.

of liberality. Since every overseas missionary but one had joined it, it carried on its shoulders the whole missionary burden of the Church it had left. It had as its leaders the ablest theologians and the most popular preachers in Scotland, and it had among its rank and file the flower of her youth. In such a situation it was small wonder that the new Church carried its head high and was not altogether free from spiritual and intellectual pride. Lord Cockburn thought that the splendour of their new position had cured all the old defects of the anti-Moderates—'except,' he adds dryly, 'fanaticism, which it will probably increase.'

'We quit,' said Chalmers in a famous passage, 'a vitiated Establishment, but would rejoice in returning to a pure one. To express it otherwise, we are the advocates for a national recognition, and a national support of religion, and we are not voluntaries.' But though the great majority shared Chalmers' view on this point, it is clear that it was not an obligatory article of belief. Soon after the Disruption the Free Church had to devise a formula which should embody its binding principle, and in that formula establishment was not included. The binding principle was 'the freedom and spirituality of the Church of Christ and her subjection to Him as her only Head, and His Word as her only standard.' The form which Chalmers' doctrine came presently to take was a belief in a national recognition of religion, an insistence upon the general duty of nations and their rulers to protect the welfare of the Church and the interests of Christianity. It may be best expressed, perhaps, in Cromwell's words: 'If any whosoever think the interests of Christians and the interests of the nation inconsistent or two different things, I wish my soul may never enter into their secret.' The Free Church did not repudiate an establishment, provided it were combined with complete spiritual independence, but its cardinal principle was the second, and it soon inclined to grow apathetic about the first. It claimed to be the continuing Church of Scotland, the direct heir of the Reformation, the true repository of the traditions of Knox and Melville and Henderson, and such credentials were not made more splendid by any nod of assent from the State.

Chalmers died and new men appeared, men without his

conservatism and deep historic sense, and sometimes without his charity. The new Church advanced from strength to strength, its missionary enterprise brought it the admiration of the world, and soon its scholarship was not less famous than its evangelical zeal. It would have been strange if in such circumstances it had not developed a certain proud exclusiveness. Not all his successors could have said truly with Chalmers, 'Who cares about the Free Church compared with the Christian good of the people of Scotland? . . . Be assured that the moral and religious well-being of the population is of infinitely higher importance than the advancement of any sect.' Toleration was not a common mood. Its battles, internal and external, were stubbornly and bitterly fought.

Meantime the Church of Scotland, dazed for some years by the shock of the Disruption, was slowly putting its house in order. Younger men were arising in its ranks—Norman Macleod, Tulloch and Caird, Charteris and Flint and Story, who had none of the old Moderate obscurantism, and who as preachers, thinkers and ecclesiastical statesmen could compare with the best in any communion. The first tasks were to get rid of compromising lumber and to awaken the Church to its proper work. Robertson of Ellon carried out a large scheme of Church extension and endowment, and the duties of education, and of home and foreign missions, were undertaken in a new spirit. In 1852 ecclesiastical tests were abolished in the universities except for theological chairs, and finally, in 1874, after many futile attempts, patronage disappeared.

No doubt there were blunders in tactics. Considering all that had gone before, it would have been well if the Church of Scotland had taken the Free Church into its confidence and carried it with it in the various stages for the abolition of what had been the original rock of stumbling. Many churchmen believed—Norman Macleod among them—that the disappearance of patronage would open the road to re-union. But the Free Church had travelled far since 1843. Towards the removal of the handicaps of the sister Church it showed itself either apathetic or hostile, so that Mr. Arthur Balfour was compelled to ask in the House of Commons whether one religious sect could have a vested interest in the abuses of another. It held, not unnaturally, that what had driven it into the wilderness should not be removed without some confession of past error, or even restitution. It feared that the now liberated Church of Scotland might draw to itself seceders from its ranks who had forgotten, or had never understood, that patronage was the occasion rather than the cause of the breach of 1843.

An inevitable outcome was a demand for disestablishment. Resolutions in its favour were carried by large majorities in the Free Church Assembly and the United Presbyterian Synod in 1874. During the next six years the agitation grew, and with the return of Mr. Gladstone to power in 1880 it became a matter of party politics. The Liberal Prime Minister was never more than half-hearted on the question, and the emergence of Irish Home Rule as the main topic of political controversy, and the consequent schism in the Liberal party, put it beyond the sphere of the practicable.

The best of the Free Church leaders advocated disestablishment because they believed that it was the only basis for an ultimate Presbyterian unity in Scotland. But others—as was shown by the opposition to the Bill introduced by Mr. Finlay (afterwards Lord Chancellor of England) to declare the exclusive right of the Church of Scotland to regulate all matters spiritual by its own courts 'not subject to interdict, reduction, suspension or any matter of review by any court of civil jurisdiction'—were influenced by the less worthy fear of losing, through the abolition of patronage, members to the other Church. To the historian it may well appear that for one communion to enlist the help of a political party, temporarily in power, in order to enforce something which another communion vehemently dislikes was the extreme of Erastianism, if that word have any meaning. It was fortunate that the movement failed, but it may be that the raising of the question had its own value, for it beaconed one perilous path, and prevented the minds of those who followed after unity from straying into fruitless fields.

During those years influences were at work in Scotland to broaden the dogmatic basis of faith and to enrich the traditional worship. There were many who in cult desired to return to the way of the first Reformers and to get rid of the alien Puritan belief that ugliness was indispensable for godliness. In matters of creed the Free Church was the pioneer. The tragic issue of the Robertson Smith case did more to liberalise its theology than if the great heresiarch had remained in its fold. It burst for good and all the bonds of a blind Scripture literalism, and his historical standpoint, in no way inconsistent with faith, became the creed of all thinking men. 'In the Bible alone I find God drawing near to man in Christ Jesus and declaring to us in Him His Will for our salvation, and this record I know to be true by the witness of His Spirit in my heart, whereby I am assured that none other than God Himself is able to speak such words to my soul.' In the Church of Scotland, too, men like John Caird were linking religion with an idealist conception of the world, and insisting that spiritual truths stood in need of constant re-statement, since creeds and theories are transient things, and no single one can be taken as the final and infallible interpretation of God's mind to man. The Church in Scotland, under the challenge of a new environment, was following the inexorable biological law and modifying its structure.

Meantime, among the non-established Churches, there had been during the century a steady drawing together. The wise course was followed whereby those closest to each other united, and thereby formed a potent centre to attract further adhesions. In 1847, the year of Chalmers' death, in Tanfield Hall, the scene of the Disruption, a new Church was born—the United Presby-terian, formed by the union of the Secession and Relief bodies—a Church at once orthodox and liberal, which was destined to play a great part in the religious life of Scotland. In 1852 the majority of the Original Seceders were received into the Free Church, and in 1876 the majority of the Reformed Presbyterians. Just as in the Free Church some form of establishment was generally accepted as desirable, but was not made a cardinal principle, so among the United Presbyterians what was known as 'voluntaryism,' while not an obligatory tenet, was the view of the majority.

Voluntaryism meant an aversion not only to State control, but to any kind of State connection. It was not the extreme atomism of Independency, for it contemplated an organised Church. On the negative side it was inclined to the view that a civil government had no concern with religion; on the positive side it laid down the duty of congregations to support the preaching of the Word by free-will gifts. This positive side alone was included in the standards of the Church; the negative side was left to the taste of individual members. It may fairly be said that the United Presbyterian Church had not in its articles any renunciation of an establishment, so long as spiritual autonomy and religious equality were safeguarded, or even of endowment, provided the duty of voluntary giving was not forgotten. And in men like John Cairns there was a burning vision of religious peace in Scotland—nay, more, of

a Church which, while separately organised in different countries, shall be one in basis and spirit, taking the Reformed Faith as its creed, simplicity as its guide in worship, and the Bible as its supreme standard, but which both in formation and administration must be independent and free from control by civil powers.[1]

Clearly no barrier of doctrine or practice stood between the Free Church and the United Presbyterian Church if establishment was not a cardinal tenet of the one or voluntaryism of the other. But this natural union was long delayed. From 1863 onward there was a second Ten Years' Conflict within the Free Church on the matter, but the efforts of the majority were thwarted by the 'Constitutional' party under Begg, and they relinquished their campaign in fear of a threatened schism. 'Disruption pride' was still too strong a thing. A tribute is due from the chronicler to the dignity and wisdom of the United Presbyterian leaders during this difficult time.

The movement was resumed in 1896, by which date both Churches had by means of declaratory acts broadened the basis of their articles of faith. This is not the place to tell the tale of the different stages in the advance to union, in which Dr. Rainy was the leader, as he had been the colleague of Candlish and Buchanan in the abortive attempt a quarter of a century before. By 1900 all difficulties had been surmounted, and on the 30th day of October of that year the Union was formally consummated. The achievement formed a happy precedent, for in the new United Free Church neither of the constituent bodies surrendered

---

[1] MacEwen, *Life of Cairns*, 301.

anything: things on which they had formerly differed remained
open questions; it was union without uniformity; the points
of contact were the fundamentals.

A section of the more conservative party in the Free Church,
mostly living in the Highlands, refused to enter the Union, and
constituted themselves the Free Church of Scotland. What
followed will be long remembered. They brought an action
at law to have themselves declared the historic Free Church and
therefore the owners of the Church's property, which was held
on trust for the principles of that Church's constitution—principles, they alleged, violated by the Union. They were un-
successful in the Scottish courts, but in August 1904 the House
of Lords on appeal, by a majority of three, gave judgment in
their favour. It is probable that future ages will regard the
verdict as at least dubious, and look to the dissenting judgments,
like Lord Lindley's, for sounder law and sounder history.

But the supreme court of the land had decided, and its
judgment must be accepted. Dr. Rainy, now within sight of
eighty, faced the crisis in the spirit of Chalmers, and in his third
Moderatorship steered his Church through the storm. Money was
collected for immediate needs, as in the days of the Disruption;
there were few words spoken of bitterness or complaint; the
help of the State was called in to redress an impossible situation:
a Royal Commission divided the property in accordance with
the needs and capacities of the two parties, and an Act of Parliament made this apportionment law. A clause in that Act gave
the Church of Scotland the right to revise its formula of sub-
scription on the lines of the declaratory acts of the other Churches.
In the General Assembly of 1905 the United Free Church in a
solemn declaration reasserted its claim to spiritual liberty, on
lines similar to the resolution of the Assembly in 1838.

The judgment of the House of Lords was the proximate cause
of Scottish Church Union. Already the main obstacles had
gone. The Covenants, with all their dangerous implications,
were now things of only antiquarian interest. The Churches
had long withdrawn themselves inside their spiritual domain
and abandoned all theocratic pretensions. The antique literalism
with which the Bible had been interpreted was discarded, and
their theology had been at once broadened and vivified. Patron-

Y

age with all its ugly concomitants had disappeared. Spiritual liberty, which involved liberty to change within certain limits, had become everywhere an accepted article of faith. There was a juster distinction made between fundamentals and 'circumstantials,' between essential tenets and open questions; and unity was conceived of as possible without a drab uniformity. This general consensus had come about in the right way, since old dogmas had not been formally renounced but had faded out of the intellectual air. A thousand matters of ancient dispute had become simply meaningless. Toleration, moreover, so far from being regarded as a soul-killing vice, was seen to be in itself a religious duty.

The events of August 1904 completed this clearing of the ground. As far back as 1767 Lord Mansfield had laid it down that voluntary Churches were 'established,' since, being tolerated, they had a place of security in the commonwealth.[1] The word was ceasing to have the sinister connotation which it had possessed since the Disruption. It was now clear that from a certain kind of establishment no Church could be free, since, if it owned property, it was bound by the terms of endowment, and, if it sought to change, might find itself compelled to choose between impoverishment and liberty. Declarations of independence were not enough; it must secure the State's co-operation in safeguarding such independence. The State had restored to the United Free Church the patrimony which it had lost through a lesser union; it might well be asked to assist in opening the way to a greater.

VI

THE GREAT WAR AND AFTER

Twice in the last century the Church of Scotland had made overtures to the Free Church for some form of co-operation which might lead to union, but the time was not ripe for so bold a venture. But after 1904 the atmosphere had changed, and the problem came out of the mists of idealism into the clearer air of the practicable. On the side of the Church of Scotland

---

[1] *Corporation of London* v. *Evans* (H. of L.), Holliday, 225.

Archibald Scott and William Mair were the protagonists, and the leaders of the United Free Church, some of whom had been active in the old disestablishment crusade, were not slow to welcome their advances. One thing was plain: the purpose must be union or nothing, for the Churches were too closely akin for mere co-operation. A long step forward was taken in 1909, when there was a general agreement that the whole ground must be examined by unrestricted conference. Meantime two men had emerged, Dr. John White of the Church of Scotland and Dr. Alexander Martin of the United Free Church, who were to lead the movement to a triumphant conclusion; while a third, Dr. Archibald Henderson, did much to create within the latter Church the atmosphere without which union was impossible.

It is important to remember the magnitude of the task which confronted the negotiators. The field had indeed been largely cleared, but, when they began their work in 1909, the difficulties still seemed almost insuperable. One Church had been formally pledged by annual resolutions for nearly half a century to disestablishment and disendowment as a policy not only of expediency but of justice, while the other clung to the historic association with the State. It is true that many of the old lines of division had grown faint, and that the identity of the two Churches in doctrine, ritual and government had become clearer. But this very admitted identity was in itself an obstacle. In the words of Lord Sands:

The differences which to a stranger seem most obscure are often the most difficult to reconcile. When two denominations are separated by some difference clear and palpable, there may be no need to justify separation. The cause is obvious. But when the difference is not of this character, it is felt that separation needs to be justified in the eyes of the world, and this leads to the attachment of immense importance to the ground of quarrel and the most tenacious and meticulous adherence to the one position or the other.

Here it is needless to trace the various steps by which the ground of difference was narrowed and the ground of agreement enlarged. The memorandum published by Lord Sands in 1912, a document which may well be called epoch-making, simplified the issue by making it clear that freedom from State control was the only possible basis of union, and that such freedom was compatible with all that the Church of Scotland valued in its relations with the State. The next step lay with the Church of Scotland, which had the task of preparing a new series of articles to declare the constitution which it regarded as its charter. It was a delicate task, and was not accomplished without controversy, but in the end it was patent that there was nothing in the creed now defined by the Church of Scotland as its basis which differed in fundamentals from that of the sister Church.

Then in August 1914 came the Great War, which proved to be the final reconciler. Co-operation there had to be, under the stress of urgent needs both in Scotland and in the field. Ministers of both communions served—after the fine Scottish fashion—not only as chaplains but as combatants, and as platoon and company commanders shed the foibles of clericalism and reached a new understanding of the ordinary man. The social duties of the Church, too often forgotten in ecclesiastical quarrels, were burned in upon such minds. The consequence was that, after the Armistice, it was found that the whole question had undergone a chemical change. The problems of reconstruction were so vast that the Church of Christ could not face them unless it possessed a united front and a unified command.

Dr. Archibald Henderson had already pointed out in 1911 the desperate needs of the new Scotland. Her population had doubled since 1843, and the two Churches did not number among their members and adherents one-half of that population. The distribution of churches was faulty, and denominational rivalry meant a grievous waste of money and power. The two Churches between them had two hundred congregations with less than fifty members, and nearly five hundred with less than a hundred each. Moreover the War, with its urgent realities, had cast many old controversial matters still further back into the antiquarian mists. Lastly, the whole conception of the State had changed. Whig individualism had given place to a deeper and more organic conception of the part of the State in the communal life. That a Church should have some kind of relation with the civil Government no longer seemed a dereliction of Christian duty.

The new draft articles of the Church of Scotland, which were in substance akin to the old 'Claim of Right,' were nine in number. The first defined the faith of the Church as Trinitarian, Evangelical and Protestant, a sufficiently wide charter, and power was given to the Church to interpret the terms. The fourth, dealing with spiritual freedom, asserted in the most emphatic terms the separate and independent government and jurisdiction of the Church, and claimed the right and power to legislate, the crucial test of autonomy. The third and sixth insisted in carefully chosen words on the national recognition of religion, not as a new principle but as part of the Church's historic identity. One passage is memorable:

This Church acknowledges the divine appointment and authority of the civil magistrate within his own sphere, and maintains its historic testimony to the duty of the nation acting in its corporate capacity to render homage to God, to acknowledge the Lord Jesus Christ as the King over the nations, to obey His laws, to reverence His ordinances, to honour His Church, and to promote in all appropriate ways the Kingdom of God. The Church and the State owe mutual duties to each other, and acting within their separate spheres may signally promote each other's welfare. The Church and the State have the right to determine each for itself all questions concerning the extent or the continuance of their mutual relations in the discharge of their duties and the obligations arising therefrom.[1]

It is a far cry from such words to the judgment of Lord President Hope, in the first Auchterarder case, that Parliament was 'the temporal head of the Church, from whose acts, and from whose acts alone, it exists as a national Church, and from whom alone it derives all its powers.'

The new articles were put in the form of a Bill which passed both Houses of Parliament without a division in the summer of 1921. The Act was not to come into operation till the articles had been adopted by a majority of the presbyteries of the Church of Scotland—which was accomplished by 1926. The next problem was the endowments. A commission was appointed

---

[1] It re-echoes in parts similar declarations made in earlier times, *e.g.* the Heads of Agreement drawn up between the Free and United Presbyterian Churches in 1869, and even the Basis of Union between Burghers and Anti-Burghers in 1820.

to examine the difficult question of the teinds, ancient property rights which it was desirable to change from the position of a fluctuating annual charge to a capital sum, which could be handed over to the Church's keeping. After much negotiation an arrangement was arrived at which became the law of the land in 1925. The Church lost in the transaction nearly one-sixth of its former revenues from this source, but won complete freedom in dealing with what was left.

The Church of Scotland was now, as to creed, status and property, on the same basis as the sister Church. There remained the slow task of securing that final ratification of union from below, from presbyteries and congregations, which is an essential part of Presbyterian democracy. This task presented no difficulty in the Church of Scotland, but in the United Free Church, where there was an appreciable dissenting minority, and where the subordinate organism was more highly integrated, it required time and a patient diplomacy. In 1926 new committees were appointed in both Churches to conduct the actual negotiations, the leaders being Dr. John White and Lord Sands for the one Church, and Principal Martin and Dr. Drummond for the other. Within a year a provisional agreement was reached on a 'Basis and Plan of Union,' which during the next two years was carefully examined by the lower Church courts. Counsel's opinion was taken on the question as to whether, in a union with the Church of Scotland on the proposed basis, the property of the United Free Church could without breach of trust be transferred to the United Church. The present Lord Macmillan held that it could, since the Churches differed neither in creed nor ecclesiastical polity, but he advised, in order to make assurance sure, that the United Free Church should, under the terms of its constitution, expressly declare that the two Churches were at one in constitution and principle.

In the Assemblies of 1928 it was evident that the opposition, never formidable, was rapidly shrinking. The Basis of Union was sent down finally under the Barrier Act to the presbyteries, kirk-sessions and congregations being also consulted. In the Church of Scotland every presbytery voted in its favour—seventy-two out of the eighty-four unanimously. In the United Free Church all the sixty-three home presbyteries approved, and there was only a small minority of dissentients among the congregations and sessions. So at long last, in May 1929, when a royal prince acted for the first time as Lord High Commissioner, the Union was ratified by the two Assemblies. In the following October, with the Duke of York again representing the King, the first Union Assembly took place. A small minority constituted a dissenting remnant. It would not have been Scotland without such a protest.

The Church thus reunited is a new type among Christian communions, and it is right to remind ourselves of its conspicuous privileges. For the first time in history we have a Church which is acknowledged by the law of the land to be wholly free: free in its government and jurisdiction, free in its faith, having power to interpret its creeds and to alter them within the wide limits of Trinitarian Protestantism, free in its use of its temporalities. And at the same time it is a historic Church, with no gap in its continuity from the first Reformers, cherishing its ancient documents of title, recognised by the State as the national representative of the faith of the Scottish people—the Church of Scotland, and not merely a Church in Scotland. The words 'established' and 'dis-established' have no longer any but an historical meaning. The Church is that far greater thing, a national Church, as it was in 1560 at its beginnings.

Looking back on the long story, it may well seem that no stage was without its beneficent purpose. Each schism, each controversy had its place in a great plan, for each emphasised a facet of the truth which was in danger of neglect. Men who seceded on one point gravely over-emphasised that point, but their secession and their over-emphasis secured for whatever it contained of substance a place in the national testimony. The extravagance of the seventeenth-century theocrats made it certain that no Church would ever command the assent of the Scottish people which was in spiritual bondage to the civil power and when this article seemed in peril the eighteenth-century seceders rose to affirm it. The 'voluntary' movement taught the economic side of autonomy and the importance of religious equality; those who clung to the establishment preserved the belief in a national recognition of religion. The strength of the nineteenth-century free communions gave a chance both for

the liberalisation of confessions and for a larger view of the social
duties of the Christian faith.

Slowly, painfully, the Church rid itself of certain sinister
heritages; it shed the mediaevalism which made it a rival of
the State; it abandoned its narrow Scriptural literalism; it
learned that toleration was not a pagan vice but a Christian
virtue, and that the path to unity did not lie through a bleak
uniformity. But all these lessons would have been vain had not
a vision of the peace and felicity of a united Jerusalem survived
among good men in each generation, even when their conscience
demanded a further disruption. The very vigour of their
scruples and their honest resolution to be loyal to what they held
to be truth made it certain that unity if attained would be no
shallow, unfeatured thing, but a living organism in which all
that was of value in old differences would be transmuted and
reconciled.

' Why else was the pause prolonged but that singing might issue
      thence?
Why rushed the discords in but that harmony should be prized? '

From the standpoint of the goal attained we can retrace the
road and see how all the pilgrims, even in their deviations,
contributed something to its attainment. One lightened the
baggage and was cast out, but in time what he had rejected was
left behind by all. Another took a course of his own in sterile
country, but his followers stumbled upon Pisgah - views and
returned to the main march with a new vision. Others stuck
by the path which ordinary folk could travel, and formed a
rallying-point to unite the stragglers.

These men, moving down through the ages, are many of
them great figures, attaining often to heroic stature, men who
had the making of their country in their hands, for the history
of Scotland is largely the history of her Church. Some are still
in our memories—Rainy and Caird and Story, with faces cast
in a mould of antique dignity. Behind them we see Norman
Macleod with his kindly sagacity and Highland fire, and the
noble head of Cunningham, and Candlish's short, gnarled figure,
and John Cairns' rugged face, and Chalmers with the brow of
the mathematician and the eyes of the visionary. . . . Further

back are the perukes of the eighteenth century—the bland
precision of Blair; the black mittens of Webster; Carlyle of
Inveresk, handsome as a pagan god; the great chin and the
bright, vivacious eyes of Principal Robertson; the Erskines, too,
with their high foreheads and lips pursed as if in an eternal
protest, and Boston of Ettrick, pale with fasting and study, and
William Carstares, heavy-wigged, heavy-browed, his fingers
crooked from the torture-chamber. . . . Beyond them are the
men of the heather, lean, wild folk, short-lived for the most part
and tragically fated, with voices shrill from hillside preaching
and eyes pale like a seaman's from hilltop watches. . . . Then
come the skull-caps and bands of the divines who saw their
Church on the pinnacle of its temporal power—the 'fair little
man,' half jurist, half dreamer, who was Samuel Rutherford,
and Alexander Henderson, his skin yellow with ague and his
eyes hollow with unsleeping thought, a statesman born in an ill
season for statesmanship. . . . Now we are among the flat caps
of the Reformers, chief of them Knox with his hawk's nose and
hawk's eye and patriarch's beard, the man who had the passionate
momentum of some great portent of nature. . . . Then the
mists descend, and we see only dim figures in proud hieratic
robes, and sometimes under the robes a gleam of steel, for they
were often of the church militant, and served in the field as well
as at the altar. . . . But in the far distance the air clears, and
against a Hebridean sky we can discern him who was called the
Dove and was both priest and prince, and who on another isle,
like John on Patmos, had visions of a peace among men which
'has its birth in mortal love, but its evening home where are the
dews of immortality.'

INDEX

Stair, James Dalrymple, Viscount, 112, 132, 171 ; John, Earl of, 113, 130, 131-145, 160, 168, 170, 171, 173, 175
Stead, W. T., 206, 210, 212
Steenkirk, 169
Stephenson, General Sir Frederick, 241, 257
Stevenson, R. L., 276, 327
Stewart, General Sir Herbert, 243, 247, 250, 252
Stewart, Colonel J. D. H., 208, 216, 221, 227, 228, 232, 233
Stubbs, Bishop, 5
Suakim, 181, 204, 207, 209, 214, 216, 218, 220, 222, 224, 227, 228, 241
Suebi, the, 58, 62, 67, 72
Suessiones, the, 64
Suetonius, 24, 104
Suez Canal, the, 185
Sugambri, the, 68
Sulla, L. Cornelius, 33, 34, 35, 36, 37, 39, 40, 43, 44, 45, 48, 50, 53
Sulpicius Rufus, 79

Tacitus, 27
Taine, H., 4, 19
Tamaai, 226
Tarbat, George Mackenzie, Viscount, 109, 111, 113, 134, 139
Taynuilt, 126
Tel-el-Kebir, 185
Tencteri, the, 67
Teviot, Viscount, see *Livingstone, Sir Thomas*
Tewfik, Khedive, 203, 204, 205, 214, 215, 219, 257
Thapsus, 90
Thucydides, 96
Tigranes, 48

Tokar, 218, 257
Toski, 257
Trebonius, 70, 99, 102
Trevelyan, Professor George, 3, 13
Treveri, the, 70, 71
Tuti Island, 253
Tweeddale, John, Marquis of, 171

Ubii, the, 68, 74
Usipetes, the, 67
Ussher, Archbishop, 314
Utica, 90

Varro, 87
Veneti, the, 65, 66, 69
Vercingetorix, 72, 73, 74, 75
Verres, 44
Vesontio, 62
Victoria, Queen, 208, 234, 254

Wad-el-Nejumi, 233, 244, 254, 257
Wadi Halfa, 181, 205, 222, 224, 242, 243, 257
Weem, Menzies of, 142, 151, 162
Wesley, John, 278
White, Dr. John, 339, 342
William III, King, 112, 114, 131, 132, 141, 142, 144, 145
Wilson, Sir Charles, 248, 252, 253
Winzet, Ninian, 307, 308
Wolseley, Lord, 195, 199, 200, 208, 209, 210, 238, 239, 240, 241, 242, 243, 248, 252
Wood, General Sir Evelyn, 200, 216

Zobeir, 196, 215, 216, 219, 221, 222, 223, 224, 225, 226, 227, 229, 234
Zwingli, 305